Lois
Remembers

Memoirs of the co-founder
of Al-Anon and wife of the co-founder of
Alcoholics Anonymous

Al-Anon Family Group Headquarters, Inc.
World Service Office for Al-Anon and Alateen, Virginia

For information and catalog of literature write to
World Service Office for Al-Anon and Alateen:

Al-Anon Family Group Headquarters, Inc.
1600 Corporate Landing Parkway
Virginia Beach, VA 23454-5617
Phone: (757) 563-1600 Fax: (757) 563-1655
Web site: www.al-anon.alateen.org
E-mail: wso@al-anon.org

Library of Congress Catalog Card No. 79-006975
ISBN-0-910034-23-0

1. Alcoholics Anonymous. 2. Al-Anon Family Group Headquarters,
Inc. 3. Alcoholics—Family relationships. 4. Alcoholics—United States-
Biography.I. Al-Anon Family Group Headquarters, Inc. II. Title

HV5279.L64 1991   362.2'92'092
                                              QBI92-20144

Approved by
World Service Conference
Al-Anon Family Groups

8-3M-02-9.50

To Bill
Who loved both alcoholics
and their families

"It takes
only one person
to start something,
but many others to
carry it out."

Lois W.
1891-1988

Al-Anon Family Groups, Inc.

For help in preparing this material, I am grateful to many people of AA and Al-Anon, among them Henrietta, Alice, and Nell. But to Barry I am particularly grateful. His editorial help has been invaluable. No one deserves blame for any flaw but myself, for the final choice of contents and of words is my own.

L.B.W.
Stepping Stones
January 24, 1979

The Al-Anon Family Groups are a fellowship of relatives and friends of alcoholics who share their experience, strength, and hope in order to solve their common problems. We believe alcoholism is a family illness and that changed attitudes can aid recovery.

Al-Anon is not allied with any sect, denomination, political entity, or organization or institution; does not engage in any controversy, neither endorses nor opposes any cause. There are no dues for membership. Al-Anon is self-supporting through its own voluntary contributions.

Al-Anon has but one purpose: to help families of alcoholics. We do this by practicing the Twelve Steps, by welcoming and giving comfort to families of alcoholics, and by giving understanding and encouragement to the alcoholic.

The Suggested Preamble to the Twelve Steps

CONTENTS

PREFACE

This account of my life and Bill's together is written in hope—hope that it will encourage those of you experiencing the same difficult periods of living with an alcoholic as I did. Even when you cannot see a way out, never give up hope. Alcoholics, though erratic, are often magnificent people, seeking in alcohol some sublime goal which inevitably eludes them. Your life can be far richer in the future because of your suffering now.

Bill's recovery came about in spite of me. Although it was what I had been working for all our married life, I had gone about it the wrong way. My love, as deep as it was, was also possessive; and my ego was so great I felt I could change him into what I thought he ought to be.

The material for this book was taken from sporadic diaries, old sketches, letters, and my memory. Many of Bill's letters have been preserved, but few of mine. Those experiences about which I have kept memoranda are told in detail while others are skipped over lightly, as they have no firmer foundation than memory. I have included situations which reveal Bill's or my interests of characteristics, or seem colorful in their own right.

A great deal of the story is centered on Bill. I'm sure you will understand that Bill *was* my life. Therefore much of this book is about Alcoholics Anonymous, since for the first seventeen years of my recovery and Bill's, there was no fellowship for the families of alcoholics. The ideas of Al-Anon germinated during this period, but Al-Anon did not take its own shape until 1951. AA was therefore my first love. Although not alcoholic, I feel even today as much a member of AA as of Al-Anon, at least in spirit.

The big lesson I have learned is that we cannot change another human being—only ourselves. By living our own lives to the best of our ability, by loving deeply and not trying to mold another to our wishes, we can help not only ourselves but that other also.

When this project began some three years ago, I was offered the services of several fine writers to ghostwrite the book from my notes. I am sure one of them could have produced a much more polished and slick literary work than I. But I wanted to write it myself, above all to share directly and honestly with readers my own personal experience in my own words, which is the Al-Anon and AA way.

These pages reflect some of the love I feel for all AAs and Al-Anons whether they read these pages or not. But for those who do, I hope my sharing will be meaningful.

Childhood Memories

It was in the fall of 1915 that Bill and I became engaged. At the depot in North Dorset, Vermont, I had just put a longtime friend who had been visiting us on his train to Montreal. Then Bill jumped off.

Surprised and delighted, we walked back together to my family's summer camp on Emerald Lake, and that evening on the shore of the lake, we told each other of our love.

We could not then foresee, of course, our path ahead: the long, difficult years of his alcoholism, the founding of Alcoholics Anonymous, the dawning of the Al-Anon Family Groups and Alateen. Nor could we dream of the great joys these worldwide Fellowships were to bring to us many years later, and to thousands upon thousands of people like us.

Then, to be in love was our entire world.

To tell how we met and who we were, let me bring to life some memories from the beginning.

Children seem to understand some great reality that is a mystery to grown-ups. As they grow out of childhood, they lose this secret knowledge.

I did not want to grow up. An invisible wall seemed to prevent adults from entering my child's world. I wanted to stay on the near side of that wall. As I inevitably climbed over it, I promised myself I would never forget what it was like to be a child. But of course I did. I remember only my desire to remember.

My childhood was an extremely happy one. Mother and Dad truly loved one another and openly showed their affection to each other and to us children. They taught us never to be afraid to tell of our love, never to go to sleep angry with anyone, always to make peace in our hearts before closing our eyes at night, and never to be ashamed to say, "I'm sorry. I was wrong."

My father, a gynecologist and surgeon, was brought up in Lancaster,

Pennsylvania, went to Franklin and Marshall College, and studied home-opathic medicine at the Hahnemann School of medicine in Philadelphia.

His interest in medicine may have come from an ordeal he'd shared with his youngest brother, Charley. Once while the two boys were out together, Charley found two sticks of phosphorus, which he put in his pants pocket. As the youngsters raced home, friction ignited the phos-phorus. Dad did everything he could to put out the flames, but Charley died as a result of the burns.

My father used to tell about one snowy day when he was a boy. A dig-nified gentleman who lived nearby and a friend, both wearing stovepipe hats, were driving past in a horse-drawn victoria. My dad couldn't resist such a perfect target. The minute the snowball knocked the neighbor's top hat into the snow, he stopped the rig, got out, chased Dad over the fields, caught him, and spanked the daylights out of him. That neighbor was ex-President James Buchanan.

Dad's father, Nathan Clark Burnham, practiced law and medicine and was also a minister of the Swedenborgian Church in Lancaster. He wrote a book, "Discrete Degrees," about the relation Swedenborg had found between the spiritual and the natural life. The Swedenborgian religion, also called the New Church or Church of the New Jerusalem, had recently come to America. Grandfather, wanting to be sure he was on firm ground, learned Hebrew in order to translate the Old Testament into English. Unfortunately he became blind soon after starting this project. He per-suaded my father to study Hebrew to help with the translation.

While the New Church has had but a small following, it did attract some well-known people, among them John Chapman (known as Johnny Apple-seed), Helen Keller, and Robert Frost.

Dad went to Brooklyn to practice medicine because his Uncle Lyman owned a big department store and knew many people there. He visited his patients on horseback from 182 Clinton Street, where he boarded. Five of us six children were born in that red brick house, built in 1848, in the very bed which is now in our bedroom here at Stepping Stones.

Originally, Dad rented the front room of the first floor to serve as bed-room and office. A pile of medical books supported one corner of his sofa bed. Later, he rented the back room for examining his patients. Then in 1888 he leased the whole house and brought his bride there.

Dad had met my mother, Matilda Hoyt Spelman, at her coming-out party at her parents' home in Brooklyn Heights.

I remember their laughing together about that party because Dad, carry-ing his medicine case, was mistaken for a musician and sent upstairs to wait with the other musicians until needed. Mother found him there and rescued him.

The oldest of four, she had gone to Miss Prentiss's Finishing School for Young Ladies. She rated all A's in her classes, much better than the marks of any of her children.

The famous and graceful Brooklyn Bridge was opened while Mother was a young girl. Before it was ready for vehicular traffic, a temporary boardwalk with a rope railing for pedestrians was placed on the permanent supporting cables which hung over the two huge stone arches. Mother was one of the adventurers of the day who climbed up the cable walk to each arch and then down, an exciting but precarious way to reach New York (Manhattan, we would say now), then a city separate from Brooklyn.

She liked dramatics and belonged to a literary club, where she put on amateur theatricals and read many papers. She also was a member of a choral club led by the composer R. Huntington Woodman. Among my most pleasant memories are of Mother's reading aloud to us youngsters before we went to bed and of her reciting poetry or a monologue as we were driving home after a long day in the open.

Absolutely without self-consciousness and totally selfless, Mother loved people and people loved her. Everyone told us youngsters that Mother was the loveliest person they knew. Her features were somewhat plain, but they were framed by curly, burnished-blond hair, and her outgoing spirit charmed everyone and made her beautiful.

Mother's people were New Englanders. Her father, William Chapman Spelman, used to tell how as a boy in Granville, Massachusetts, he worked out a plan to escape Sunday restrictions. The Spelmans, his Congregationalist grandparents, lived at the top of the hill and celebrated their Sabbath on Sunday. His Cooley grandparents, at the bottom of the hill, were Seventh-Day Adventists, and their holy day was Saturday. So, living in between, he climbed up the hill on Saturday to the Congregationalists to spend the day as he chose; and on Sunday he sped down the hill to visit with the Adventist grandparents, where he was free the whole day.

Granddad's first cousin, Laura Spelman, married John D. Rockefeller Sr. I remember being taken for a weekend visit to the Rockefeller estate at Pocantico Hills by my great-aunt, Granddad's sister, Eliza Spelman Williams, since childhood a companion of her cousin Laura's. I slept in a trundle bed pulled out from beneath the magnificent four-poster Aunt Eliza slept in. I recall John D. standing with his elbow on the mantel in a long living room with green and gold furniture.

My grandparents lived on Willow Street in Brooklyn, where my mother was born. Sarah Hoyt Spelman, my grandmother, had come from a lovely, elm-shaded village, locally called "the Street," in Manchester, Vermont. At her death when I was a small child, my father bought the house and all its beautiful antique furnishings from my grandfather. A long time before, the house had been an inn. A dance floor built so it would sway when trodden on was fun for us youngsters to run across, so we'd hear the furniture creak and the bric-a-brac rattle. We were told the inn had once been painted black to lure business away from its popular rival, the Black Tavern, down the road. We kids scraped off some of the white paint but found no black beneath.

Of my parents' six children, Rogers, Barbara, Katharine, Lyman and Matilda came after me. Matilda lived only a year. At the proper age, each of us went to the well-known Pratt Institute in Brooklyn. Pratt may have been the first school in this country to use a new type of preschool education imported from Germany—the kindergarten. Each day a school brougham collected a handful of us neighborhood youngsters. Once a little boy somehow fell out of the carriage, cutting his head badly. I remember feeling very grown-up mothering him as we drove to the hospital.

From Pratt I went to Friends School. When I was in first grade, the Quakers (Society of Friends) permitted neither singing nor dancing. But later all this was changed. The pupils sang happily at assembly and were even taught to dance.

Elise Valentine and I sat next to each other at school for thirteen years, eight of which were at Friends School and five at Packer Collegiate Institute. Elise was occasionally driven to school by a little boy whose pair of goats pulled them in a tiny cart.

When we first went to Packer, Elise and I felt very superior to the girls there. *We* had gone to a school with boys, since the Quakers have always believed in coeducation. Boys were just boys to us, not the great adventure that the Packer girls seemed to find them. We were amused at our classmates' telling how the Polytechnic youths, as they strolled past the Packer garden, tried to flirt with them. We felt we knew boys through and through and they were nothing to get excited about.

At home Sundays were special. After attending morning service, a visiting minister or other guests from the church very often came to dinner. Various wines were served, which Dad chose from the large stock of alcoholic beverages given him by grateful patients (GPs, we called them). Before a meal we always said a blessing while holding hands. At its close we kissed the hands we held. Our guests, although sometimes slightly nonplussed by this custom, joined in self-consciously.

Some Sundays three or four of us youngsters would walk the mile or so to Fort Green Place, where our Great-Aunts Emma and Annie lived. Uncle Lyman had died too long ago for us to remember him. Aunt Emma, his widow, wore white curls hanging down on her forehead from under a lace cap, but spinster Aunt Annie's thin gray hair was pulled straight back. They had come from England on a sailing vessel when they were little girls, and I have a Circassian walnut writing desk which accompanied them on that long voyage. Their brother, Edward Molineux, was a general in our Civil War. His room-sized flag with thirty-eight stars was left to me.

Sunday afternoons Dad often drove us out to Prospect Park in our smart, yellow-wheeled, horse-drawn rig. Mother and Dad each had a special tree they liked to pass. Dad's was an old, gnarled, spreading oak, whereas Mother's was a tall, straight tulip tree.

My father was on the staff of the Cumberland Street Hospital and operated there. He was a bright, quick, energetic, do-it-now person with a great zest for life but a poor memory. He left many of the humdrum things for Mother to do. Typical remarks of his were: "Shake a leg, Laddy" and "Matilda, have I read this book?" Very generous, he attended many patients to whom he sent no bill. I remember Mother's asking him often when she was making out the bills, "What shall I charge such and such a family?" and Dad's saying, "Oh, we won't send them a bill now; maybe if they get sick again. . . ."

Dad was not only a stubborn but a very self-assured gentleman; he never could admit to us children that he was wrong. As a youngster I thought he was perfect, but as I grew up I recognized these characteristics. I remember one evening saying, "Dad, you *could* be wrong." But no; he *knew* he was right. "You are always right," I said. "Is that human? Isn't it possible that sometime you might be wrong?" We kept this up for hours, all in good humor. I, you see, was just as obstinate as he.

About 1908 Dad had a patient who was an executive in an early movie company. The executive persuaded the whole family to go to the studio of the American Multiscope and Biography Company, located in Long Island City, and act out four reels of ad-lib farces.

At the time we felt too silly even to show these "movies" to friends. Recently I came across the oaken, sewing-machine-like box (patented 1895-1898) and brought it out of storage for the amusement of my friends. A handle turns the reels, and a mirror on top focuses the light on pictures as the leaves flash by. The farces were titled "The Proposal," "The Holdup," "Song and Dance," and "The Family."

Ben Foster, later well known as an artist, was a close friend of Mother and Dad's. In his youth, he had applied to my grandfather for a job in his store. Upon discovering that the boy was unusually gifted, Granddad sent him to art school. At his peak "Uncle Ben," as we children lovingly called him, was considered among the first ten American landscape painters. One or two of his paintings hang in the Metropolitan Museum of Art in New York City. The walls of our house were covered with his landscapes. He gave the family a picture on every celebration. There are some lovely ones still at Stepping Stones.

Dad's determination and endurance, even when he was well on in years,

5

were demonstrated one summer when he went to visit Uncle Ben in Arizona and stopped off at the Grand Canyon. Disdaining a guide, he trotted the eight miles down the Bright Angel Trail to the very bottom, where characteristically he then swam across the Colorado River. Upon his return, about three-quarters of the way up the canyon wall, he met a man who was apparently having a heart attack. So Dad hoisted him on his back and carried him up the rest of the way.

During my childhood in those days of large families and large houses, many people had house help. We children loved most of ours. Maggie Fay, a jolly, fat, Irish cook, worked for Mother and Dad for twenty-five years. She used to tell of a silly thing I said as a small child. She must have given me some milk in a bowl instead of in my silver baby cup, for she reported that I lisped, "Poor Pois, you give her milk like a cat."

Maggie was a wonderful cook and quite a philosopher. When I had grown old enough to have beaux, she warned me not to marry anyone that the servants didn't like, because she said they could judge the true caliber of a person better than anyone else.

The first coachman I remember was Edward Lord, the son of Betty, the lovely old "colored mammy" who took care of most of us youngsters. Betty had been a slave and was one of the truest, finest people I knew. Then there was Alfred Withington, who looked very handsome sitting on the box in his coachman's uniform. He was followed by Elias Green.

Green, as we called him, was one-quarter American Indian, the rest black. He hoped that the state of New York would give him his share of property on Long Island originally owned by his ancestors, the Shinnecock Indians. Many years later, after I was married, Bill (who had studied law) tried to help Green get back his land, but with no success.

Starting out as coachman, Green shortly turned into chauffeur. The first car Dad and Mother bought was a Stevens Duryea with running boards but no windshield. My brother Rogers, as a teenager, soon learned to drive it. He also studied its mechanism and became the most expert mechanic and driver I have ever run into. I wasn't interested enough then to learn to drive the car; and besides, Dad or Rogers or my sister Kitty was always at the wheel. Brother Lyman learned as a mere child, sitting on cushions. But when I began to have a beau or two, I learned from whoever had a car.

In addition to driving and taking care of the car, Green had indoor duties. Our house was heated by two built-in stoves, one in the front and one in the rear, on different floors. The kitchen had its own large range and gas stove plus a brick Dutch oven. Green used to come daily to fill up the stoves with coal, take out the ashes, sweep the areaway, and "polish up the handle of the big front door."

When Bill and I had to leave the old house for good in 1939, Green and

I held tight to each other's hands while tears streamed down our faces. This was the end of our living in the old homestead and of his contact with the Burnham family. He died several months later.

Mother and Dad paid rent on the Clinton Street house for many years. In the middle of their lives they thought, "We could have bought the house several times over with the rent we have paid." So they bought it. But there were still monthly payments to be made to the mortgage company. Dad's income, although increasing, could not keep up with the increasing expenses as the family grew. In the end the mortgage company got the house.

We children were all sent to private schools and colleges. Besides this educational expense there were salaries for the children's nurse, an office nurse, a cook, a waitress, and a chauffeur, and the upkeep of two homes.

Our family spent nearly half the year in our summer home in Manchester, Vermont. Mother used to have our teachers give her our spring and fall lessons so she could tutor us. Thus, we could stay in Vermont from May to November, without dropping back in our grades. Our outdoor life made healthy youngsters of us all. Because many of Dad's patients followed him to Manchester, he could afford to take a long vacation there.

Manchester was a summer resort, and my parents entered into much of its social life. When a golf course was needed, Dad and other residents called on a well-known professional golfer, Walter Travis, to plan one. Robert Todd Lincoln, President Lincoln's son, and others donated the land. Mr. Lincoln owned a beautiful estate nearby, and his grandchildren, Peggy Beckwith and Lincoln Isham, were among our playmates.

The T.'s, from Albany, also regular summer visitors, and were family friends. Pa T., as everyone called George T. Sr., had five sons. Edwin, the youngest—Ebby to us—was a pal of my brother Rogers and later played a crucial role in my life and Bill's.

Two very old and wrinkled Indian women named Icey and Vicey Palmer lived at the poorhouse and used to visit the homes of the summer people. Also at the poorhouse lived two Civil War veterans. On the Fourth of July they marched down the center of the street in their tattered uniforms, playing the fife and drum. Only boys joined their parade, however; little girls ran the other way when they saw tall John, the fifer. He always tried to kiss them.

All of us children went barefoot in the summer, but I was called a tomboy because I rode a bicycle when I was five, climbed trees, and never gave a thought to how I looked.

One day while sitting in an apple tree, I wanted to tell something to my friend Esther Congdon, who lived in a boardinghouse at the other end of town. Jumping down, I tore my dress and lost my hair ribbon, loosening my long, dark braid. This did not concern me, although I had to walk past the very proper Equinox House, where smartly dressed guests sat in rocking chairs on the lawn. Before going to Esther's room I stopped to chat with her aunt, Miss Dennison, who was sitting among others on the boardinghouse porch.

Many years afterward Miss Dennison told me that at the time I spoke to her, a social worker who had come to study the welfare needs in Vermont said the only person she had observed in need of help in Manchester was the little girl with the torn dress, dirty face, and flying hair who had come to see Miss Dennison's niece.

When I was about eight years old and playing in the orchard, I heard horrible screams coming from the house. They were so terrifying I was afraid to go in. In truth a calamity had happened. My sister Barbara, two years old, had noticed that when people struck one of the sticks from a little red china shoe, a beautiful flame arose. She thought she'd try it. She must have known it was wrong, because she hid under a table and pulled a couple of chairs down around her before lighting the match. Her starched white dress immediately caught fire.

Annie, the cook, the only adult in the house, heard Barbara's screams, dashed in, pulled her out and threw rugs over her to douse the flames. Annie suffered burns herself but saved Barbara's life.

Barb's face and hands were deeply seared and required much treatment and many grafts. Dad, without using any anesthetic, once sliced skin from his own leg to graft on Barbara's face. He called her *his* child after that, because part of her had literally been part of him.

Most of the grafting skin, however, was cut from her own arms and legs. She recovered remarkably well, and the scar on her face hardly shows. She has made a very happy life for herself, and when we talk about those Vermont summers now, it is the happy times that we recall.

My parents always spent much of the season outdoors. At first they rode a tandem bicycle with a basket on the handlebars for little Lois, and later, after Alfred had hitched the horses to the long buckboard, the increased family drove off with a full picnic basket for an all-day outing. Mother and Dad knew every back road for miles around. They used to stop at any farmhouse that looked as though it might contain antiques. Offering a generous price to the owner, they picked up many beautiful pieces of Colonial furniture, china and glass, which enhanced our city house as well as the Manchester one.

One day as the buckboard was coming down steep Peru Mountain, the axle broke on a particularly high thank-you-ma'am. (A thank-you-ma'am, in case city-dwellers don't know, is a mounded ridge across a dirt road on a hill, for drainage and to rest the horses while the wheels are supported by the ridge. Driving up this notoriously steep grade, we always got out and walked to save the horses.)

The sun was sinking behind the mountains. There was no house within miles on this lonely road, but Dad was equal to the occasion. He had no ax (ever afterward we carried one on the wagon), so with his penknife he laboriously cut down a good-sized birch tree and tied it so it supported the back axle. Limping home, we arrived after midnight. This was an exciting adventure for Rogers and me, especially the staying-up-late part. The younger ones had fallen asleep in the buckboard many hours before.

Early one summer when the family stopped at one of their usual picnic sites under a big elm beside Dorset Pond (afterward named Emerald Lake), Dad was annoyed to find somebody had built a bungalow there. How dare anyone build on his favorite picnic spot! He immediately bought the bungalow. We used the Camp, as we named it, all that summer on weekends. The next year when we came up, there was another bungalow not far from the first one. Dad, of course, had to buy that, too. It gave us room to entertain guests, and we called it the Other House.

Social life in Manchester had become too demanding for Mother and Dad, and the bungalows presented a delightful escape. They decided to spend the next summer at the lake and rent the Manchester house. That would give the children a wonderful opportunity to live informally in this wild, beautiful spot and would bring in some money besides.

We youngsters swam, boated, wandered in the woods, or drove to Manchester for tennis, golf, or dancing. Many of our friends visited us.

We all loved Jerry, a black Shetland pony Dad had found in the kitchen of a patient's house in Coney Island. Jerry had performed in circuses. On our many outings, one of us youngsters rode the pony while Dad drove abreast our three horses, Bolus, Quinia, and Bess. Even the little ones learned to ride Jerry.

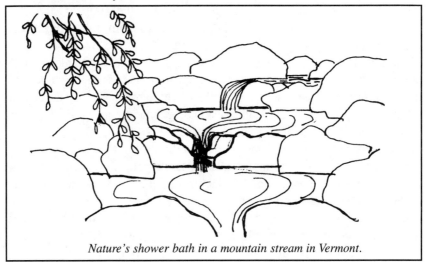

Nature's shower bath in a mountain stream in Vermont.

We left Jerry and Bess in Vermont during the winter but took Bolus and Quinia to New York with us. We drove the buckboard to Albany, then all of us, including the horses, steamed down the Hudson on the night boat.

Jerry loved to tease the cow with which he shared the pasture. Day in and day out he chased that poor cow. Finally the cow returned his attentions and threw him over the fence, goring him badly. Dad had to take many stitches in the teaser's side.

We were driving up to the Camp one day when Mother suddenly realized she had forgotten the keys. Rogers rode back on Jerry to get them while we waited in what we thoughtlessly called "the dummies" home. The owner and his wife were both deaf and dumb. Aunt Edith, who fortunately was with us, knew the sign language of the deaf, and while she and the lady of the house carried on a labored conversation, the lady took down her long hair and brushed it. Later we were told this surprising informality was an old-world folk custom, a way of honoring guests by making them feel at home. I wonder whether this could be the source of the expression "let your hair down."

When Jerry got old and gray, he was put out to pasture at the Camp, where he roamed the hillsides. If anything edible was left on the back porch overnight, it was gone in the morning. Unless the kitchen door was locked, he would push it open, walk into the house and help himself. Jerry knew his way around kitchens.

Each year when my tomboy summer was over and I went back to Brooklyn and to school, time seemed to be going by faster. Although I was small, I was agile and strong; according to a gym test I had the strongest back and next-to-strongest legs in the school. In spite of this, when I was nineteen my brother Lyman, only eight years old, challenged me to a wrestling match at the Camp, and we scrambled in the dust in front of the garage. He won!

I played guard for four years on the basketball team, the only athletic game the Packer Collegiate Institute played at that time. We wore middy blouses and bloomers in the gym and white blouses with ankle-length skirts to class. We wore ribbon bows in our hair, one at the nape and perhaps another at the end of the braid. We could hardly wait to put our hair up in a pompadour, thus signifying we had become young ladies. By then, my attitude about growing up had changed.

My senior year at Packer, comparable to the sophomore year at college, was a lot of fun in spite of having to wear to chapel every morning a mortarboard on my pompadour and a black robe set off by a white Peter Pan collar and black velvet pussycat-whisker bow.

My closest friends were Edith Roberts, president of the class, Elise Valentine, vice-president, and Helen Cruden, treasurer. I was secretary.

At sunset Elise and I often used to walk to the foot of Montague Street on the heights above New York Harbor. It was a spectacular sight. As the lights came on in the office buildings in the Wall Street area of lower Manhattan and the ships steamed past the Statue of Liberty, we watched the color spread across the sky and water while the sun sank behind the New Jersey shore.

There were many fine residences in Brooklyn Heights, a quiet, tree-shaded area where financial, political, and professional people lived. The brownstone or red brick houses along Clinton Street were inhabited by many other doctors and their families.

My school friends and I read books by such authors as Charles Dickens, Sir Walter Scott, William M. Thackeray, Jane Austen, Louisa May Alcott, Bret Harte, and Rudyard Kipling.

I had taken dancing and music lessons as a child and loved to sing in the glee club and to dance at the many coming-out parties. But neither Elise nor I wanted a coming-out party of our own. We felt only "social butterflies" came out.

In fact, we were quite snobbish about a number of things. We disapproved of jazz and vaudeville but loved to go to concerts of classical music, to the opera, to the theater, and to the occasional high-class musical comedy such as *The Pink Lady* and *H.M.S. Pinafore*.

But we did go to the vaudeville once, to see the aging Sarah Bernhardt in a short skit; but unfortunately she was ill that night, so we never saw her. I still have a girlhood scrapbook that includes such programs as Joseph Jefferson in *Rip Van Winkle*; Laurette Taylor in *Peg o' My Heart*; Maude Adams in *Peter Pan*, *What Every Woman Knows*, and *The Little Minister*; and John Barrymore, as well as his sister, Ethel Barrymore, in several plays. There were E. H. Sothern and Julia Marlowe in *Twelfth Night*, *As You Like It*, *The Merchant of Venice* and *Much Ado About Nothing*. At the Metropolitan Opera I heard Caruso in *Aïda* and in *Samson and Delilah* with Louise Homer; also Geraldine Farrar and Lucrezia Bori in *Carmen*. I saw Anna Pavlova dance and heard violin recitals by Fritz Kreisler, Mischa Elman, and Jascha Heifetz.

My family or school friends or occasionally a beau accompanied me to these performances. Elise and I had grown past the stage where "boys were just boys," and young men now occupied quite a bit of our thoughts and conversation. Several girls in the class had already become engaged to be married. On the subject of "spooning" (the pastime later called "necking"), we had very strong opinions about its impropriety before engagement. We guessed, however, that many of the other girls were not so strict. Elise was prettier than I and had more beaux. She never had any desire to spoon with any man until she met Frank Shaw. Her beaux sensed this and seldom tried. She fell deeply in love with Frank, and they were married.

But I was different. There were several young men to whom I was attracted physically, yet I knew I didn't love them. Sometimes it was hard for me to keep to our strict rules. When young men sat with me all evening long in the front parlor, they frequently tried to spoon. But I did hold quite faithfully to our conventions, although it was often difficult to find lively enough conversation to interest a young man otherwise. If the guest hadn't gone by eleven o'clock, Mother always called down from the top of the stairs that it was time for my friend to leave.

In 1912, after I had graduated from Packer, I spent two consecutive fall terms learning to draw in charcoal with live models at the New York School of Fine and Applied Art. Upon completing the second term I felt I should earn my own living. I found a job at the Central Branch of the Young Women's Christian Association in Brooklyn. For a short time I was receptionist. Then the head of the employment bureau asked me to help her. Her assistant, Ethel Smith, was planning to be married, and Miss Metcalf wanted Ethel to train me for her job before she left.

Ethel and I became friends. She had been engaged for three years, but her half-knowledge about sex so scared her that she could not bring herself to set a wedding date. At her request I explained some of the facts of life. My doctor father believed in informing his children about how babies were conceived and born. She soon married and often told me that her husband was understanding and kind.

In 1915 I accepted a job transfer to the Y's Eastern District Branch as girl's-work secretary. It was a long way to commute from home, but I enjoyed planning the children's activities and being with the youngsters.

My years with the Y ended when I moved to New Jersey to work for my Aunt Marian. Left with four children to bring up after her husband had run off with another woman, Aunt Marian had started a small private school in her home in Short Hills. She asked me to help her, and I went there to live and teach in January 1917. It was the era of progressive education and individual instruction. We taught no regular classes; each child had lessons especially suited to his or her stage of development. This took much time in preparation.

I left Aunt Marian's home to get married.

2

Strawberries and Kerosene

My brother Rogers kept talking enthusiastically about his friend Bill. When I finally met this Bill, the only impression he made on me was that he was tall and lanky. After all I was a young lady of twenty-two and he but a teenager, a whole four years younger.

Bill and his sister, Dorothy, lived with their grandparents in East Dorset about three miles south of Emerald Lake. Bill's parents were divorced, and his mother, who was an osteopath in Boston, used to vacation in East Dorset.

During the summer of 1913 Bill, his mother, and his sister camped at the other end of Emerald Lake from where we had our bungalows. My grandfather had given us a skiff with an attachable mast and sail, and I liked to cruise on the lake. Bill liked sailing, too. With a rigged-up sail on a hired rowboat, he almost beat me in spite of my superior craft. He had learned about sailing from studying his grandfather's big dictionary. In fact he knew the name and purpose of every line on a sailing vessel.

The small lake, only about three-quarters of a mile long, lies between two ranges, the Green Mountain and the Taconic. At the north end, they almost touch each other; yet interestingly they are of entirely different age and composition. Marble is plentiful on the Taconic Range, but none exists in the Green Mountains. The Emerald Lake water is a clear, deep green all year round because, it is said, of the chemical effect of the marble dust in it. Otter Creek, which flows through the lake, once brought in the dust from a nearby marble mill. Although the mill has been shut down these many years, the green color of Emerald Lake remains. An island in its center is set off by white birches along the shore, where a necklace of boulders encircles it.

Although Bill and I had fun competing in sailing, I still wasn't especially interested in him.

When the next summer rolled around, Rogers and Bill's sister were going together. Dorothy and Rog, my sister Barbara and a beau, and Bill and I, who at first just went along for the ride, had a glorious vacation picnicking, hiking and taking all-day drives. Long before the end of the season, however, I thought Bill the most interesting, the most knowledgeable, and the finest man I knew. I forgot all about the difference in our ages.

Bill was what we "summer people" called a "native," and there was quite a noticeable feeling between the two groups. The natives felt themselves to be more genuine than the summer people, and the summer people knew the natives did not "belong." Ridiculous!

Bill liked to pitch baseball. He would practice anywhere by picking up a stone and aiming at some target. The tall chimney of the old disused marble mill across the tracks from his home was a pet target, and it became shorter and shorter as Bill hit one brick after another. (As a result, in later life he had what they call a "tennis elbow" and could not completely straighten out his arm.) He pitched for the Equinox ball team in Manchester, winning many games.

One day in August the summer people gathered at the Bennington ball park for a game between Manchester and Bennington. Everybody was eagerly awaiting the famous Equinox pitcher. Rogers was supposed to drive Bill the twenty-six dusty miles from East Dorset to Bennington in my father's Stevens Duryea, the car that had no windshield. When they finally arrived, they were a sight. A blown tire had delayed them, adding layers of dirt to their faces and clothes.

Bill tried to make up for the delay by clowning. He put on a little red cap at funny angles, making a fool of him so the audience would laugh and relax. But the onlookers were not amused, just irritated. This began to affect Bill's pitching. He lost confidence and did badly. It was a fiasco for the Equinox team and for Bill. Suddenly I realized it was a fiasco for me, too. What hurt Bill also hurt me, and I became provoked with my Bennington friends for not appreciating Bill's humor and pitching.

One night Rog and I drove to Manchester for a dance. While waltzing I noticed Bill standing at the open door with other local folks watching the summer visitors cavort. I hoped he would break through and ask me to dance, but he never did. He told me later how badly he had wanted to, but he had no confidence in his social demeanor, especially in his dancing.

We were together often, though, after I opened what I called a tea arbor at the north end of Emerald Lake, in order to have some work to do in the summer. In 1915 automobiles had not completely replaced horses, and many people enjoyed driving their teams to a pleasant spot for a cup of tea in the afternoon. Only nine miles from Manchester, a tea arbor on the hill where it could be seen from the road would be, I hoped, such a place. It was an open-sided arbor, the roof supported by evenly spaced birch poles. Rustic chairs and tables were handmade of maple. The floor was painted green. I trained vines up the poles and placed plants and flowers in between. It was charming.

Business, however, was very slow. It was hard to cross the brook to the arbor, and I hadn't put up signs or done any other advertising. Only a few people learned about the place by word of mouth.

But Bill used to stop there many afternoons after peddling burners for kerosene lamps through nearby villages. He didn't sell many burners and I didn't sell much tea; but we had wonderful visits. Often I would give him a treat of wild strawberries or fried picked-on-the-hillside mushrooms on toast.

During these long afternoons he told me much about himself. It had meant a lot to him to go to Gettysburg in 1913 with his grandfather Griffith. At this celebration of the battle's fiftieth anniversary, his grandfather showed him just where the Vermonters outflanked Pickett's charge up the hill and helped decide the outcome of the battle.

Bill's mother, who had taught school until she married, was a brilliant, positive, confident person. His father, on the other hand, was easygoing and likable and often drank with the boys on Saturday nights. Having a great sense of humor, he was an irresistible storyteller.

As foreman of a marble company on Dorset Mountain, he quarried the marble for the New York Public Library and for the Soldiers and Sailors Monument on Riverside Drive in New York. At one time he was in charge of the excavating for a part of the Boston subway.

Bill could remember many happy times with his family. They drove out together in the buggy on Sundays, and he often played ball with his father in the backyard. They liked to sing folk songs together in the evenings while his mother played the accompaniments on the melodeon. His father had a good voice and often sang Figaro's aria from *The Barber of Seville*, amusing the children with his gestures.

After Bill's parents were divorced, his dad was offered a job in a quarry in British Columbia. He was so well liked that his Vermont crew followed him west. As he and another man traveled by horse and wagon, they mainly feared being attacked by Indians when they bedded down to sleep under the wagon. One night when their blankets were suddenly twitched away, they were sure the Indians were upon them. But they soon discovered the blankets were caught in the wheels of the wagon, which was sliding down the hill by itself.

Bill knew very little about the cause of the divorce but thought it came about because his father drank a great deal. It had been a traumatic experience for Bill—he had practically lost both his parents at once. His mother had left the two children with her parents in East Dorset while she studied and later practiced osteopathy in Boston. Although Bill and Dorothy loved their grandparents, who were very good to them, they felt abandoned. Bill was especially devoted to his father and badly missed him after he moved to the West. Bill was only eight or nine years old when this happened, so the separation made him feel set apart and inferior to youngsters who lived with a mother and father.

That summer of 1915 was a memorable one for me. Several years before, I had made the acquaintance of Norman, a young man from Canada, at our church conventions of young people, where he had squired me around a number of times. While my family and I were vacationing at the Camp, he wrote and asked whether he could come down to see me. My parents invited him to stay with us.

Norman was nice-looking, intelligent and a good person; ordinarily I enjoyed being with him. But now I begrudged the time spent with him. I was longing every minute to be with Bill. As I took Norman to the station at the end of our week together, he asked me to marry him. I had to tell him no.

Just as Norman stepped on the train for Montreal, Bill jumped off. We walked back to the lake together. We didn't hold hands; that would not have been proper. But somehow our fingers often seemed to brush against each other.

That same evening we told each other of our love.

There were only a few days left before I had to go back to my job in Brooklyn, so we made the most of them. Every morning Bill walked along the railroad tracks the three miles from East Dorset to Emerald Lake, and then back again at night.

At first we didn't tell anyone about our engagement, because prospects of an early marriage were dim. Bill was a student at Norwich University, a military college in Northfield, Vermont. Founded in 1819, it was considered second only to West Point in the quality of its military training. By this time the First World War had started in Europe, and it seemed that the United States might get into it at any moment and call up the Army.

From my parents' standpoint Bill was hardly a brilliant prospect as a son-in-law. He was only twenty years old, still in college, with no profession in view except the Army. But they liked him. Everybody did. And they loved me, their daughter, and respected my choice. When we told them about our engagement, they seemed surprised but happy.

Bill spent that fall and early winter with his grandparents in East Dorset. He had had a severe depression the previous winter, because of the death of a girl he had been very fond of at Burr and Burton High School. The ensuing absence from the university had dropped him back a grade. That meant he did not return to complete his freshman year until February 1916.

*"My God, what a rookery,"
said the angular Irish cook
when she beheld the Camp,
different indeed from the elegant
stone residence where she
worked at the other end of
Emerald Lake.*

From Brooklyn I wrote him so many letters (at least one a day) that his grandmother said, at the rate they were coming, there'd soon be enough to wallpaper the kitchen!

Of course I anxiously awaited Bill's letters. There weren't as many as I wished, and they were sometimes apologetic for missing the evening mail train. The reasons would be that he and Rog had been arguing about atoms and ions, or he had been practicing with the new bow my dad had sent him for the violin obbligato he was to play to a soprano solo on a Sunday evening. However, his letters were most satisfying when they came, often lively with such whimsies as "Figuratively speaking, I shall always wear cowhide boots and smoke a corncob pipe," and "Her dog forgot to put on his gloves before handling a porcupine."

Emil, a friend of mine, came to our house one evening to take me to the movies. I didn't want to go; I was afraid of missing a phone call from Bill. Emil didn't know about my engagement, so he repeatedly urged me, and I was so irritated that I threw a book at him. In my school yearbook I had been voted the most amiable girl in the class. Little did they know! When I was a child, flashes of temper occasionally caused me to be shut up in a closet for hours. I hope now, at last, I have learned to control them.

During Bill's enforced leave from Norwich, he had earned money by surveying for the telephone company and chopping wood. By January he had accumulated enough to come to Brooklyn to see his gal, to buy an

17

engagement ring, and to rig himself out in a new suit, overcoat and hat.

The first thing, of course, was to get the ring, for which he had set aside twenty-five dollars. He had heard that Tiffany's was the best jeweler in New York. I persuaded him to try several wholesale places first, but nothing there suited him. He was determined to go to Tiffany's where we finally found a beautiful amethyst ring suitable for my practical hands and priced exactly right. I gave him my Packer school ring in exchange.

Back at Norwich, where he studied electrical engineering, Bill had a spring recess in March of 1916. So I took a long weekend off from my job, and we spent it together at the Camp with Mother. The ice on the lake was beginning to wake up and become alive; and it snored and groaned as it stretched itself. The brook beside the Camp gushed down the mountainside and supplied background music to all our activities.

Soon after Bill's return to college, Pancho Villa began acting up on our Mexican border. Many volunteers joined the Norwich University Reserves. Bill drilled recruits at Fort Ethan Allen near Burlington most of the summer. At one moment he expected to be sent immediately to Mexico, and the next he was sure the trouble would be over before they could get ready.

Meanwhile, at commencement time, Bill and the student troops were called back to Norwich, where he witnessed a hazing incident—some freshmen being dunked in a pool. When questioned, however, Bill refused to tell who was responsible, so he and the entire sophomore class were suspended for a term.

Since he was again not in college, Bill could visit us in Brooklyn over Thanksgiving. That was always a big time for the Burnham family. Relatives whom we seldom saw joined us for dinner.

On Saturday morning, Bill and I took subway, ferry, bus, and trolley into the wilds of Staten Island. We selected a protected spot for our cookout and raked away the nearby leaves to prevent the spread of fire. After we had enjoyed our delicious, broiled-just-right steak, however, the wind changed. A big gust whirled down the gully, scattering the embers. Staten Island was afire! We tried to smother the flames with our coats, but soon the fire was beyond our control, and we ran to the nearest house for help. Fortunately it didn't take the fire department long to put it out.

In the meantime our new friends (the people in the house) had dug into an old trunk in the cellar and found a black velvet hat with a feather. Thoughtfully, they gave it to me. In those days, every woman *had* to wear a hat.

Bill's jacket had been burned in the fire, so he wore his badly scorched topcoat over his shirt and trousers. As soon as we sat down on our return routine of trolley, bus, ferry, and subway, the neighboring passengers moved away from us. Did you ever smell singed wool?

It was a memorable night for other people, too. It was the first time that a woman—Ruth Law, I believe her name was—flew solo over New York Harbor. The event was being celebrated with lights, rockets and sirens. From the ferry we were able to watch the acrobatics of the daring pilot.

That night Mother and Dad held a reception to introduce their prospective son-in-law. It was Bill's *only* suit jacket that had been burned, and a new one could not be bought on a Saturday night. But my father was always equal to any emergency. Although of medium height, he insisted his striped cutaway coat was just the thing for Bill. Luckily Bill was not clothes-conscious, because he certainly was an odd sight that evening. His long, skinny wrists protruded at least six inches from the sleeves, and the jacket's waistline hit him just a little below the chest. But the back was perfect; the cutaway tails exactly covered his bottom.

However, I learned that Bill did have certain definite nos about dress. He would *not* wear a derby! He told me that he had once gone to buy a new suit at a Rutland clothing shop owned by a cousin. When Bill left, his cousin generously presented him with a derby. Bill politely accepted it, but the minute the train left Rutland he threw it out the window.

The following month, I learned still more about my husband-to-be and his forebears. I spent a pleasant Christmas vacation with Bill, Dot, his mother, and his grandparents at their home in East Dorset, where they told me many family stories.

For instance, Grandpa Griffith's older brother Marley had hiked all the way to Pike's Peak in Colorado at the time of the gold rush. He wrote such glowing accounts to the family that Gramp, then a teenager, started out on his own. But he got lost for three days in the swamps of Michigan, where he went to escape wolves, so he never reached Pike's Peak.

When Bill was a little tot, his mother told me, he spent hours looking at illustrations in their big dictionary. One day when he asked what it said underneath a picture, she replied, "Cantilever bridge." Soon afterward she took him by train to New York. Standing up on the seat as they approached Poughkeepsie on the Hudson River, Bill shouted in excitement, "Oh Mom, there's a cantilever bridge!" Everyone turned to look at the smart little boy who could recognize the engineering feature.

One day in the country school Bill attended, the classroom was in an uproar when Mary Milotte, the new teacher, appeared. Without saying a word, she picked up a log of wood and threw it into the chunk stove so hard that it thrust through the back end of the stove. This show of authority and strength immediately quelled the disturbance, and she held sway thereafter. Mary Milotte remained an authority all through Bill's life, and he often quoted her.

Bill always liked to work with tools. As a boy he had made bows and arrows, skis, jack jumpers, and sleds. One day his grandfather told him that only the Australians could make a boomerang, a weapon that would return to the thrower Bill determined to be the first American to make and throw a boomerang. After that no schoolwork was done, no wood brought in; boomerangs were the order of each day. Morning, night and noon, Bill was either studying books on Australia or hacking away in the shop on a piece of wood. Time after time he thought he had solved the puzzle, but the weapon didn't return.

After about six months of failure he was going to bed in his attic room one night when he noticed the grain in the headboard of his bed. It was just the thing he needed. He ran for his saw and cut the piece out. Since he had already burned part of the headboard in an earlier experiment, he didn't think Gram would scold him.

When this boomerang was cut and sanded, his grandfather watched as Bill threw it across the churchyard; Gramp had to jump to save his neck. The boomerang returned to its thrower the way a genuine Australian one would. Bill was sure he was the first American to accomplish this feat. After his previous sense of inferiority and awkwardness, it was great to feel he was the number one man in boomerang-making.

To encourage Bill's interest in science, his Uncle George gave him a chemical kit. Bill started his experimenting in the back shed by mixing sulfuric and nitric acids. Just as he was dipping strips of paper into the mixture, his father appeared and was appalled. As a quarry foreman he was well aware of how close Bill's mixture was to nitroglycerin, the chief component of dynamite. Quickly but most gingerly he lifted the dish, carried it outdoors, and buried the frightening stuff in a hole in the ground.

When Bill was about eight years old, his family moved to Rutland, where he and another boy learned the Morse code and set up a wireless telegraph system between their homes.

At another time, Bill's grandfather told him his Uncle Clarence had played the fiddle very well. He said Bill probably wouldn't be able to play it, but it was stored in the attic after Clarence's death. This was enough to stampede Bill into the attic. He laboriously taught himself to play the violin and nearly drove the family mad in the process.

On the neck of the instrument, under the strings, he pasted a diagram of the position of the notes, which he had found in an old hymnal. He had Dorothy hit a key on the melodeon as he searched for its duplicate on the strings. He persisted with this, as he did with other interests, until he became really proficient.

Later he partly supported himself at Norwich University by playing the fiddle or cello (which he preferred) at dances with a small college orchestra, and often accompanied the glee club at concerts in nearby towns.

20

Bill and I both enjoyed music. I knew enough piano to accompany him when he played the violin or cello. We loved to practice Beethoven's Violin Concerto in D major. All through our lives many happy hours were spent together playing or listening to fine music.

Bill's calculus course had given him trouble. He told me that intricate problems are solved by selecting and applying the right formulas or theorems. You just have to know which to use on which problem. Bill was always curious about bows and whys, so he asked the teacher how the theorems had evolved. The teacher did not know; he said no one had ever asked him that before. So Bill raided the library to find the answer. At the end of the semester he told the teacher how the formulas had been worked out. But even so, he flunked the course.

He said later that this drive may not have been entirely in search of pure knowledge. A desire to prove himself smarter than the teacher may have entered into it.

In 1917 all academic work at Norwich halted because of the war. Only military training was given, and students automatically became members of the U.S. Reserve Forces. Bill was sent to the first Officers Training Camp at Plattsburg, New York.

When his grandmother, Dorothy, and I visited him there, Bill and I kept trying to sidetrack the others so we could be alone for a few minutes, but we didn't have much luck.

Bill chose the heavy artillery branch of the Army, because it challenged his scientific curiosity. However, he recognized that many soldiers considered this the safest arm because it was farthest from the front. So once again he was nagged by inferiority feelings, a fear that he might be cowardly.

In June he was sent to Fortress Montroe for training. My parents let me visit him there unchaperoned. Their understanding and their trust in Bill and me were very unusual during that conventional era.

One day by the sea at Monroe stands out in my memory. After a storm the retreating waves had left great heaps of froth on the beach. As the wind rolled balls of this foam along the sand and tossed them into the air, we laughingly raced to catch and throw them.

In August Bill was commissioned a second lieutenant in the 66th Coast Artillery Corps and stationed at Fort Rodman at New Bedford, Massachusetts. I visited him there several times, staying at a boardinghouse in town. The trip on the Fall River night boat was made without any trouble, although the night boat did have a shady reputation. I felt it was a woman's fault if undesired advances were made to her. It was her attitude, conscious or unconscious, that affected a man one way or the other, I believed.

My job at the Y had often included evening gatherings. I had trolleyed safely unattended at night through a somewhat hoodlum part of Brooklyn and had traveled alone to Bill's various posts. The slight trouble I did have I later analyzed as my own fault. A desire for attention on my part caused the reaction from others.

Although we were separated much of the time, I working in Brooklyn and Short Hills, and Bill chopping wood on the mountain, studying at Norwich, and drilling in the Army, we had many wonderful times together during the two and a half years of our engagement.

It was in January 1918 that I left Aunt Marian's school in Short Hills, where I had been teaching, and Bill and I were married on the 24th. Our wedding day had been set for February 1, but when Bill heard rumors that his regiment was to be sent overseas immediately, we decided to be married as soon as possible. Invitations were changed to announcements, and there was much scurrying around to get ready for the big church wedding a week earlier than planned. Family and friends called up guests, and the seamstress put aside everything else to finish my dress.

Elise Valentine Shaw was matron of honor, and my sisters, Barbara and Katharine, and two of my schoolmates were bridesmaids. My brother Rogers, the best man, arrived from Camp Devens too late to change his heavy-duty boots before stomping up the aisle.

After a small reception at Clinton Street, Bill and I left on the night train to visit his mother and sister, Dorothy, in Boston. I had asked Dorothy to be a bridesmaid, but because of bad colds neither she nor her mother could come. After a brief visit with them we caught the train for our new home in New Bedford.

A great welcome awaited us at the furnished apartment Bill had rented. Flowers and plants were everywhere, and people dropped in continuously to congratulate us. Bill was very popular on the post.

New Bedford was a cotton-manufacturing town with much wealth and social life, and the hostesses entertained the Army men lavishly with parties.

Bill had been warned since childhood not to touch alcohol. His mother had divorced his father largely because of drink, he thought. His paternal grandfather had also had bad drinking episodes, but through some kind of transforming experience had stopped drinking completely. If Bill once began, he had been warned, he, too, might get into trouble. He believed this and decided not to drink. Later I marveled that this had been enough reason for a man like Bill, whose independent spirit always led him into experimenting.

During our engagement he had gone with the boys to the saloons, but while they drank beer, he sipped ginger ale, sarsaparilla, or birch beer. I was proud of his great willpower. Therefore it was a great shock to me when I looked for Bill during one of these affairs in New Bedford, and his Army buddies told me they had dragged him home and put him to bed. There I found him, dead to the world, with a bucket by his head.

His drinking had started shortly before we were married. It didn't occur too often and usually began at parties. I used to tease him by saying that he could resist the boys who offered him a drink, but not the gals. I was only slightly unhappy about this drinking, because I felt confident I could persuade him to return to his former abstinence. I could "fix" him. Living with me would be such an inspiration, I was sure, he would not need alcohol!

We dreamed about our future—the family we would raise and all the great things we would accomplish. He told me how he longed to help humanity. Sometimes his goal would be in one field, sometimes another, but always it was to benefit others. These dreams sprang from a deep love of his fellowman. I always believed Bill was uniquely special, his heart warmer, his mind clearer, and his ideals higher than those of others.

I, too, had ambitions. I wanted to be the best possible wife and mother, as much like my own mother as possible. When Bill, knowing I idolized Mother, wanted to please me, he would say, "You're just like your mommie."

In April Bill's battery was transferred to Fort Adams in Newport, Rhode Island. We wives had to live off the post there, and the men came home only on weekends. But we could ferry over to the fort and visit them during any leisure time they might have.

I especially remember when Bill, appointed adjutant for the day, drilled the troops. He appeared late on the field, wearing his old campaign hat with a bullet hole in its crown, pulled way down over his eyes. I don't know how the bullet hole got there; he had probably used the hat as a target. But he was very military in spite of the odd-looking campaign hat. I was extremely proud and thrilled at his performance. The band played "The Stars and Stripes Forever," and to this day I cannot hear Sousa's great march without hearing Bill's booming voice and seeing him in my mind's eye, standing out there in the field commanding the men.

To honor the troops preparing to go overseas, the Curtis Jameses invited the whole battery to a celebration on their magnificent Newport estate. It was held in a miniature Swiss village, complete with chalets, registered cattle and pretty dairymaids. The officers' wives were asked to wear peasant costume and help serve.

In spite of Bill's drinking too much occasionally, we had a very happy six months together before he went overseas. Besides members of my family, Bill's dad visited us. He wanted to see what kind of girl his son had married. I loved him immediately.

Bill and I never forgot the night in August before his regiment left for overseas. After dinner with other couples, he and I strolled off by ourselves and climbed a great crag overlooking the sea. There, alone beneath a bright moon, we again pledged our love to each other.

In the morning on the station platform, there was much weeping. Running along beside the moving train, we wives clung as long as we could to our men's hands as they leaned out the window. I didn't cry until the train was out of sight.

3

Maine Blueberries and Brook-Jumping

When the submarine alert sounded, the transport Lancashire, bearing Bill and the 66th Coast Artillery from Boston, was nearing the coast of England. The men were all asleep in bunks packed solid on the decks. To prevent panic, officers were stationed at every hatch on every deck. Bill was on night watch down in the hold, where the men would be the last to be rescued in case of accident. Standing on a platform near the foot of the ladder, he was under orders to shoot anyone who tried to climb out before permission was granted.

Bill was trying to keep awake when suddenly there was a terrific impact against the hull of the ship. "This is it!" someone yelled. Bill pulled out his gun as the men started to panic and run for the ladder. But he was able to calm them with his words without much difficulty. This reassured him as much as it did the men, for he discovered he was not the coward he had feared he might be. Until then he had always doubted his courage.

He later learned a German submarine had fired a torpedo at the Lancashire, but it missed. A nearby U.S. escort destroyer returned the fire with a so-called ash can; it exploded underwater so closes that it made the shattering blow against the ship's hull.

Soon after his arrival in Southampton, Bill wrote me also about an experience he had in Winchester Cathedral. He was feeling depressed and lonely, fearful of what lay ahead; but upon entering the cathedral, its atmosphere seemed to take possession of him, and he was lifted up into a sort of ecstasy. Although he was not a conscious believer in God at the time, he felt a mighty assurance that things were all right and would continue to be.

In a daze, he strolled out into the churchyard. Suddenly he was brought down to earth by the name on a headstone, Thomas Thatcher. Perhaps an ancestor of his good friend Ebby T. had been buried there. Bill smiled broadly as he read part of the epitaph:

> Here lies a Hampshire grenadier
> Who caught his death drinking cold small beer.
> A good soldier is ne'er forgot
> Whether he dieth by musket or by pot.

His mood was changed, but the effect of the uplifting experience at the cathedral clung to him ever after.

In those months when an ocean lay between us, I tried to get the Y to send me abroad as an aide to the wounded. I hoped I could at least be on the same continent with him. But the National Board of the YWCA refused because of my religion. Their letter of rejection stated that Swedenborgians (the sect to which I belonged) and Unitarians were not considered Christians! When I objected, I was told I should have known, since I had worked for the YW for some time. This seemed to me not only narrow but illogical; a "non-Christian" could instruct children but could not aid wounded soldiers.

Of course their viewpoint has long since changed and even then obviously was not held by the less orthodox branches where I had worked.

During Army post life, I had become especially friendly with Iva Chamberlain, the wife of a buddy of Bill's. After the boys had gone overseas, we heard about a new method of aiding recovery of the war-wounded, called occupational therapy. We immediately signed up with the first training course in the new profession, the Mansfield War Services Classes in New York.

Besides instruction in a variety of crafts, we were taught discipline, hospital routine and a certain amount of practical psychology. As the wounded boys were pouring home into the hospitals, there was a great need for speed, so our intensive courses accomplished in two months what later would take nearly a year. I was sent to the New York Presbyterian Hospital for two weeks' training. After graduation my assignment was to the shell-shock ward (for those suffering what was later called "battle fatigue" in World War II) in Walter Reed Hospital in Washington, D.C. The experience there was often heartbreaking, for I saw at close hand what war does to young men, and I kept wondering what it was doing to Bill.

Evidently his drinking did not interfere much with his military career. He was recommended several times for promotion but didn't get it, not because of alcohol, but because of a mistake in names, as he learned later. A man with the same surname received the promotion meant for Bill.

Upon leaving France the men of his battery paid him special honor. His letter of January 3, 1919, read: "Quite a touching thing happened yesterday. The men presented Captain Sackville and me each with a watch, chain, and ring. The whole battery was lined up, and I tell you it was equal to promo-

26

tion and decoration by J. J. Pershing himself! Coming as it did from a clear sky, it was quite overwhelming. Wouldn't have changed insignia with a brigadier general. It means so much more than promotion. Insofar as I know, we are the only people in the regiment who have been so honored. I'm sure you will be as happy and proud as I am." Of course I was.

His drinking did prevent his writing as many letters as I longed for. There was never enough mail from overseas. One day, however, a letter brought the great news that he would return soon on the troopship Powhatan, docking at Norfolk, Virginia. Immediately resigning my job in Washington, I took my luggage home to Brooklyn, then dashed down to Norfolk, only to learn the Powhatan was to dock in Hoboken, New Jersey! Back again I chased, getting there just in time to see Bill running toward me through the iron grill gates.

The joy of his homecoming completely swamped the slight strangeness we both felt at getting together again after living intense experiences apart.

After Bill was mustered out at Camp Devens in May 1919, we stayed with Mother and Dad in Brooklyn. Soon my brother Rogers also returned from overseas. One day, to celebrate, he and Bill went down to the cellar and raided the store of liquor given to Dad by his grateful patients, his GPs. Rogers seldom got drunk, but this day he and Bill made a shambles of the cellar and got deathly sick. It upset the whole household, but the returned heroes were readily forgiven.

Bill had completed no vocational training and didn't know what he wanted to do. He considered staying in the Army, but Army life was not appealing in peacetime. He had great dreams for his future, but like many returned veterans, he had a hard time adjusting to civilian living.

He got various jobs, such as decoding cablegrams for an exporting firm at twenty dollars a week and working as a laborer on the docks of the New York Central Railroad at sixty-one cents an hour. He was so unsuited for these kinds of employment that he stayed only a few weeks with each.

Something had to be done. To think things over, we decided to take an extended walking trip through Maine, New Hampshire, and Vermont. This started a lifelong habit. When we were tired or unable to solve some problem, we would go off by ourselves in the woods or occasionally by the sea. It did not always solve the problem, but we were better able to think clearly after such a renewal of body and soul.

So Bill and I, carrying packs on our backs, set off from Portland, Maine. Few people took cross-country walking trips in those days, nor did women wear knickerbockers as I did on this hike. So we were objects of much curiosity shown by staring adults and giggling youngsters.

We had many small adventures in that exhilarating month. We set a fishing line at night on Lake Ossipee, New Hampshire, and caught a thirty-three-inch wiggly eel, enough to feed us for a week. After washing and scraping it thoroughly, Bill chopped off pieces with a hatchet for me to fry. It tasted delicious the first two days. But by the time we got to the third camp, the odor was overpowering, so we fed the remaining two feet to the birds and worms. No matter how much we scrubbed the pots and ourselves, we couldn't get rid of the persistent odor. After that neither of us was ever able to bear the thought of eels. We learned later that the peculiarly penetrating odor is in the skin, which we had not known enough to remove.

I kept a diary on this trip. One day Bill, feeling silly, wanted to write in it. This was the result:

"Made a very early start this morning—about one hour after noon. We are en route to Great Pond and lying on the roadside. Under way one hour and sixteen minutes, we are exactly 325 feet from where we camped. We now belong to the school of contemplative philosophy, outstanding feature of its code being an unwavering conviction of the great possibilities of life spent in the horizontal or recumbent position. Even the high cost of living gives us no concern. We have consumed this week five whole dollars' worth of supplies, which is a perfectly outrageous expenditure.

"The following discovery is of no more credit to us than was the discovery of the great Anaconda Copper Lode to the pig that unearthed it while rooting for acorns. In fact, the greater credit should be awarded to the pig, for he was grubbing for his living. As we were climbing the fence, Lois suddenly slipped and fell. We looked at once for the banana peel but saw only a large, slimy blue spludge about the size of a saucer. Upon probing, it developed that the cause of her accident was a blueberry of most extraordinary size. To our utter astonishment we perceived that blueberries hung about in the greatest profusion. Naturally our next thought was 'Let us pick and eat.' Whereupon we fell to, and after gathering enough for our supper and two meals thereafter and having eaten all we could hold, we still had made no visible impression on the berries left on the bushes. Thus, by our toil and foresight, we feel we have earned another day of repose and contemplation.

"Set to paper this 6th day of August, 1919. W. G. W."

"Dictated to me by W. G. W. while under the influence of sunshine and two quarts of Maine blueberries. I disclaim all responsibility for the above and will not vouch for its authenticity. Signed L. B. W."

We usually bought milk and vegetables from farmers near our camping ground. But sometimes, if a plentiful garden presented itself and there was no farmhouse nearby at which to ask permission, we would help ourselves to enough for a meal. Among the entries in my diary were:

"For supper we ate swiped-peas-and-beans with honest bacon and lots of free berries. . . .

"Met an ultra modest red-haired man with his shirttail hanging out through a hole in the back of his pants, who, most properly, kept his eyes away from the shocking spectacle of a woman in knickers. When asked about the Saco River, he said it was three miles down the road but that he hadn't been that far this summer. . . .

"We got a fairly early start but stopped at the first brook we came to and took our morning baths. Although almost in the center of a place called Ross's Corners, we managed somehow to find a secluded spot. An auto with a horse hitched on behind passed us. Later we ran into acquaintances we had met the previous evening, one of whom told us, 'I git poisoned terrible by them horned pouts and also by mercury, that is to say running' ivory.' (Poison ivy?) 'I'd like haying fine if it weren't fur that.'

"The only remark the other man made was to say, 'I like turtle soup fine. Turtles got four different kinds of meat in 'em.'

"'Ye can hef all the turtles ye want but ye'll hef to excuse me,' retorted the other. . . .

"Spent the night on the shores of Lake Winnepesaukee. We spied a mink hunting among the rocks and heard a loon calling in the stillness. The northern lights were wonderful on this cold night. . . .

"We met a joyous farmer with a broad-brimmed calico hat, who sang to his team as he drove them down the hill. He explained to us his singing encouraged the horses not to stumble. . . .

"Helping ourselves most bountifully to corn from a nearby field, we pitched our tent on the shores of tiny Niger Pond, with white water lilies and a stunning purple water plant floating on its surface. While munching roasted corn, we watched a procession of shorn cobs float past, and saw a white heron stalking among the cardinal flowers at the edge of the water. . . .

"A catbird always seems to be practicing his imitations wherever we camp. Tonight on the shores of New Found Lake, it was a thrush he was aping. White clematis and purple-fringed orchids delicately tinted the bank near our tent. . . .

"That night, a whippoorwill sang for us until we fell asleep. In the morning Bill knocked a log into the water for us to ride on. Trying to climb on it caused much glee, for it kept rolling over in the water and we couldn't hang on. . . .

"Most of the morning we sloshed along in the rain until we came to Alexandria, where we bought new sneakers, having outwalked our old ones. The storekeeper and his pals stopped their conversation to stare. We ate our lunch of crackers and cheese amid stony silence while gazing at the cattle-auction posters on the wall. . . .

"Before reaching Danbury, we met an old man and woman who wanted to know if we were walking for money. They complained that a wholesale coffin maker from Boston had told them that the local undertaker had profiteered during the flu epidemic, making ten dollars on every coffin he sold, that the doctors and nurses and other town members gave their services and it was a shame the undertaker could not have been equally kind. . . .

"Another old man came up to us as we were resting on the roadside and said he was terribly surprised to see two such nice-looking people (grins from us both) with nothing better to do than sit beside the road in the rain. (The grins vanished.) . . .

"It was a long hike into Canaan, where we were quite the curiosity of the town. While we were purchasing sody-water, onions and steak, Bill ran into a weather-beaten old major who, at Norwich University, had tried to teach him calculus, Bill's second attempt. This teacher was not the one Bill had asked, 'How come the formula?'

"Major Ethan Allen Shaw was in charge of a girls' camp five miles away and invited us to pitch our tent there. As he did not offer to give us a lift, we added another five miles to our day's hike. The next afternoon Ethan Allen gave us the use of a canoe and told the girls to observe how well we handled it. (We thought we did, too!) Having paddled out of sight of the girls, we got careless, and the canoe overturned. As we couldn't seem to right it, we started swimming it to shore. This was quite an undertaking, as the lake was big and we were right in the middle. A group of boy scouts, however, did their good deed for the day by helping us. What an embarrassing contrast to our cocky start was our bedraggled return. And to lower our spirits still more, it began to rain again. . . .

"On the Long Trail near the top of Mt. Killington, wet and cold, we reached a silo-like rest house after dark. Hearing voices within, we knocked and found four boy scouts getting ready for bed. After warming ourselves before the stove and eating supper, we laid our sleeping bag on a bed of spruce boughs. It was the first time I had ever slept in a room with five males. I slept beautifully."

The hike was considered so unusual that I was later interviewed by a reporter from a Boston paper. A long article, complete with photo, was signed with my name as if I had written it.

After a month on the hoof, Bill still did not know what he wanted to do. Cy Jones, my sister Barbara's fiancé, had a good position in the insurance department of the New York Central Railroad. He arranged to have Bill put in charge of the office and work as a bookkeeper at $105 per month.

Because of his carelessness and lack of interest, Bill came home at night with his hands and shirt covered with ink. He told me his books and desk at the office were in the same inky condition. The job lasted several months until he and the New York Central agreed it was best to part.

I had been doing volunteer occupational therapy at Roosevelt Hospital in New York City. But in February 1920 I got a paying job with the Red Cross as occupational therapy aide at the Brooklyn Naval Hospital. Because of my experience at Walter Reed, I was assigned to the psychopathic wards.

Now that I had a job, we could manage a home of our own; so we moved to a one-room furnished apartment on State Street, around the corner from my parents' house. The bed alcove was so small there was only enough space on one side of the three-quarter cot for each in turn to slide in crabwise. The cot had to be pushed from one side to the other in order to make it, and its butt end stuck out awkwardly into the living room.

Not finding what he wanted to do, Bill was restless and his drinking increased. A friend tried to get him a job in physical training at the YMCA, but this did not work out. He was athletic enough but had had no experience in gymnastics.

To "get away from it all" we took another camping trip when I had my vacation in July. This time it was on the 300-mile Long Trail along the tops of the Green Mountains in Vermont. The trail was started in 1910 by the Green Mountain Club. Members pledged themselves to construct sections of the trail. My dad, brother Rogers, and a longtime friend, Herbert Congdon (who used to take me to concerts before my engagement to Bill), had helped to clear a section of the trail.

Primitive log cabins had been erected at the end of an average day's hike, sometimes five miles apart, sometimes ten or twelve, according to the terrain. Most of the trail was very steep and rugged. The law of the camp required occupants to leave enough cut wood for the next traveler and to replace with something similar any food found and eaten in the cabin. If drinking water was not at hand, there were instructions.

This trip did help Bill reach a decision. His grandfather had always been anxious for him to become a lawyer. So by the time we returned home, he had decided to study law. Although not sure he wanted to be an attorney, he felt knowledge of the law would always be useful whether or not he became a lawyer. He resolved to enroll in a night course at the Brooklyn Law School, a division of St. Lawrence University. He kept at it conscientiously for four years until his graduation in 1924. After paying the fifteen-dollar fee for his diploma, he was too drunk to leave the apartment the next day to pick it up. He never bothered to get it. It could still be there.

It was not strange that he should have been influenced by his grandfather's ambitions for him. Bill's sense of homeland was always very strong. He liked to go back to East Dorset. He loved visiting with "the folks," as he called his Griffith grandparents and his Grandmother W., a charming lady who lived up the hill. And he loved to have long discussions with his old friend Mark Whalon, the local mail carrier, a genuine philosopher. I

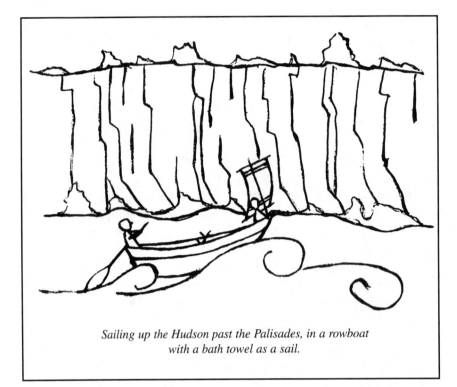

*Sailing up the Hudson past the Palisades, in a rowboat
with a bath towel as a sail.*

believe Bill never felt the same kind of friendship for any other man that
he felt for Mark. They spent hours tramping the woods together, and it was
Mark whom Bill first told about his interest in me.

Ten years older than Bill, Mark never wanted to change his simple country life, although he was a university graduate and trained as a pilot in
World War I. Bill often urged him to come to New York, but a job there
had no appeal for him. His mail route gave him time to think, to observe,
to meet backwoods characters whom he enjoyed, and to write poetry, a little of which was published.

Then there was Charley Richie, who played the fiddle. Charley, a French
Canadian, couldn't read or write but had helped Bill's grandfather work his
farm at the foot of the mountain. When Grandfather moved to the village,
Charley looked after the farm. He was soon calling it "my farm."

Charley used to drive his horse and buggy miles to a dance. Holding the
fiddle against his ribs, he would tap out the time with his foot. He knew all
the jigs and reels and could call as well as play for square dances. He used
to put fresh sawdust inside his violin— "to sweeten the tone," he'd say.

Charley constantly needed a housekeeper. Whenever one left him,
Charley would advertise in the local papers for another. One time one of
them got sick, and Charley sold her to two Polish brothers for two dol-

lars—whereupon she promptly died. A question then arose about who should pay for the burial. The Poles argued that Charley had sold them damaged goods, so they were not responsible. Charley insisted that the woman had been their property, as the bargain was sealed by the exchange of two dollars.

However, Charley had known very well that she had heart trouble, because he had told Bill her symptoms were the same as those of a horse he had once kept alive for a long time by giving it digitalis. Charley had figured he could do the same for the woman. The horse dose worked fine for a while, but suddenly she began to fail. Fearful she might die, he sold her to the Polish brothers.

Bill, called in to settle the argument, wrote her relatives that he would give them fifty dollars to come get the body. After some time, much too long for the comfort of the Poles, a funeral procession arrived and took the body back to Massachusetts.

People often turned to Bill for such help, even before he began studying law. From his early teacher, Mary Milotte, his dictionary studying and his voluminous reading, he had acquired a tremendous range of overall knowledge. His spelling was practically perfect, and he knew the capital, major cities, principal industry, rivers, mountains, lakes, volcanoes, and population of every country in the world. Years later, when he used one of these facts in conversation, he would say, "Well, at least that's the way Mary Milotte said it was."

In 1921 after Bill finished his law course, he was looking for work when he saw an ad stating that young men with broad general knowledge could compete for a job by taking a certain test. This turned out to be the first of the famous Edison tests, the theory being that better researchers could be found among people with a backlog of general information, on which specific training could be laid. Bill went to New Jersey to take the test and was intrigued to see Thomas A. Edison handing out the long test sheets. Several weeks later Edison offered Bill a job. Bill was very much surprised, since he had taken much longer to finish than most of the others. A reporter came to the house, and an interview with Bill was published in the *New York Times*.

But, by then, Bill had found a job as investigator of fraud and embezzlement for the United States Fidelity and Guaranty Company. This involved dealing with shady lawyers who were defending criminals charged with bribery and blackmail. The experience convinced him he did not want to become a lawyer. However, time proved he had been wise to study law. It was a help to him in many ways, especially years later in setting up AA's service structure.

It was also in 1921 that I changed jobs and we found a new home. While living in our furnished room on State Street, we heard of a very reasonable attic apartment of three rooms in a fine old residence on Amity Street. Prices had gone down in this section, recently occupied by Syrian immigrants. When the landlord, Salem Ghiz, showed us the rooms, we were as much taken with him and his wife, Sheba, as with the apartment itself. Bill started painting it and fixing it up with a few pieces of furniture Mother and Dad gave us. In September we moved in.

I had enjoyed my work at the Naval Hospital, but the Red Cross pay was below average. So in February 1921 I took a similar but better-paid job in the women's psychiatric ward at Bellevue Hospital. Mental defectives, alcoholics, epileptics, and psychopaths of many kinds were all mixed in the same ward. My work with them was absorbing, and I stayed there until September 1922.

That summer I became pregnant. It was the first of three ectopic pregnancies (growth of an impregnated ovum outside the uterus—in my case, in a fallopian tube). My dad recognized immediately what was the matter and put me to bed in the old home on Clinton Street, where he could look after me. He knew that a healthy body such as mine could often recover naturally without an operation, even after the bursting of a tube. The first time, that is what happened. The following July, I had another ectopic in the other tube. This time, Dad sent me immediately to the Skene Sanitarium, where he was on the staff. A colleague of Dad's operated on me, and I went to the Camp in Vermont to recuperate under Dad's supervision.

But instead of recovering, I kept feeling worse and worse. I wanted so badly to return to Bill that I pretended I was improving, and Dad finally let me go home.

Bill put me right to bed, where I stayed for several weeks. When he realized I was not getting better, he called Leonard Strong, his doctor brother-in-law, who recognized that a cyst had developed on what was left of the ovary after the operation. He suggested we call the surgeon who had operated. After a cursory examination this doctor advised a laxative, assuming that I was simply constipated. Bill knew better than that and immediately called Dad in Vermont. Dad jumped on the train, and in no time I was back in the Skene Sanitarium for the removal of an ovarian cyst. Then recovery was rapid.

In May 1923 the improbable happened—a third ectopic. I was tutoring a young girl in Latin when I felt the first symptoms. After another operation I made a quick recovery. By then both tubes and the complete cystic ovary had been removed. A small portion of the other ovary was kept so that I might retain my feminine characteristics, it was said. Bill was often too drunk, for days at a time, to come to see me in the hospital.

We had both deeply desired a family. But after my second ectopic, Bill and I knew positively that we could never have children. My tubes had apparently been closed since birth. Bill, even when drunk, took this overwhelming disappointment with grace and with kindness to me. But his drinking had been increasing steadily. It seemed that after all hope of having children had died, his bouts with alcohol had become even more frequent.

I knew I had done nothing to prevent our having children; yet somehow I could not help feeling guilty. So how could I blame him for the increase in his drinking?

This kind of thinking made me try harder to understand him and to be tolerant when he was drunk. But there were many times when I lost my temper. He never hit me, but I hit him. I remember with shame one time toward the end of his drinking, when I was so angry as he lay drunk on the bed that I beat his chest with both my fists as hard as I could.

Several years after we learned we could never have children of our own, and when we felt financially able, we applied to the Spence-Chapin child-adoption agency for a baby. As time went on and we heard nothing, we inquired several times, and the agency always replied that the suitable child had not yet been found.

But Bill was always sure that the real reason was his drinking. Only a short time ago, in 1974, I learned that this was so. We had given to Spence-Chapin the names of a few of our friends as references. One of my best and oldest friends responded to the agency by saying she considered that we would not make reliable parents because Bill drank to excess.

In those years, however, our world was not completely closed in by alcoholism. We had many interests, and our lives seemed full.

One of Bill's hobbies provided a welcome distraction for me. While living at Clinton Street in 1919, I had had a great thrill. To surprise me Bill placed on my ears the phones of a crystal radio set he had built. I knew nothing about radio and for a few fantastic moments thought I was hearing the "music of the spheres."

Bill enjoyed my excitement and then told me about radio waves. What I had heard was gramophone music sent over the air by an amateur operator in Schenectady, experimenting with sending as Bill was with receiving. Even now the mystery of radio haunts me. What other great forces may there be, unseen and unknown?

When we moved to Amity Street, Bill built a bigger and better set—a superheterodyne, it was called. On a chart we kept from 1923 to 1925, there were thirty-seven stations we could reach, all amateur and as far away as Montreal, Savannah, Dallas, Minneapolis, and Los Angeles, Our friends came to the apartment to hear this great novelty. Bill built several other sets, gave one to my parents and one to his grandfather, and sold a few.

While I was convalescing from the last operation, I helped him make these sets by doing some of the mechanical work. One of these superheterodynes was perfectly good when we moved to Bedford Hills, twenty years later.

I also studied Braille and transcribed several stories from the *Saturday Evening Post*, such as Arthur Train's "Tutt and Mr. Tutt," which I sent to the Library of Congress for circulation among the blind. I so greatly love seeing the beauties of the natural world that I have always been particularly sorry for those who cannot see.

It was not until October 1923 that I returned to work. I went back to the Naval Hospital at an increased salary, because the civil service had taken over the occupational therapy department.

Even without transportation of our own, we managed somehow to get outdoors on weekends. We would hike in Van Cortland Park; take the train to Croton-on-Hudson and walk back along the aqueduct; or sail on the Hudson River in a rented rowboat with a bath towel for a sail, hitched to an oar for a mast. One time, to find a breeze and outwit the mosquitoes, we slept on the bottom of the boat while it was anchored at the edge of the steamship channel—a mighty risky business!

We had a favorite spot on a brook not too far from a New Jersey village called Haledon, in an area that was then pure country and could be reached by ferry, trolley, and hoof. It is almost impossible to believe now, when it is all built up, that we used to camp there under a spreading oak. The early morning jumps *au naturel* into the brook were so stimulating that Bill coined the phrase "brook-jumper," an expression we used all the rest of our lives to signify the joy of living.

To me, getting away for the weekend also meant getting away from liquor; but Bill always seemed as happy as I was to spend time in the open. It was fun just being together, enjoying the same things. Maybe part of the reason we liked it was that neither of us was entirely grown-up. We liked to play games, not serious games like cards or chess, but silly games of our own devising.

We had exhausted most of the inexpensive nearby trips and wished we had a car, but knew we couldn't afford one. So we compromised and bought a Harley-Davidson motorcycle with a sidecar.

The three-wheeler turned out to be a godsend. We drove up to Vermont to see Bill's grandfather just before he died, and were able to spend splendid weekends in the country sections of New Jersey, Connecticut, and Westchester and Long Island in New York. There was a neck of land extending out into Long Island Sound at Northport, Long Island, where we loved to dig clams for supper before spending the night on the beach.

One time we took Mother there in the sidecar and had a grand clam and flounder feast. She went to bed in the tent while Bill and I slept on the sand under the stars.

Another time we took one of the sailors from the Naval Hospital with us, an Englishman who had joined our Navy and enjoyed outdoor life.

Once we drove to Vermont on a cold winter night. I can still see the gorgeous sunrise and feel the cold air sting my face as we sped up Storm King Mountain. Our Syrian landlord had given us a bottle of arrack, a potent liquor, to warm us on the motorcycle. Bill shared the bottle with me and behaved very well.

However, when he made dandelion wine in East Dorset or bathtub gin at Amity Street during Prohibition, he could never leave it alone long enough to mature. It was always raw when he drank it. It made him sick as well as drunk.

Bill's work for the United States Fidelity and Guaranty Company often took him to Wall Street, where he made contacts with several brokerage houses. He felt strongly that customers as well as brokers ought to know more about the companies whose stocks they dealt in. People gambled with stocks as they would with poker chips. When Bill's grandfather wanted to purchase a cow, he went to look at the cow, feel its legs, and inquire about how much milk it gave, its age, forebears, and so on. Why shouldn't these same precautions be applied to buying stocks?

For some time Bill had wanted to do this sort of investigating. Though none of his Wall Street friends encouraged him, his own conviction was so strong that he decided in 1925 to take a year to test his theory.

I wanted to get away, too, but my reasons were different. I was so concerned about Bill's drinking that I wanted to get him away from New York and its bars. I felt sure that during a year in the open I would be able to straighten him out.

So in April 1925, in spite of advice from many of our family and friends who thought we were crazy, we gave up our jobs and our apartment on Amity Street and made the motorcycle ready to be our home for many a day.

From Sears Roebuck, we bought a 7' x 7' explorer's tent with a canvas bottom and an entrance covered by a mosquito-netting and a flap. I put a window in it like those in more expensive tents. A mattress filled with kapok, was warm and soft and yet so light it could be rolled into a small bundle. Seven army blankets were sewn together on three sides to make a fine sleeping bag, better than the store variety, for we could choose the proper layer according to the weather, sleeping under one on warm nights and four or five on cold ones. Each morning the blankets could be turned inside out to air and to rotate their use. A toilet-article kit was made out of black oilcloth, lined with rubber and bound with gray tape, looking quite stylish. It had plenty of room for pajamas and towels in addition to the toilet articles. Waterproof oiled-silk bags, which occupied very little space, carried our food. Rainy weather would not bother us too much; I had made for both of us waterproof, zippered coveralls to keep out wind and wet; and waterproof covers for every box and bundle were laboriously fashioned out of army-shelter halves.

We took along four huge Moody's manuals on industry; each as large as an unabridged Webster, for Bill's study of the companies he wanted to investigate. And before taking off, he bought two shares each of General Electric and Giant Portland Cement, expecting to soon look into the GE plant at Schenectady and the Giant at Egypt, Pennsylvania.

We felt well-prepared for anything. Crazy or not, it was fun to anticipate the open road and unknown adventures ahead. The next two chapters are excerpts from a diary I kept on this trip, but since I sent it home weekly to Mother, I avoided any mention of Bill's drinking—which luckily turned out to be infrequent. This misled me into thinking he wasn't going to drink much in the future.

4

Two Motorcycle Hoboes

Off at last! What a time we had hitching and tying our duffle on the motorcycle! Passersby must have thought we were bound for the Arctic with presents for all the Eskimos. In the bow of the sidecar, on its rear, behind the driver or between the two seats, we found niches for everything—books, radio, gasoline stove, basket of provisions, seven army blankets, a mattress, a small trunk of clothes, a tent, and many odds and ends. Each of us wore several layers of underwear and many strata of sweaters. We had both tossed up good jobs and had only eighty dollars for a long trip. However, we planned to stop and earn money whenever our slim funds ran out.

It was mighty cold in April riding a motorcycle without a windshield, but breathing in the ozone as we whizzed along was so invigorating we hardly felt it. As I sat in the driver's seat and turned on the gas, the sense of power—somehow mine, not the machine's—was tremendous.

Near Poughkeepsie, New York, we found a splendid spot for our first camp, a glade in the woods beside a brook, sheltered from the wind. Yellow and blue violets spattered the grass in front of the tent, and bloodroots whitened the hillside.

After studying the whims of our new gasoline cooking stove and lighting it many times only to have it blown out by the wind, we finally caught the knack and enjoyed a hot supper in front of a log fire. We could hardly wait until dark to try out the tent's electric light, which Bill hooked up to the motorcycle battery. Right after supper we crawled under the blankets to read for several hours while listening to the radio Bill had built. Such comfort and luxury for motorcycle hoboes!

Just after dawn we took our baths in the brook while the sun was drawing the frost from the ground and making a great steam about it in the treetops. The spot was so lovely we dawdled over our breakfast.

The next evening we pitched our tent at Emerald Lake. Although the night sky had been studded with beautiful stars, we awoke to six inches of snow. Gritting our teeth, we ran down to the lake and plunged in. Surprisingly the water was warmer than the air, but we didn't loiter and hurried back to the warm tent. After a vigorous rubdown we tingled and glowed all over.

Then we got the keys from Charley, the local handyman, and made ourselves at home at the Camp. Bill's grandfather had died the previous summer in nearby East Dorset, and we planned to stay a week or so to find and tie together the loose ends of his estate.

The next morning I noticed a clumsy insect on a rock near the lake. With wings tightly furled it was emerging from a hard, beetle-like case. For years I had wondered what funny little bugs came from those ugly, brown shells seen in the spring near the water's edge. So I carried it to the porch to watch. Its six legs were out, and I could see where they and the folded wings had fitted into their housing. Slowly drawing its rather chunky body free of the casing, it began to teeter and seesaw. To my astonishment its body lengthened and grew thinner until it was twice as long as the shell it had discarded. At last, apparently satisfied with its slender length, it began to unfurl its crumpled wings, which soon became smooth and transparent. Then before my eyes the dragonfly lifted high four glistening, iridescent green wings, so beautiful, bright, and shimmery they took my breath away. Fluttering them experimentally a few times, the dragonfly flew several feet to the porch railing, where it poised a moment before plunging into the big world. It soared only a few yards before a phoebe bird darted down and gobbled it up. I sat down and cried.

There had been so much rain that our brook gushed and foamed down the mountainside. I was using one of its shallow pools as an icebox. One morning the cupboard was bare. I found butter and bacon way down under a bridge, but a quart of milk had disappeared entirely, swept out to sea, no doubt.

It took Bill much longer than we had expected to tie up the loose ends of Gramp's estate, and the prolonged stay ate up most of our eighty dollars. We had to find work immediately.

Bill hoped to get a job at the General Electric Company in Schenectady, New York, where he had a double purpose: to learn about the company and to earn enough money for another leg of our journey. But on the way he wanted first to look into the waterpower development on top of the Green Mountains near Readsboro, Vermont.

We found what we thought was a perfect spot to camp with a lovely view, but perfection was short-lived. Late that evening a thunderstorm came up, and it rained all night. This was a chance to test our new tent's waterproof floor. We had always dug a ditch around our pup tent for drainage, but we thought this unnecessary with the new explorer's tent.

About three in the morning I felt dampness seeping through from the bottom and awakened Bill. He discovered the tent was standing in a small lake three inches deep. After sponging up the water and pushing a mass of ferns under the tent floor to raise it, we belatedly dug a ditch and slept fairly dry the rest of the night.

What pleased us, though, about the test run of the tent was that the window I had meticulously made, with mosquito-screen netting and a waterproof shade, had not leaked a drop.

In the morning the sun and the wind dried everything thoroughly. But we had learned a lesson: always dig a ditch around a tent, even one with a canvas bottom—and a window!

Near Schenectady, New York, we got permission to camp on an attractive farm owned by a Polish family named Morowski.

The following day we both looked for jobs in town, as our capital had by now sunk to four dollars. Work was slack, and other companies as well as General Electric were laying off employees.

I tried for a salesclerk's job in a department store, but the man would not take me on my face alone; he said that I should come back with references, and if I had experience in selling linens, he would take me immediately. My selling experience being as nonexistent as my references, I was out of luck.

A sign hung in front of a restaurant saying "Dishwasher Wanted," but I could not bring myself to go in. Before this I'd had a theory that it would be interesting to take any job for the experience as well as the pay. But reality often explodes theory. After three days neither of us had found work.

The youngest Morowski boy, Leon, was obviously subnormal and decidedly unprepossessing, but he was a big help, bringing water and keeping stray cows and little boys from disturbing our things. His conversation mainly comprised "You wop?" and "When ya goin' git married?" We later guessed how his interest in matrimony had arisen. When his mother visited us, she talked only about her friends' marriages, the chances of her daughters' marrying, her own marriage, and just matrimony in general.

The next morning she came running out in the rain waving a newspaper, containing a want ad for a farmhand. We set out immediately. The rain simply poured down, causing a short circuit in the motorcycle. We hated taking the time to fix it, scared someone else would nab the job.

No one else did—but neither did we. The farmer, however, told us about neighbors, the Goldfoots, who might need two people.

Upon arriving at this second farm we must have looked so wet and bedraggled that we were engaged out of pity, for the folks kept reiterating they should not spend money for help that season. Bill's boast that he was a good milker clinched the matter in our favor. So we became hired help at seventy-five dollars a month for both, with board and keep. I was to assist with the housework; Bill, to milk and work in the fields.

For several days we could barely keep up with our bosses. Mrs. G. was a human dynamo. As I was willing to do all the housework, she was free to work in the fields, which she loved. She was worth three of her husband. Though tireless, he was a putterer, going around in circles. He had little mechanical sense, so most of Bill's time those rainy days (when he wasn't milking ten of the twenty cows night and morning) was spent doctoring broken machinery and tools. When we first came, no haying could be done. But soon Bill had repaired the hay-wagon pole, the tedder (the big fork that lifted hay into the barn by horse pulley), and the mowing machine.

Robert, a wistful, cowed, and overworked youngster about eleven years old, was an orphan being brought up by the Goldfoots. They were good-natured and kind, but they didn't seem to realize that a young boy needs something besides work, work, work. Robert constantly plied Bill with whys and wherefores.

He was so timid he was afraid to do anything but eat. When asked whether he wanted to drive the hay rake or do something mildly adventurous, his one reply would be "I daresn't take a chancet." He did enjoy being treated to a motorcycle ride, but he held on tight all the way.

Besides helping with the milking, haying, churning, and water carrying, Robert's particular job was feeding the livestock: four horses, hundreds of chickens, eight pigs, twenty cows, one bull, twelve calves, six cats, and one dog. The cats were the favorites of the establishment and had to be fed hot potatoes mashed up in either gravy or warm milk. No cold, dried-up stuff for them!

Never having made a pie before in my life, I made two on my first attempt, a blackberry and a custard, as well as six blackberry tarts. They were darn good if I do say so. I hoped my luck would continue, for I had not confessed my ignorance to my boss. Mother had tucked a little cook-book into our duffle, and that saved the day.

Such appetites! One day I spent an hour frying forty-eight slices of squash. And so many potatoes! We ate potatoes three times a day, some-times sliced and fried, sometimes diced and fried, sometimes baked, creamed, mashed, or just plain boiled. We even had potato cakes. I would not Frenchfry them for that bunch, because I would have been at the stove all night. I grew sick of potatoes!

On Saturday we were exceptionally busy. At night the folks were still in the fields, haying by lantern light. It was midnight before the dishes were washed. By then three meals had been prepared, three sets of dishes washed, a pudding, two pies, and a cake with icing made for the weekend, nine milk pails and a separator washed in the morning and again at night, windows and lamp chimneys cleaned, lamps and oilstone filled, range blackened, floor swept twice and mopped thoroughly, rugs and porch swept, and my knickers mended.

When we had first arrived, we had gotten terribly tired, but by the end of the week we were beginning to really enjoy it. After supper each night Bill went up to our room (Mrs. G. called it "the office") and studied his books, the four Moody's manuals, while I wrote and Mr. and Mrs. G. listened to our radio, which Bill had rigged up for them.

Sunday was ours—except for morning and evening chores. The first thing we did was to take a bath in a nearby stream. It was certainly great to wash in something larger than a basin.

Afterward we visited the Adirondack Light and Power steam plant on the Mohawk River, an experimental station for GE, and then drove on to Amsterdam in such holiday spirit that we hunted for something reckless to do. Nothing more exciting turned up than gorging ourselves on three ice-cream sodas apiece. Shocking!

Driving home under a flaming sunset sky, we reached the farm just in time for the milking.

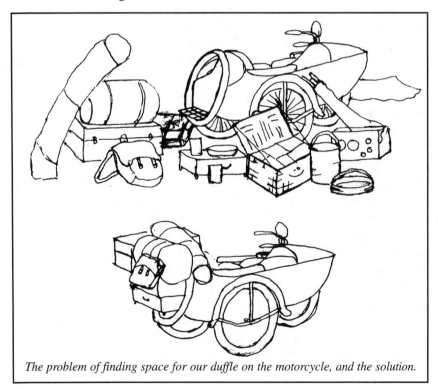

The problem of finding space for our duffle on the motorcycle, and the solution.

Our first week as farmhands had ended.

The next day Bill was astonished by the missus saying she had to kill a calf to take to market. Sure enough, before the men finished milking, she had caught and killed one and strung it up on a pulley, all quartered and ready to go to town. Nothing fazed her. She certainly was the "swash-buckler" Bill called her.

Bill and I often had a hard time keeping our faces straight when we were listening to our male boss. He talked incessantly; everything he said was parenthetic to something else, which he seldom reached. Trying to decide whether to water the horses before or after supper, he changed his mind a dozen times and then ended by "asking Ella" (Mrs. G.). One night when there was an unexpected letter for them, Pa strode to the door for light, read out loud an invitation to a "variety shower" and was obviously puzzled. Coming back to the table, he sat quietly while I explained what a variety shower was. Then, thinking of some point he wanted to verify, he went to the door again to reread the note. Discussing the matter and starting to sit down, he didn't quite make it before another point took him to the door again. He must have done this at least five times. We stuffed potatoes into our mouths to keep from howling.

The old man could not rake a straight row of hay to save his life. Bill said he tried to rake his name in hay. When an appealing wisp at a distance caught his eye, he headed for it, but a still more irresistible bit off at an angle changed his course again. Bill, the missus, and Robbie laughed all one afternoon at his capers, until he finally turned the rake at too sharp an angle and broke it.

One day the boss had a couple of teeth out. When he complained, the missus' replied, "Why don't ya keep ya mouth shet? Ya go around chin-waggin' all day, and ya mouth gits full of fog."

Robert said funny things, too. He called bunching hay after it had been raked "doodling the hay." One time when it looked like rain, Robbie said, "Oh, dear! We jest doodled the hay, and now we got to undoodle it all."

Robert changed greatly in our first two weeks, often smiling and even getting the giggles when Bill played with him. While haying, Bill would say, "Sock 'em, Robbie," or "Stomp 'em down, Robbie." When Robert mumbled sulkily, Bill would say, "Speak up like a man, Robbie," and Robbie smiled and spoke up. He followed Bill everywhere.

When we left the Goldfoots, the ninety-three dollars and seventy-five cents we received seemed pretty big to us after having been so flat broke. But believe me we worked for every penny of it. We did hate to leave Robbie and wished we had more to give him than one of our Ernest Thompson Seton nature books.

We then headed for Hudson, where Bill looked into a couple of cement plants. One was fine; the other, second-rate. At our new camping spot the tent was pitched under a cedar tree with a barberry bush at its base.

I took this opportunity to do our week's washing and hung it on a low line. Upon our return from a walk I noticed a lot of grasshoppers on the clothes. Closer inspection showed the woolens and silks—animal products—were simply riddled with tiny holes, while the cottons—vegetable matter—were not eaten at all. I caught a couple of grasshoppers in the act of devouring my only pair of silk stockings. How pure their taste—nothing cheap or sleazy for them! What a terrible thing that plague of locusts mentioned in the Bible must have been.

Bill had been very much interested in the stock of the Giant Portland Cement Company, so our next stop was Egypt, Pennsylvania. With permission from the owners of a field near the town, we pitched our tent there, overlooking a valley where red spires of sumac and purple asters complemented each other.

It rained and blew every minute of the four days of our stay. For about one hundred hours we slept, dressed, read, wrote, listened to the radio, received visitors, cooked, ate, and washed dishes—and Bill drank—in that seven-by-seven area. The tent and its appurtenances, including us, began to show wear and tear.

Bill drank most on the rainy day when a neighbor with a bottle came to visit us. Bill kept him company drink for drink, then went to town for another bottle after the neighbor left. Bill continued to drink some until the rain stopped.

I took several walks in the rain, and Bill somehow managed to go to the plant almost every day. When he wasn't drinking, he used every spare moment to write a detailed report on Giant—its management, efficiency, production, labor situation, and prospects for future growth—to send to Frank Shaw, the only one of his Wall Street friends who might be interested in paying for such a service. And Bill bought a little stock himself, giving two shares (thirty-seven dollars' worth) to Mother and Dad for Christmas.

We continued our journey south. When we reached Washington, a friend directed us to a hotel, where we reveled in hot baths and clean clothes before dining with him at the University Club. It seemed queer to be so grand after having been so . . . otherwise.

I wanted to go to Walter Reed Hospital to visit the occupational therapy department, where I had worked during the war. Before going, I called a friend, Peggy Beckwith, President Lincoln's great-granddaughter, who spent her summers in Manchester. Peggy and I first visited the Corcoran Art Gallery, then had lunch at her home, a fascinating, two-story, white house with green shutters and fir trees on either side of the front door—it looked just like a Christmas card. One of the oldest in Georgetown, the house had a passageway to the Potomac, used, they said, to help slaves escape during the Underground Railroad days.

Afterward she drove me to the hospital. Unfortunately occupational therapy was over for the week. Although we had a great day, I missed my sentimental reminiscing in the OT department.

Bill spent hours at the Patent Office and the Congressional Library and was excited about all he learned. However, living in Washington cost too much, and we soon hit the road again.

Everybody in the South lived up to its reputation for cordiality, but the "sunny South" seemed a myth to us. After we left Washington, it grew dark and began to pour, so we were forced to crawl all the way into Fredericksburg, Virginia, on slippery, red-clay roads, between endless, tall, dark pines.

We ate rabbit for the first time at an old-fashioned boardinghouse, and when we were finally bedded down for the night, I continued to feel as if I were still riding the motorcycle. I kept seeing the reflecting silver screen of raindrops between walls of tall, dark pines until at last I fell asleep.

The next day on the road a car with a New York license passed us, its occupants shouting, "See you in Miami." Later they stopped. When we asked whether they needed help, they hollered back that we could help make away with their extra hot coffee and sandwiches. We felt as much excitement and camaraderie among those en route to Florida as if we had all been seeking our fortunes in the Klondike.

Virginia was heavily wooded—pines and pines and almost tropical tangles of briar and southern smilax, reminding me of Brer Rabbit and Uncle Remus. It was also the "shootin'est" place. You'd have thought by the sound that each day was the Fourth of July. Every other man and boy carried a gun. It was the Christmas season, and making as much noise as possible seemed part of the celebration.

When we reached Danville, almost on the North Carolina border, we found lots of mail and a big Christmas package from home, filled with all sorts of good things. Even more important was a check from Frank Shaw, with a letter congratulating Bill on his Giant Cement report and promising to buy some of the stock and put it in Bill's name. He suggested that Bill continue his investigations and make reports on other companies. Bill wasn't particularly surprised, because he had always felt this would happen, and I was delighted that his efforts were being recognized.

Noticing a pine grove on a sidehill out of the wind, we inquired at a log cabin if we could camp there. The folks seemed pleased, and an old man, Mr. Brown, and his grandsons helped set up our camp. So there we were, ensconced in a tent—to spend Christmas. Although it was bitter cold, we hoped to be cozy enough with the aid of newspapers, heated stones, and our faithful hot-water bottle.

Early Christmas morning old Mr. Brown came over to invite us to Christmas dinner. Such hospitality! And we did not learn its full extent until we had been there several days.

The senior Browns lived in one log cabin; the juniors and their children in another. My tall Bill had to bend to enter the low doors. There was one small window in each room, and the whitewash on the log walls helped only slightly to lighten the dark interior.

The whole family gathered around the grandparents' kitchen table for Christmas dinner; five of the six children had to stand, as there were not enough chairs. Salt pork, turnip greens, sweet-potato custard, corn pone (coarse white cornmeal, salt and water stirred together, then baked in a frying pan), cake decorated with jellybeans, and the vilest coffee we'd ever tasted. We learned later that coffee beans bought green had been roasted and ground, and the brew (I cannot again call it coffee) had grown bitterer as it was reboiled over and over. The old grounds mounted until, of necessity, they had to be emptied; even then half an inch of used grounds was kept to "sweeten the pot."

The children were too excited to eat anything but cake, jellybeans, and custard, although they drank that awful brew. Probably they had dessert only at Christmas, so were allowed to make the most of it.

Sharecropping tobacco for a living, the Robert Lee Browns were paid only when the crop was sold, generally after Christmas. If the yield was poor, very little money remained after their rent was deducted. Mr. Brown took us into one of the delightfully fragrant tobacco barns—a small, log building with big, crinkled leaves hanging from every rafter. Chimney pipes from the brick fireplace ran around inside the shack to dry the tobacco.

In spite of being terribly hard up, they were a jolly crowd, apparently quite free of self-pity. As the children had received no Christmas presents that year, other than a little knitted cap given the baby by his grandfather and a few jellybeans for the others, Mrs. Junior hoped to get a doll for Barna with the first dollar she could spare. She had had eight children and looked older than my mother, yet she was about my age, in her early thirties. A cheerful, capable soul, she was always coming up with a bright answer or a joke.

Saturday we dined at the Juniors' on the identical menu we'd had on Christmas, the old folks bringing the food over with them. Robert Lee Jr. was away looking for Santa Claus. His search must have been successful, for he returned slightly "aweather." His Santa was an uncle who had a still in the bush.

We felt both couples would be really hurt if we refused their invitations to dinner. The next day we took over much of the food Mother had sent

us, including a greatly enjoyed canned plum pudding. Perhaps not surprisingly the kids had never before tasted it, nor butter, nor celery. They
oohed and aahed over the candy, crackers, and peanuts (known here as
"goobers"), as well as the Christmas cards, fancy wrappings, and ribbons
from our gift box.

In the evenings, with the baby crawling on the warm floorboards before
us, we all sat around the open fire, telling stories. Flickering flames silhouetted dancing giants on the rear wall. The men chewed dried tobacco leaves,
kept in a jar on the mantel, while the women gnawed on sticks of snuff. The
hiss of spitting into the fire was continuous, and all the honors for aim and
distance were held by the old lady. Several times passersby stopped for hot
water to thaw their radiators and were invited to join the circle.

Both families urged us to sleep inside. They said the cold had seldom
been so intense. The bluebird we saw hadn't expected this cold either. We
also saw lots of cardinals and, of course, plenty of buzzards, one or more
of which had circled over our heads all the way down from Washington.

When we left "Camp Robert Lee," the family all turned out to see us off.
They surely were good to us and seemed sorry to have us go.

As soon as we reached Charlotte, we got a room in a small hotel and
took long, hot baths while work was being done on the motorcycle. The
next morning we found an inch and a half of snow on the windowsill.
Our machine skidded badly in the snow, so we didn't dare start south.
Snowbound!

I spent the time fixing up a box for the Browns: a doll for Barna, ten-
cent-store toys for the boys and a little knitted jacket for the baby, to match
the cap her grandfather had given her.

Bill called on a few odd bankers (not that these were any odder than any
other bankers). One had phoned another that "Mr. W — — of New York
is here." The magic words, the open sesame, everywhere in the South
seemed to be "New York." On the other hand the people insisted that the
growth of the South was entirely due to their own energies and imagination. They would stoutly say, "This town is growing from within, without
any help from the outside."

Although the snow persisted on the ground, we were spending so much
money for room and food and for movies on three nights, a real extrava-
gance, that we simply had to go camping again. So daringly on we went
down the slippery roads to the Southern Power Company's steam plant at
Mount Holly on the Catawba River. The fine big layout pleased Bill. Then,
before driving into Gastonia, we shoveled away snow and put boughs
underneath the tent at a not-very-good camping place in piney woods.

Gastonia was called the "City of Spindles," because it had at that time
more cotton mills than any other city in the South. Bill, wearing his knit-

ted cap and his traveling coveralls ("uber-alles," we called them), much tattered and generally disreputable, strode into the chamber of commerce office and asked for pamphlets about the city. The clerk, looking him up and down, inquired superciliously what he could possibly want with them.

The next day the sun was bright, the sky a deep blue, and the ground and mountains white with snow as we climbed the Blue Ridge through gorgeous scenery. The road wound, circled, horseshoed, and tied itself in knots all the way from Chimney Rock to Asheville.

The mountains, not in long ranges as they are in Vermont, poked up here and there in separate peaks. Asheville, on a high plateau with a circle of mountain caps around it, was like a huge pie with a crinkly crust. The higgledy-piggledy city was dingy, but the surrounding scenery was superb.

As we climbed down from the plateau, wonderful vistas across deep gorges took our breath away. The birds were lovely, too. The vireo, with its haunting song that one also hears on mountaintops in the North, filled us with nostalgia.

That night, sitting around the fire, we were startled by the most unearthly scream. It had to be some creature in its death throes—perhaps a horse in mortal agony or a hog being butchered. However, when we heard the anguished sound again in the morning, it hit a chord from Bill's Army days. It was the braying of a mule. How could he ever have forgotten it!

The cold was so severe that water froze on the dishes before I could wipe them; Bill's dampened hair stiffened upright before he could comb it; and with each mouthful of bread we bit off butter from the unspreadable stick.

Bill spent nearly one whole day writing a letter to Frank Shaw, thirty-odd pages. Before he finished, while the sun sparkled on snow and water, we walked up an old wood road over a rickety bridge across a stream overhung with rhododendrons.

Upon our return I tied two shelter halves to trees around the fire, making a cave for myself, and took a grand old bath while Bill wrote.

Several mornings the inside of the tent was covered with tiny crystals—from our breath, I imagine. Living in a tent can be far from dull. When a car went by at night, its lights turned objects in between into fantastic silhouettes on the fabric of the tent; in moonlight grasses and boughs sketched decorative patterns on the walls; and seen from the outside when our electric light was lit inside, the green, translucent tent seemed eerie, like a fairy habitation that might fly away at any moment.

5

Seashells and Flat Tires

We broke camp and drove the eight miles into Marion because Bill wanted to see James Lake, a tremendous storage reservoir for the Southern Power Company. Its 150 miles of shoreline were being considered for a real-estate development. When we questioned a caretaker, he answered, "No, there ain't many summer people coming here yet, praise be! They and the campers that don't do any real work are the ruination of the country!" That for us!

We camped that night in a stunning wild spot near a place named Tuccoa-on-the-Tugalo. The clear brook, rippling over the rocks, reminded us of Vermont.

In South Carolina the next day, the roads worsened until, upon reaching Georgia, they became unspeakable. Pushing on in order to make Atlanta before the prophesied rain, we traveled through parts of three states and wound up at ten o'clock at night in a mudhole called Alto, and I mean literally a hole of mud. The sidecar where I sat was sunk completely out of sight, so that my elbows were level with the mud, while the motorcycle itself stood on terra firma. The machine was tilted at such an angle that Bill, a leaning tower above me, was in imminent danger of tottering off the seat.

When he walked into the little town for help, all were abed. However, he did find a huge beam and a plank. After unloading everything from the machine, we began to dig. The clay mud was so sticky it kept sucking my shoes off. Finally succeeding in getting a path dug, we put down the plank, and while Bill pried the bike with the beam, I pushed—and out she came. It was then after midnight, and as the road ahead probably was no better, we pitched the tent right there, between the road and the railroad tracks, and fell asleep immediately. Soon we were awakened by the nostalgic sound of a train whistling in the distance. Then we were terrified by its onward rush—it seemed to be coming right into our tent.

In the morning we were so anxious to decamp that we didn't even bother to look for water to wash or make coffee. But we seemed glued to the area. After moving less than 100 yards we bogged down again. Later we learned there was a perfectly good detour used by the well-informed, but no one had bothered to put up signs.

All this red mud grew tiresome to look at as well as dig at. Fields of cotton and corn had to be terraced to prevent erosion. Many deep red gashes scarred the countryside. The terraced effect of the fields, however, was picturesque.

Georgia seemed flat and rockless. So before we reached Atlanta, it was astonishing to see the tremendous Stone Mountain rising almost perpendicularly from the plain, a most fitting and majestic national monument! Three men, held by ropes to steel shafts sunk in the rock face, were carving with electric drills, but only General Lee's head was finished. The work appeared both perilous and costly.

As soon as we arrived in Atlanta, Bill called up an old friend from East Dorset, Joe Reed, who knew everyone.

The friendliness of the people was the nicest thing in the South. Everyone spoke to you; old gentlemen touched their hats as we passed. When I remarked to Joe how charming I found this custom, he told me it was dying out because Northern women, misunderstanding, refused to return the bow. Soon after, while I was walking alone, a man in a car took off his hat to me and bowed. Not to be thought a stuffy Northerner, I nodded my head slightly. He immediately stopped his car and said, "How about a ride, kiddo?"

In bowing—as in everything else—discretion is necessary, I learned.

After leaving there we camped near Griffin in a beautiful pine grove under a romantic full moon. Spanish moss veiling the trees deepened the mystery of the woods. Being an air plant, it drapes itself on anything handy, telephone wires or fence rails. But it kills the fruit trees, they said. Bill heard of a cement plant at Clinchfield, Georgia, about twenty miles away. He asked an old codger how to get there. The man said he didn't know, because he had never been there, adding, "I never go any place where I haven't been before."

When we finally did get to Clinchfield, the boss of the cement plant was away, to return the next day. We set up housekeeping in another pine grove, where the cones were nearly a foot long, their scales spread out like the petals of a flower.

In the morning Bill went to the cement plant and found it both modern and efficient. The quarries contained more clay and sand and less rock than those in the North. Wages were lower and production was easier, therefore cheaper.

Upon entering Florida we expected there would at least be decent roads, since a land boom was going on. But instead we bumped over washboard and crawled in low gear for nearly twenty miles. The endless swamps were monotonous, but what really depressed us was that this terrain was all staked out for building lots.

While we were eating a snack beside the road, an old black hog tried to join the party. Pigs in the South were either brown, black, or spotted black and tan, like the limerick's Hottentot man. So-called domestic animals turned up in the strangest places. Cows, hogs, and goats ran wild through woods and swamps. On the road you never knew when an animal would pop out in front of you.

A fine hard-top road led into Jacksonville, but the tourist camp where we stayed for several days was miserable, crowded with all sorts of harum-scarum people. Nothing was safe if left outside. Many people lived there from week to week. Some had jobs, but most had no money and could neither go home nor travel farther south. Like Mr. Micawber, they were waiting for something to turn up.

We found much kindness there, too. A little girl had died in camp, and the other tourists chipped in for her burial. One man's tent burned down, and the campers joined forces to buy him an even better one.

Leaving the tourist camp and crossing the toll bridge to Ormond Beach, I let the motor out all the way, and we whizzed along on the magnificent hard sand until suddenly we stopped dead. Looking down, I saw the carburetor hanging by a thread. We had nearly lost it.

The next day, just at suppertime, we arrived in Orlando at the home of Percy and Dora Strobel, son and daughter-in-law of Bill's stepfather, Dr. Charles Strobel. They were expecting us to stay with them a few days.

Saturday our hosts and their two boys took us for a picnic on Cocoa Beach. We saw many kinds of heron stalking the black waters of the cypress swamps while mud turtles basked in the sun. The blue sky and gray moss set off the delicious new red of the maples. While we ate lunch on the beach, sandpipers gingerly picked their way along the water's edge, and pelicans plummeted for fish offshore.

Florida seemed either intensely cultivated or wasteland. The soil in the swamps, however, was said to be rich. It would be necessary only to cut down the trees, dig out the stumps, drain, plow and fertilize the soil, and sow the seeds to start a fine truck farm. No trouble? The yield from the resulting excellent vegetables was said to be worth it. But what about the birds, the mud turtles, and the small animals? Where would they go?

Much of the Florida peninsula has a coral base, and we were told water would bubble up anywhere a twenty-foot hole was dug; but if digging went down 300 feet, water would run out, and a swamp could be drained.

Most confusing but, we were assured, absolutely true.

After a pleasant visit with Dora and Percy, we hit the road again. Near Haines City we had the first of four blowouts.

Thinking a broken spoke had pierced a tube, Bill patched the tire, but it soon blew again. Once more he patched, and once more it blew, all on the back wheel, the hardest to handle because the wheel itself had to be removed and both mudguard and brake loosened.

After walking about a mile to buy patches, we found patches wouldn't do, so we put on the spare tire. All luggage on the rear had to be removed and then put back again. A man in a Ford stopped to help. But the spare lasted only a short distance before wham!—it, too, blew out. We could hardly believe it. A new tire was a necessity, so I started off to look for one while Bill and the man continued to tinker.

A beautiful sunset brightened but did not shorten my two-and-a-half-mile hike into Winter Haven. Trudging from garage to garage, I could find no suitable tires, but I did spy a parked delivery-box motorcycle. A little girl told me the driver was downtown and I would recognize him immediately because of his red sweater and fat cheeks.

Sure enough I did, and he drove me, riding on top of the delivery box, to still another garage, where again there was no success. However, an officer in a police station across the way volunteered to drive me back to Bill, who was terribly worried, as I had been gone more than two and a half hours and it was pitch dark.

The helpful man in the Ford, who had made an unsuccessful search for me in town, had learned where two tires could be bought, and the cop drove Bill to get them. People were certainly kind wherever we went.

My, but we were glad to reach Fort Myers that night! Bill's mother and Dr. Strobel had supper waiting.

Their double-decker houseboat, painted yellow with white trim, was most attractive. Purple bougainvillea covered a trellis over the gangplank, edged with flowerboxes. A living room, kitchen, and bath all with modern conveniences were on the lower deck, with two bedrooms above. Three folding double beds, one in each bedroom and one in the living room, and built-in chests, desk and wardrobes were all highly compact. Bill's mother had put flowered cretonne on the chairs and at the windows, and decorated with sea fans, starfish, coral, and dried grasses.

On the afterdeck she fed flocks of hungry wild ducks. A few came to her hand when she called, but most were very shy and scattered at the least noise or unusual motion, so it had taken much patience and a long time to win over even a few.

Both Henry Ford and Thomas A. Edison lived in Fort Myers; their nearby homes appeared to be unpretentious, old-fashioned New England houses, but dense foliage made them almost invisible from road or water.

We spent our time chatting with the folks, basking in the glorious sunshine, riding around the countryside, observing the sights, and enjoying loafing after our strenuous trip.

A plan was afoot to fill in this part of the Caloosahatchee River in order to make a causeway and a bridge on the as yet unfinished Tamiami Trail. This meant the houseboat would have to tie up elsewhere.

The men who were to tow us to the new pier delayed from day to day. Meanwhile the carpenters took the heavy flower boxes from the gangplank and placed them on one side of the deck. This, of course, caused the boat to list. Consequently the oil would not feed into the stove; the icebox door hung open; and the water pipe was broken.

While we were all away one day, the iceman, climbing over the makeshift gangplank, dropped the ice into the river. He never showed up again!

I was pressing Bill's pants when the iron suddenly went cold. An electrician had cut the wires. But before nightfall Bill had spliced them, and we were in business again.

To complicate matters, Dora and Percy Strobel and their two boys arrived to spend the night. Percy had just received a raise and a transfer, and naturally wanted to tell his father about it. But we had no water, no food, and no clean sheets, and as this was Sunday, none could be bought.

It was the worst possible time for four unexpected guests, and Bill's mother was upset. She hated housekeeping anyway but felt still worse not to be gracious and not to have the house neat and clean, with plenty of good food. So we lugged in water, washed sheets, pillowcases and towels, hung them in the quick-drying sun, and took our guests to a cafeteria for supper.

At last we had the fun of being pulled up the river by a tiny motorboat. The towing man claimed to know the channels and tides of the Caloosahatchee, but about a hundred feet from the new pier, the boat got stuck on a shoal, and he could not budge it. So he left us there, stranded for the night.

About 2:00 AM Dr. Strobel, feeling the rise of the tide, began to pole the boat ahead. Before long, with the aid of the rest of us, the boat was tied up at the new platform.

One day we drove to Punta Rassa, a tiny fishing village on the gulf, where the news had first arrived of the sinking of the battleship Maine. Every post of the pier was decorated by a pelican finial. A fishing boat was throwing refuse overboard, and we were fascinated by the pelicans diving to catch it in their huge beaks before it touched the water.

Another day the four of us were ferried in a launch about five miles on the Gulf of Mexico to Sanibel Island. Fourteen miles long, it was undeveloped except for a few cottages, a small hotel, and a tanning factory for shark and porpoise skins.

On the beach, noted for its beautiful and unusual shells, there was no one around except two girls. One of them knew the shells by name, such as butterfly, angel wing, turkey wing, and devil's toenail. I found a stunning orange sea fan, a huge starfish, and a big conch shell with a beastie inside, its foot used as a door to lock itself in.

While Bill and I played along the beach, a big ship hove into view. After it cast anchor, a motorboat shoved off toward the beach. Having heard rumors that Henry Ford had arrived in Fort Myers, we guessed it was his yacht. Sure enough, after the boat eased up to the beach, I recognized his lanky figure in straw katy and long, flowing duster. His party of six, all with baskets, began busily picking up shells, and the two girls and I helped them find unique specimens. Mrs. Ford told us their friends had never before been to the seashore, so she wanted the shells for them.

Bill would not go near the Ford party, saying, "I won't intrude on the daddy of all flivvers."

The Fords were gracious and friendly, and when the girls and I gave them most of our collections and mentioned we were from New York, Henry smiled pleasantly and replied, "We are from Detroit." As if we hadn't guessed.

Later Bill ran into a man who said, "It must be very shallow for your yacht out there." His mistake was understandable, as Bill and Henry were both tall and lanky.

Our attempt to get away from the mosquitoes in order to sleep on a spit of land jutting out into the Hudson River proved impossible. We switched from the hard earth to the still harder bottom of our rowboat anchored in the busy, dangerous channel of the river where, mosquitoless, we were put to sleep by the boat's gentle rocking.

We sped home across the bay just at sunset. Pelicans flying low in line were silhouetted against the sinking sun. The foam in the boat's wake reflected a lovely shade of lavender, with the peaks of the waves touched with orange. It had been a glorious day.

One afternoon a gusty wind bounced the houseboat around so gaily on the choppy waves that Bill did his studying in the motorcycle on the stable pier. Once in a while the boat gave Willie the willies.

We hated to leave Fort Myers, but it was time to start north. Near Arcadia smudge pots hung on the orange trees to prevent fruit from freezing. A bad frost had already killed young beans and other vegetables.

The few orange buds that were out were enough to sweeten the air. Blue water hyacinths colored many of the drains that paralleled the roads. The swamps were blue with iris, and I picked violets in the woods. Spring had chosen her blue-flowered dress.

The American Cyanamid Company owned and ran the town of Brewster. Mr. Curry, the assistant manager, gave us permission to camp nearby. When he drove us to the company's mines, he picked up a bit of rock, saying, "This is probably a part of a tooth of an ichthyosaurus. Anthropologists claim that the bones of the three-toed horse (about the size of a shepherd dog) and the three-horned rhinoceros have been found here." Bones were everywhere, and we picked up a few curious ones ourselves. One evening Mr. Curry showed us a perfect specimen he had dug up of a little, crablike trilobite over 400,000,000 years old.

Bill was interested to see that the powerhouse at the Cyanamid plant was using only General Electric equipment, and he was pleased with the efficiency of the establishment. He seemed to have the knack of painlessly extracting succulent scraps of information from company officials.

Our next stop was Tampa, where Bill wanted to look into the phosphate business. Along the Tampa River, we came to a grove of moss-covered oaks, a charming camping location, deserted except for one large tent. After our tent neighbors had lent us planks to build an outdoor table and bench and given us a bushel of oranges, we felt quite settled.

Mockingbirds sang all day long and whippoorwills called every night. Bill was intrigued when the mockingbirds sang on the wing. A little brown bird yodeling from a treetop, first a high note then a low one, amused us by seesawing back and forth in rhythm.

One day in Tampa, Bill and I heard a voice say, "Well, if that doesn't look like Lois Burnham." There, on a porch, sat Hortense Lopez, an old schoolmate of mine. We reminisced during lunch, after which she drove us to new Davis Island, recently made of sand pumped from the bottom of the bay.

In one of Bill's many letters to Frank Shaw, he explained the motive behind his work thus:

"This trip has given me the time and material to indulge in what is to me the greatest pastime in the world—the construction of theories. Nothing seems to give me as great joy as evolving a theory from a set of facts, and then seeing it justified. Maybe that is simply satisfying my personal vanity. But whatever it is, I certainly do enjoy it."

As we were getting low on funds, Bill had written Frank to wire us some cash, but no word came for ten days. Bill would sit day after day on a park bench between half-hourly calls at both telegraph offices, Postal Telegraph Service and Western Union. While he waited and wrote, I watched the passersby and wished I could sketch some of them. The old country couples must have made easy prey for real-estate sharks. Every day the same folks just sat and talked and talked and sat. They depressed me as much as the abandoned subdivisions depressed Bill.

We might have been getting very hungry if we had not had a lot of staples on hand, such as oatmeal. Each day we thought, "Tomorrow we will have a feast." One night our neighbors invited us to supper. I guess they suspected our lack of funds, because Ed offered to lend us ten dollars, which Bill refused, of course.

This family was a type entirely new to us—professional itinerants. Ed, a truck driver, was a follower of oil booms. His sweet little ten-year-old girl, Vera, had developed hip-joint disease. On several rainy afternoons, she and I made doll clothes and baskets together.

When Bill went to town on the tenth day, he made a great hullabaloo at Western Union. At first the clerk maintained there was nothing, but at Bill's insistence he looked again and found a notice from Postal that a wire was being held there. Bill flew over, and a wire from Frank's office revealed that Frank was in the hospital with appendicitis and asked Bill to telegraph how much he wanted. Bill did so immediately and sat right there for almost three hours until the money came. Why Postal hadn't given him the wire earlier remained a mystery.

With our long-awaited cash, dinner and movies in town were a wonderful spree. I bought Vera a toy hand-sewing machine that really worked. Although she and her mother had fun with it, Ed seemed to enjoy it most and played with it several evenings.

We were enchanted by Ed's tales of the West, told in picturesque language. He had run into many of the notorious badmen as well as marshals and rangers. For Bill, hearing Ed talk was better than eating. Among Ed's stories was one about a well-known oilman, who started his career by sinking all his money in a small well, and when it turned out "dusty," shot his toe off and used the insurance payment to drill a second well—a gusher!

After leaving Tampa we set up camp on a farm outside of the little phosphate-mining town of Coronet. We never could be lonely there, for five children played all day round the tent, which we had set up overlooking a duck pond. Every kind of domestic animal and a number of undomesticated ones were near at hand. The boys said a small alligator lived in the pond, besides several water moccasins and hundreds of frogs. The baby frogs squeaked; the grown-ups honked; and the big old granddaddies grunted just like pigs. What a cacophony they made at dusk!

Our hosts, the Englishes, seemed to work just as hard and long as the farmers up north. Old man English had sixteen children, ten by a previous wife. Among the six by this one were adorable two-year-old Rita, spoiled by everyone, and boy twins, Lloyd and Moyd. Moyd was a bit void in the upper story but was sweet and likable.

While the boys paddled in the pond one day, we saw a big water moccasin swimming as straight as an arrow with its head sticking up. The boys weren't a bit scared, they said, because a moccasin could not strike while in the water.

Coronet Village and the plant were owned by the Coronet Phosphate Company. After inspecting their Hopewell and Pembroke mines, Bill had learned all he needed, and we moved on.

It was dark when we found a place to camp on a farm in Florida's panhandle. Bill went off to get water, and it seemed to be taking him a long time (because the old black farmer had only a two-quart pail to let down into his well, some distance away, I learned later).

I had started to get supper while waiting, when I heard a car drive up and stop. I turned my lamp to see what was up. Coming through the bushes, with my light gleaming on his black and white stripes, was a big, burly, black prisoner. Believe me my heart jumped. I managed to walk to where I could put my hand on Bill's army pistol and said as calmly as I could, "Good evening, and what can I do for you?"

Politely returning my greeting, he replied, "Is y'all in trouble?"

I told him we were just camping for the night, whereupon a white man's voice from the car said, "All right, Harry. Come along." The car turned around, went down the road a short distance, and stopped.

Then I really began to be scared. Constantly hearing noises in the bushes, I threw my light this way and that. Once, positive that something was moving nearby, I got panicky. But it was only an old sow walking sedately down the road.

It seemed Bill would never come. Then, definitely hearing someone walking up the road, I called, "Bill?" There was just a guttural response, so I called again.

This time a voice answered, "Who-all is you?" I said I had made a mistake, and the footsteps continued up the road.

By the time Bill finally came, I had worked myself into a dither. Taking the pistol in one hand and me in the other, he walked us down the road to see what this was all about. We were greatly relieved to find that, unknowingly, we had set up our tent near a black prisoner camp and that my visitor was not a dangerous fugitive loose in the woods. The guard, seeing our light and hearing the motorcycle climbing the bank, probably had thought we were in some kind of trouble, so he had sent "Harry" to investigate.

At Birmingham, Alabama, our next stop, we were taken through a tremendous steel plant devoted entirely to the making of rails. It was owned by the Tennessee Coal, Iron and Railroad Company, a subsidiary of U.S. Steel. Workmen handled four-ton, red-hot ingots of steel as if they were made of rubber, shot them here and there, turned them over and drew them out into long rails with miraculous skill and speed. Bill was very much impressed by it all. It was exciting and terrifying to watch several hundred tons of molten metal pour out of a Bessemer converter into a waiting railroad car. In one place we saw water showered on a full car of hot coke to cool it, causing so much steam one would have thought the whole town was afire.

We heard there was coal under one-seventh of the land in Alabama. We were camped right over a mine, and toward the evening we could see men with black faces and little lights on their caps come out of a hole in the ground at the foot of our hill. It was spooky. I wanted to go down into a mine, but Bill knew we couldn't get permission.

Although there were several other plants Bill would have liked to investigate, time was getting short for us to reach home for sister Kitty's wedding on June 17. We decided to head straight for Brooklyn.

When we reached the Tennessee River, we ferried across on the strangest boat, resembling a rugged, awkward duck. Its rear paddle wheel was like a huge tail, and it held aloft flapping wings on either side. The shore had no pier, so the duck turned sidewise as it approached the bank and let down one of its wings, and ashore we rolled. More fun!

Just outside of Dayton, Tennessee, I was driving on a sandy road, which seemed to run straight ahead. Suddenly it made a sharp right turn, which I hadn't seen because of a large barn. I tried to force the wheel, but the sand was too deep, and over we went. Bill, in the sidecar, was thrown over my head, breaking his collarbone; I twisted my leg, causing water on the knee; the equipment flew in every direction; and the trunk burst open.

Luckily, a man soon came along and drove us both—dazed, scratched, and bruised—to a doctor in town, who set Bill's collarbone, bandaged my knee, and settled us in a hotel room over his office. There was no hospital.

During our ten-day stay Bill and I tried to picture what the town of Dayton had been like the year before during the Scopes evolution trial, which the whole country had been talking about. Scopes was a young teacher charged with teaching a nonbiblical version of the creation of man.

The trial lawyer Clarence Darrow defended Scopes. Opposed was William Jennings Bryan, the famous orator, who insisted that only the Fundamentalist Bible version should be taught in the public schools and that the theory of evolution was anti-God. Looking at the hotel's five balconies, railed with fancy grillwork, we imagined William Jennings Bryan pacing back and forth on one of them as he rehearsed his speech, and Clarence Darrow with his chair tilted back against the wall and his feet on the rail, haranguing a coterie of youths, while the streets were crowded with visitors come to hear the great orator and see the show.

As soon as we were able, we returned to the fateful corner. The man who had picked us up had collected our entire duffle, as he said he would, and put it and the motorcycle into the same barn that had obstructed my view. Although the barn door was left open and more than a week had passed, not a single article was missing; even such attractive and available items as a traveling clock, a compass, and a radio were all there.

We made arrangements to have the motorcycle and gear shipped to Brooklyn. In a few days, when the doctor said we could travel, we took the train for home. I made a sorry-looking matron of honor at my sister's wedding. Red gashes decorated my face as I limped up the aisle.

Still the trip had been worth it. Besides the fun, Bill's investigations proved to be a financial success. The trip was also a partial success from my standpoint, for it had slowed down Bill's drinking. There were only three or four bad episodes. One was on the rainy day the neighbor spent with us in our tent in Egypt, Pennsylvania. At another time, while we were camping off by ourselves, Bill provided himself with a supply of liquor for the weekend. As there was no one to see me get potted, I thought it was an opportunity to hold a mirror up to him and show him what a fool a person appears when drunk.

However, Bill had had enough to drink to look on my drinking as a great game, and he encouraged me more and more until I was so sick I couldn't hold up my head. Two fools instead of one. In the morning, nipping the hair of the dog that bit him, he had only a slight hangover while mine was excruciating—and all for nothing!

But that year on the motorcycle was a highlight in our lives, and we often reminisced about it.

6

Halfway to Hell

We had recovered quickly from our motorcycle accident, with little permanent injury to Bill except a bump on his collarbone; but several times later my knee gave me considerable trouble. The minor damage to the motorcycle was repaired.

Bill had decided to check on the operations of the Giant Portland Cement Company, so we left my father's house in Brooklyn, where we were living temporarily, and again took off on our motorcycle, for Pennsylvania.

The open road and living close to nature always put us in fine fettle. We seemed to absorb a certain invigorating something from the very earth itself. When we were in the city, we often felt stodgy and stupid, but a night or two in the open always set us up again.

The country was so colorful at that time of year. Tawny patches of wheat and the light green fields of oats patterned the distance; near at hand wild roses tinted the hedgerows and sweetened the air.

Bill finished his study of the Giant, and soon he and his friend Frank Shaw had a new interest, the American Writing Paper Company, which was then in receivership under the management of a Mr. Willson. So we drove to Holyoke, Massachusetts.

We arrived in time to locate the paper factory and find a splendid place to set up our living quarters about a mile from town—on top of a hill, of course! From our tent, we could see what appeared to be a large river running parallel to the Connecticut River, and we wondered what it could be. At night Mount Tom, our hilltop's nearest neighbor, wore a crown of lights, and the moon rose large and red over the city.

When we woke up in the morning, our tent was floating in a sea of mist. However, Bill left for the plant in high glee, all dressed up in his neatly pressed old suit, to interview the president of the paper company.

Papermaking had always sounded dull to me until we went to Holyoke and learned that it is an art—and a very complicated one. Bill took me through one of the plants, where they made red photographic paper for Eastman Kodak and blue paper for phonograph records. The company also had a government contract for postcards and envelopes.

One afternoon Mr. Willson, the president, asked us to go up Mount Tom with him. No road climbed the mountain, so Mr. Willson's chauffeur left us at a cable car that rose to the summit. There, through a telescope, we spotted our tent with a bath towel hung out to dry, saw Amherst and Smith Colleges, and discovered that what I had thought was another river paralleling the Connecticut was actually a series of fine tobacco fields covered with white, sun-reflecting cheesecloth to keep the bees from cross-fertilizing the blossoms.

After we had watched the magnificent sunset, Mr. Willson took us to the Top Restaurant for a good dinner, a whole broiled lobster apiece!

We descended in the cable car and watched the dancing at the amusement park at the foot of the mountain. Mr. Willson said he had never danced there but would like to if I would. So off we went. Even my husband, never too keen about dancing, was moved to waltz with me, so we stayed for a couple of hours. It was a regular Coney Island crowd, with kids dancing the Charleston and making it all the more fun.

While I was writing on our hilltop one afternoon, a large orange butterfly lit on my shoe, remaining perfectly still with its back to the sun until it took off to chase another butterfly. After circling around awhile it came back to my shoe. It kept this up all afternoon, sometimes flying completely out of sight, but always coming back to the same spot and always perching with its back to the sun. I had no idea that a butterfly had such a sense of location. (Note added in 1975: I have just learned from an article in *Natural History* Magazine that some species of butterfly periodically return to the same roosting station in their territory. Often, a number of them will gather at the same roost, particularly at night. Perhaps I had disturbed such a station, and the promontory of my shoe was the closest substitute.)

There were hundreds of mushrooms on the hill. One day I thought I would try out a cousin's formula for identifying edible mushrooms: those that smell good and taste good are safe to eat. I picked and smelled and tasted until I struck one that burned the minute it touched my tongue. Believe me I spat and spat and spat. Horrible visions flashed before my eyes of Bill finding me curled up in agony under a bush. At our tent that night only safe puffballs were served, and I have never experimented with my cousin's formula since then.

The superintendent of the company, a Mr. Yoerg, had offered Bill the use of his bungalow on the river. While we were eating at our camp, he and his wife arrived unexpectedly to conduct us there, bag and baggage.

We just dumped things into their car and our motorcycle and departed, leaving the rest of our supper for the birds.

I always marvel at how good people are. The Yoergs, who had never laid eyes on us until two days before, lent us the slickest, coziest, most convenient little cabin, equipped with heat, running water, telephone, ice, and a lovely view of Mount Tom. They did everything to make us comfortable—even supplying clean linen.

The next morning, with not a soul around, we skinny-dipped in the river.

One night when Bill and I went to the movies in town, there were clouds of tiny white moths swarming around the lights, whitening the ground and making a snow-like pile at the foot of every lamppost. We had never seen anything like it, so we inquired and learned that this was an invasion of gypsy moths, a great menace to trees.

Bill was very much impressed with the ability and personality of Mr. Willson, and as well as making a report about costs and profits, he wrote Frank about the power of one man to make a success of a company that had previously failed. As I had my portable typewriter along, I typed his report.

When we got back to Brooklyn, there was a barely literate note from Pa Goldfoot in Scotia, New York, the farmer we had worked for at the start of our motorcycle trip. He wanted us to go back to work for him for a couple of months, and the pay would be better than the year before. We were flattered by his offer but felt we didn't need that kind of work now.

Frank was so pleased with the paper company report that he decided to give Bill a regular salary of fifty dollars a week as well as options on stock. We were thus sufficiently secure financially to buy a secondhand car for $250, making our trips for Bill's work much easier.

In early October we headed for the North in our new-to-us Dodge. About thirty miles south of Keysville, Vermont, we found that the "pullman" arrangements we had concocted for sleeping in the car worked very well.

After crossing the border into Canada, we spent the night at a French tavern in Laprairie, just this side of Montreal. Traveling in Quebec was terribly expensive; gas was anywhere from thirty-four to thirty-nine cents a gallon. No wonder we saw so many horses and bicycles. Every few miles there was a toll bridge or an expensive ferry. Montreal is on an island, and you couldn't leave it in a car without spending sixty cents.

From the border to Laprairie, it was like traveling in the southern U.S. again. The farmers lived in log cabins and used mules instead of horses. Pigs and sheep roamed wild; we would come upon them unexpectedly, lying in the middle of the road. Along the St. Lawrence River the soil was richer, and the farms looked more prosperous and well-kept. Fancy filigree trimmed the cornices of the painted houses, and red doors and window frames spruced up the long, whitewashed barns. And the churches! Even the smallest hamlet had an impressive church. Distant spires beckoned the traveler from one town to the next; wayside crosses and shrines appeared every few miles; and there were priests and monks everywhere.

As we crossed the St. Lawrence River from Sorel to Berthierville, an old-world monk with a kind, lovable face was aboard the steamer. He wore sandals and a long, brown, coarse-cloth robe with a hood and a rope girdle. His head was shaved except for a crown of hair around the rim of his scalp. He constantly said his beads and read his prayer book. We later saw several others like him. Perhaps because they were so unfamiliar, they all seemed fascinating.

On the way to Quebec City we stopped at Shawinigan Falls to look through the plant of the Aluminum Company of America. Bill was impressed by the management of the plant; I, by its stunning location near the falls.

Armed with letters of introduction from Frank and a Montreal friend, we arrived in Quebec City on a Saturday evening and parked in the tourists' camp.

The city was all confusion, hubbub, and postponement because of a big convention of bankers at the Chateau Frontenac. Bill had expected to see a man who would give him letters of introduction to officials at the Aluminum Company's development on the Saguenay River near Lake St. John. He learned that the man might be found in a room at the Frontenac and wasted most of the day trying to locate him. Meanwhile I wandered about the city.

The next day the man was at his office, but he was much the worse for wear, and Bill could get nothing out of him. The man did promise to have the letters the next day. That meant putting off our leaving for still another twenty-four hours. By Wednesday the gentleman was in better shape and gave Bill several helpful letters. He apologized for his previous condition and said, "A bankers' convention doesn't happen every day."

We wondered whether the convention ever did convene. Most of the time, it seemed to be a grand hurrah-boys-let's-have-another-drink, interspersed with a few visits to local points of interest, a dinner at the governor-general's mansion, and numerous trips to the golf course.

Quebec City is a charming place, and our lengthened stay was no punishment. The chateau is situated on a high bluff overlooking Murray Bay, which is formed by the confluence of the St. Lawrence and Charles Rivers. Mountains with little villages snuggled at their feet rise sharply from the bay. On the same bluff as the Frontenac stands the Citadel, the old fort built by the English in 1759 after General Wolfe had taken the city from Montcalm. Quebec had been a walled town even before that, and some of

Ma Morowski, a lady of charming curves, helped us find a job while we were camping on her grounds near Schenectady.

the walls and gates are still standing. The old section is built on a sidehill with narrow, twisting alleys running hither and yon, making the area intriguing and picturesque.

We slept in our Dodge in the dingy tourist camp, but during the day, for convenience, we parked the car in front of the elegant Frontenac Hotel. How easy to don the cloak of affluence.

At last we were on our way by train to the aluminum plant. We had planned to take a boat up the Saguenay River, but the boats ran sporadically, were more expensive, and took longer. There was no auto road, so we left our car at the tourist camp. As we sped through the wild, unpopulated country, we glimpsed forests, rocks, rivers, mountains, lakes—I never saw so many heavenly lakes! And the autumn foliage painted flaming color over it all.

After spending the night in Chicoutimi on the Saguenay, we continued by train to Ile Maligne, where the aluminum company's huge power plant was situated. Bill had a letter to one of its executives but thought we had better take a look at the plant before getting in touch with him. We were impressed by the efficient layout. Lucky we had that preview, for the man turned out to be a prude and a clam, and Bill would never have learned much by depending on him.

Our returning train for Quebec wasn't to leave for several hours, so we walked nine miles to the station, arriving hungry and with no eating place in sight. When a freight train hove into view, the station agent told us we could ride on it as far as Hébertville, where there was a hotel. We climbed into the caboose for a novel but unsociable five-mile ride. The trainmen could neither speak English nor understand Bill's overseas French. He got along well enough with the city French Canadians, but not with those in the wilds. My schoolbook French didn't work at all.

Hébertville was a little prairie village of shacks, something like Bret Harte's Mud Flats, I imagine. Anyway we managed to get a good meal in its one hotel. In the narrow dining room, red ribbons held back the long, lace window curtains; bright chromos of fruits and flowers hung on the walls; and a statue of a nymph bathing in a pool stood on the mantel. There was no bill of fare, and as we were unable to understand a single word the little French waitress said, some people at a neighboring table kindly helped us out. During the meal a mother hummed a lullaby to her baby in the kitchen. Sometimes one or two other voices chimed in. The song stopped whenever our waitress appeared.

After dinner we finally boarded the train for Quebec, where later we picked up our car. After an uneventful drive along the St. Lawrence River back to Montreal, we heard that Queen Marie of Rumania was in town. While I was waiting in the car for Bill, crocheting (I always carried some handwork), I heard a great blowing of horns and roaring of police motorcycles. Along streamed a cavalcade: the Queen, her two children, the mayor, and various hangers-on.

Reading in the newspaper that she was going to attend the opera that night (Chaliapin in *The Barber of Seville*), Bill and I blew ourselves to standing-room tickets for a dollar-sixty-five each. The opera was fine. But the aging Chaliapin had such a small part, you could hardly tell what his voice was like; the orchestra was thin; the soprano was splendid except when she couldn't quite reach the high notes. Sitting beside the gorgeous Queen, poor little Princess Ileana looked drab and tired. But we felt very gay!

On the way south we stopped at a wayside guesthouse. The man of the house, a diabetic, had broken his leg in June and developed gangrene. Hospital, doctor, and insulin bills were eating up the family's small capital. His wife was strong and capable. Beneath a huge head of moth-eaten, hennaed hair, her moon face was plastered white with powder like a clown's, except for a large pug nose worn red and shiny by a cold.

She, her husband, and a cousin continually joked and kidded with each other, sometimes quite cleverly. The cousin was short and fat, with the skin drawn tightly across his face and neck; when he laughed, the blood rushed to his head in such a surge I feared the skin would burst. But laugh they all did, no doubt to bolster one another's courage.

"Oh, the people!" as Bill was always saying. How interesting we all are!

Just as we were about to cross the bridge from Canada to the United States, Bill said he wanted to get some cigarettes. I realized this was nonsense, since cigarettes were more expensive in Canada. But liquor was cheaper and more easily available than in the U.S. of those Prohibition days. Since Bill had been sober this whole trip, he had both car keys and money with him. So I could do nothing but wait and wait, hour after worried hour, parked on that bridge plaza. Finally, as it was getting dark, I started out to find him. In the very last saloon in the area there he was, hardly able to navigate. Our money had all but vanished.

This episode was only a harbinger of the deeper troubles ahead. Bill's earning capabilities were not lost until several years later. Ever since he had sold Frank Shaw and a few other market investors the idea of looking into a business before buying its stock, Frank and the others often "carried" Bill for a number of shares in part payment for an investigation. Bill himself invested when he became financially able. The stocks he recommended and held often increased in value, and our financial status kept pace.

Upon our returning home from Canada, Bill continued this strategy of thoroughly examining the many angles of a company's management and the probable future worth of its stock. His interest was aroused by the action of the stock market or by analyzing financial statements in Moody's manuals. He naturally sought stocks that were low-priced in relation to what he considered their potential value.

Friends and relatives of Bill's often asked his advice about investing, and he would recommend certain buys.

When he learned that his sister, Dorothy, and her husband had bought a considerable amount of Penick and Ford stock, a corn products company about which he was enthusiastic, he wrote the brokerage house that he would assume any loss their account might sustain in that stock. He took that responsibility for stocks he had recommended to my dad, too.

Bill and I traveled to Washington. D.C.; Holyoke, Massachusetts; Rochester, Clifton Springs, Syracuse, and Messina, New York; Houston and Dallas, Texas; New Orleans, Louisiana; Birmingham, Alabama; and many places in Canada. The stocks he investigated included the International Match Company, the Southern Power Company, the Virginia Railroad, the Southern Baking Company, the Houston Oil Company, and Penick and Ford, besides those mentioned elsewhere.

During the winter Bill sometimes made these investigating trips himself, traveling by train. Occasionally he didn't call me to tell me where he was. Then I would know he was drinking. In January 1927 he wrote me that "there will be no booze in 1927." Alas, this good resolution was short-lived.

We spent the winter of 1926-27 primarily in Brooklyn. But at the first sign of spring we hit the road in the Dodge. Bill wanted to inspect the American Cyanamid plant at Niagara Falls and the Casein Company at Bainbridge, New York. This was before the era of plastics, and I was intrigued by the idea that household utensils could be made out of milk, through a new process being developed by Casein.

When we reached Niagara, the mounds of ice below the falls were nearly as high as the falls themselves. We were dazzled by the sun shimmering on icicles dripping from the spray-wet trees. And at night, lit by colored lights, the falls were breathtaking.

Because waterpower was cheap, Buffalo was overrun with factories. Bill procured a really reliable picture of the waterpower situation there and of the Cyanamid Company. A few months later, when he could afford it, he bought stock in that company.

When Bill had to go to Niagara again, we found that Chamberlain, a First World War ace, was flying passengers over and around the falls for ten dollars a couple. I was thrilled with my first flight; immediately upon reaching terra firma I asked Bill if he had another ten dollars. I wanted to go right up again!

After our return from Buffalo we again lived at Clinton Street with Mother and Dad, until Bill became interested in Cuban sugar. An on-the-spot investigation was, of course, the only thing. Once more we fixed up the Dodge so we could sleep in it, and we started south. We reached Florida in better time than we had on the motorcycle. The roads were smoother and less muddy, and there was no tent to put up and take down.

But being unable to resist driving on the marvelous hard sand of Ormond Beach, we again got mired there. I'd hit one of the few soft spots, and the more we dug the deeper the wheels sunk. We finally had to wait for low tide in the middle of the night to work ourselves out.

At Miami Beach we had hoped to see Bill's father, but he and Christine, his second wife, and their little daughter Helen had gone to Jacksonville, because he was building seawalls near there.

We had an exciting month in Cuba, in spite of Bill's heavy drinking. Upon our arrival we were besieged by guides. Just for the fun of it, Bill said to the most persistent one, "No, Mr. Flynn is going to show us around."

The man looked flabbergasted. "Who you say, boss?"

"Mr. Flynn," Bill repeated.

"Boss, you sure sittin' strong. You sittin' strong as Morro Castle!"

Mr. Flynn, to whom Bill had letters of introduction, was vice-president of the Bowman Hotels and a political "power behind the throne" in Cuba. He put his car and chauffeur at our disposal for days at a time. We were driven down to Matanzas to watch the natives diving for sponges. He also lent us his motorboat, in which we had some marvelous rides on the Gulf of Mexico.

It was a frustrating time for me, though, because of Bill's drinking. One day, to keep him from going down to the bar, I threw one of his shoes out the window, but this did no good. It landed on a nearby roof, and Bill simply called the porter to retrieve it. In no time he was down at the bar wearing both shoes.

The United States ambassador to Cuba was on vacation, but his substitute, a hard-drinking, fun person, escorted us around town, especially into bars! Why he rushed us I never knew—possibly because he was bored or because he hoped to get some inside information about the stock market or maybe just because he liked Bill. He was with us morning, noon, and night. One day he took us to his home, where he was very rude to his mother when she urged him not to miss an appointment at the British embassy. Bill was so shocked by the man's attitude toward his mother that we avoided him as much as possible after that. However, on the day of our departure he completely took over our embarkation, waving away customs officials and introducing us to the captain of the ship.

Bill had made several visits to sugar plantations, and he sent in his report on them; but I'm afraid that because of the drinking, Cuban sugar was not one of his most successful investigations.

When we reached Miami Beach, Bill's father and the family had returned, and we enjoyed several days with them. Construction had started on the Overseas Highway, the system of bridges and cause-ways connecting the Florida mainland and the Keys. Dad W., as a quarry man, had a contract to cut rock for foundations. Five years later, the Bonus Marchers, unemployed World War I veterans, were sent down from Washington by President Hoover to work on this highway. Bill's dad was home in Miami for the Labor Day holiday of that year, when a tremendous hurricane swept the shore where he had been and the marchers were then camping. Almost no one survived.

Upon returning to Brooklyn we rented a fine, three-room apartment at 38 Livingston Street in a good residential neighborhood. Bill was beginning to feel his financial oats; so when a neighbor moved out of the apartment next door, we took on that, too, and had the in-between wall pulled down. A three-year lease and a promise to pay for replacing the wall were necessary. Bill, although flush at the time, was well aware that he was in an unstable business. So he offered to pay the three years' rent in advance, but this was refused. We now had two bedrooms, two baths, two kitchens, and one tremendous living room. That was the point of it all—Bill loved big living rooms. A grand piano was needed, of course, to help fill the expanded space. Bill bought a Mason and Hamlin, and I recently came across the old bill—$1,600.

Randolph, the elevator man in our building, was a Rosicrucian from the West Indies. He devoted himself tirelessly to helping Bill keep sober, and not only with oral persuasion and theological tracts. When Bill was late coming home, Randolph would search him out in the nearby bars. Bill was grateful for all Randolph did. Upon learning that Randolph's daughter was studying music, Bill gave him a check to buy a piano for her.

Even after Bill had sobered up and we had moved to Bedford Hills, Randolph still wrote us and sent us Rosicrucian books. He took deep pleasure in believing that God had worked through him to help Bill. Perhaps that was so.

I had had no paid job since leaving the Brooklyn Naval Hospital in 1925, but I volunteered at my old stand, the Central YWCA, to serve on the Adult Education and other committees. I also held a class for young homemakers, explaining the principals of interior decorating.

Bill suffered increasingly from his inability to control his drinking. By the end of 1927 he was so depressed by his own behavior that he said, "I'm halfway to hell now and going strong." He then signed over to me "all rights, title, and interest" in his accounts with his stockbrokers, Baylis and Company, and Tobey and Kirk.

How he was able to conduct his investigations, to buy wisely in the market and at the same time drink so much, I will never know. Of course, the great bull market of that period was a big help. But his drinking kept pace with his improving finances, and I grew more and more discouraged.

Night after night he didn't come home until the wee small hours, and then he would be so drunk he'd either fall down just inside the front door or I'd have to help him to bed.

One night, in a burst of anguish, after walking the floor for hours, I wrote the following. I quote it here word for word, baring my heart, in the hope that those of you in the shadow, who are going through distress similar to mine, can have hope that the sun will shine for you as it did for me.

"Come home to me. My heart is breaking. How can we go on like this day after day! What's to become of us? I love you so, and yet my love doesn't seem to do you any good. Still I have faith that it must, someday. God grant that day may be soon, for it doesn't seem as if I could go on like this, night after night, waiting for you hour after hour. Oh, that I had the wisdom to know what would help you, for I'm sure you could be helped if only I knew how. I'd do anything, dear, that would help you. I put faith in love, love, love—and patience. Oh, I hope I'll have the patience to go through with it, for it seems each night as though I couldn't stand another—and yet another comes, and still another, until my heart is like a stone. A great dullness spreads over me until all things, good and bad, seem to taste alike.

"God help me to help him, my husband, my boy, who is more than life to me. God give me wisdom and strength and patience, for I love him, I love him, I love him."

I was going to do the job, with God's help, of course. But I thought that I, because of my love for Bill, could change him. His years of continued drinking after this showed me how wrong I was.

7

Ebby and the Mountaintop

While Bill was overseas, his desire for liquor never seemed to interfere with his military duties; and for quite a long period after his return, it didn't bother either of us too much. Whenever we were away from the city—camping, hiking, or taking investigation trips on the motorcycle or in the Dodge—he seldom drank. Then upon our return to the city he would get drunk every night. So I would arrange as many weekends outdoors as possible. He loved these outings but didn't want to live in the country, even in Vermont.

Bill rarely drank socially or moderately. Once he started, he seldom stopped until he became so drunk he fell inert, He was not violent when in his cups and was deeply remorseful afterward. When he finally realized he couldn't stop, he begged me to help him, and we fought the alcohol battle together. We did not know at the time that he had a physical, mental, and spiritual illness. The traditional theory that drunkenness was only a moral weakness kept us both from thinking clearly on the subject. Yet Bill was morally strong. His sense of right and wrong was vivid, extending even to little things, and his respect for the rights of other people was extraordinary. For example, he wouldn't walk across another person's lawn, though I often would. He had plenty of willpower to do anything in which he was interested; but it wouldn't work against alcohol even when he was interested.

Perhaps he could have stopped drinking in the beginning if he had realized that great dangers lay ahead and that alcoholism is a progressive disease. But "perhaps" and "if" are useless assumptions.

I suppose the pattern of his tolerance to alcohol was like that of many alcoholics. At first liquor affected him quickly; later he became able to drink more and more without showing it; but then suddenly his tolerance dramatically diminished. Even a little liquor made him intoxicated.

As the drinking increased, we kept mostly to ourselves. My brother

Rogers had upbraided me for allowing Bill, who was only slightly drunk on these occasions, to go with the family to a Woodman Choral Club concert in which Mother sang, and to other social events. So we seldom met with our family or friends. I even kept away from my oldest and closest friend, Elise Shaw. Many years later, when she had become one of Bill's ardent admirers, she told me that she had been so disgusted with him because of his drinking, she was sure he would never amount to anything.

With Frank Shaw, Elise's husband, for whom Bill did many stock investigations, he was honest about his drinking. Frank was very tolerant, and it never seemed to affect their relationship. They kept a mutual admiration for each other until Frank's death in the 1950's.

Frank was a fine-looking, dignified man, reserved and uncommunicative. His favorite remark was "We'll see. Maybe." He seldom drank, but when he did, one drink would make him lose his reticence, and he became charming. So the image that I saw in the bottle and the one Elise saw were probably both as distorted as those from the crazy mirrors at Coney Island, and the emotions the bottle aroused in Elise and in me were poles apart. A firecracker can be fun but can be hurtful. Elise and I held this firecracker by opposite ends. She was pleased when her husband took a drink; I, holding the other end, was most unhappy when mine did.

Bill almost always found his way home no matter how drunk he was. At Amity Street I could hear him stumbling up the stairs to our attic apartment. At Livingston Street I listened for the elevator to stop at our floor. Later at Clinton Street, when his drinking was almost continuous, he often fell insensible just inside the front door. Usually I would struggle to get him upstairs to bed, but sometimes I would just cover him with a coat and leave him where he fell.

While I was waiting for him at night, I would set myself some project hard enough to require great concentration, so I wouldn't have time to think. But of course there was no real escape from thought.

Was I to blame for his drinking? He had once told me that when he was a little boy, he was given a small ax for Christmas and immediately tried it out on Susie, his rubber doll. Thereafter, every time he looked into the toy box and saw the doll's head dangling by a thread, he would weep and say, "Poor Susie! I nearly cut off her head."

As he later sometimes called me Susie, I wondered just where this placed me. Could he hold a subconscious resentment against me for some subtle reason? Or was the reason perhaps something obvious that I was doing wrong? It was highly puzzling and confusing, so I would try hard not to let myself be discouraged and to rivet my attention on the job I was doing.

Probably this is how my habit began of trying to construct something out of practically nothing. I'd make over for myself one of Mother's discarded dresses, reupholster a chair from the webbing to the finishing gimp or cut out a blouse from such scant material I had to work it this way and that to get the fabric all going in the right direction.

One night I tried to reweave a hole in an old Oriental rug. Finally at dawn I fell asleep over my work. I was awakened by the telephone—the police! Bill had been arrested the night before for drunkenness, was in a Manhattan West Side jail and could be released if I came for him. Relieved it was no worse, I hurried to the police station and got him out. Many years later, when Bill and I were on the train from Bedford Hills to New York, he pointed out the forlorn Naomi Hotel in Harlem, where he had found himself one morning in the early '30's. Those were two nights he didn't come home.

Besides working for Frank Shaw, Bill made investigations for a colorful Wall Street operator named Joe Hirshhorn, who has become famous as a collector of fine art. The new, circular Hirshhorn Museum on the Mall in Washington, D.C., was built by the Smithsonian Institution to house his collection, a gift from him to the United States Government. (When Bill saw the plans in 1970, he kidded Joe about his "stone doughnut.")

Joe's interest in art started when he was a poor boy in Brownsville, Brooklyn. He found in the street a beautiful picture on a calendar and gave it to his mother for her birthday. His first job was as a runner on Wall Street. Then he started trading for himself on the curb market and soon had amassed a large fortune. Bill had met him through a drinking companion, Clint, who worked for Joe.

We were invited to a party at Joe's place on Long Island. I hadn't a thing to wear, and the "proper" side of Fulton Street, Brooklyn's shopping center, had closed for the night, as it was late. So I walked with trepidation down the "shady" side where, it was rumored, only "naughty women" shopped. However, I found a beautiful, long, red taffeta dress, which I kept for many years. Bill's getting drunk at the party is all that I remember about it, except that Clint's wife had to drive us home. It took Clint seventeen more years of drinking before he joined AA, but he has been sober now for over twenty years.

Later, during the Depression, Joe moved to Toronto and made his investments from there. Bill, half drunk, followed him to Toronto and for several days slept on a sofa in Joe's suite without registering at the hotel. Bill drank so much that he was of no help to Joe, who finally had to take him down on the service elevator and send him home.

Bill didn't see Joe again until many years later. We were waiting in Kennedy Airport when Bill recognized him walking by with what looked like a birdcage wrapped in newspaper under his arm. They had a great reunion. By then Joe was well on his way as an art collector and was bringing home some treasure. He was glad to learn about Bill's sobriety, but later always got AA mixed up with the American Automobile Association. During the years we called on Joe and his wife, Olga, at Greenwich, Connecticut, he never failed to ask Bill how he was getting on with his "AAA."

Dorothy Strong, Bill's sister, had recovered from the flu and needed a rest, so Bill sent her and me to Bermuda for a couple of weeks. We stayed on Harrington Sound and had a delightful time cycling on the auto-free roads and rowing along the shore, investigating caves in the rocks and tiny hidden beaches between rocky promontories. We both came home greatly refreshed.

Soon after I returned, Bill and I were walking up Broadway to a movie, and as we passed a Packard showroom, Bill was entranced by a good-looking convertible in the window. Entering the showroom, we found the car was secondhand, with little mileage on it but a good big price; nevertheless, we bought it then and there. We were so excited we didn't see much of the movie.

We had lots of fun with the car in spite of the endless trouble that developed in its insides. Bill surmised it must have been driven off a bridge into a stream and rusted out its innards. When we were to spend a weekend in Dobbs Ferry with the Strongs, Bill thought it was a good opportunity to take the Packard to a garageman there, whom he trusted. I went up earlier by train.

Suppertime came, but no Bill. Dot, Leonard and I whiled away the time playing three-handed bridge. Finally we went to bed. But for me there was no sleep. At about 4:00 a.m. the doorbell rang. I dashed to the front door, and so did Leonard. There on the doorstep was a shocking sight: a cold, shivering Bill without shoes or pants.

Of course all kinds of ideas went through my head until he told us what had happened. He had arrived at the garage with a bottle, and he and the mechanic worked on it more than they did on the car. When the bottle was finished, Bill started on foot for the Strongs'. On the way he got sleepy and lay down in an empty lot, taking off his pants and shoes. About dawn, awakened by the cold, he continued his trek. Suddenly realizing he hadn't put on his pants, he dodged from tree to tree the rest of the way. In the morning we drove to the field, and there were his trousers, folded neatly, with his shoes placed carefully beside them.

Whenever his work took him near Albany, Bill would stop in to see his old friend Ebby, and they always got drunk together. On one of these sprees a brilliant idea hit them. Ebby had heard that a new airfield was about to be opened by the Equinox House in Manchester, Vermont. They hired a plane, wired the time of arrival to Mrs. Orvis, owner of the hotel, and stocked up well for the flight.

This was a gala day for Manchester. Mrs. Orvis called out the band to greet the first plane to arrive at the new airport and the town fathers all gathered at the airfield. The plane flew in; the band played lustily; the welcoming committee got on the ready; and Bill and Ebby stepped down from the plane and fell flat on their faces, dead drunk.

At this distance such escapades may sound amusing. When they happened, they were not funny to me. Nor did I recognize them for what they were: symptoms of a progressively worsening illness.

In the spring of 1929 I was so distraught by Bill's incessant drinking and the many distressing incidents it caused that I poured it all out on paper, trying to analyze what was best for me to do. The following is a quote from my outpouring:

"What is one to think or do after so many failures? Is my theory of the importance of love and faith nothing but bunk? Is it best to recognize life as it seems—a series of failures? and that my husband is a weak, spineless creature who is never going to get over his drinking?

"If I should lose my love and faith, what then? As I see it now, there is nothing but emptiness, bickering, taunts, and selfishness, each of us trying to get as much out of the other as possible in order to forget our lost ideals.

"I love my husband more than words can tell, and I know he loves me. He is a splendid, fine man—in fact an unusual man with qualities that could make him reach the top. His personality is endearing; everybody loves him; and he is a born leader. Most kindly and bighearted, he would give away his last penny. He is honest almost to a fault.

"Having a delightful, whimsical sense of humor and an unusual vocabulary, he employs unique phrases which make him an interesting talker and a compelling one as well, for in every gathering people listen to him intently. His remarkable memory has retained an unusual fund of knowledge. Minute details bore him to death, his mind being of the farseeing, long-perspective kind. Extremely careless about small things, he never knows which pocket his matches or keys are in. Around the house I am forever picking up after him. But these are trivial matters. The morning after he has been drunk, he is so penitent, self-derogatory, and sweet that it takes the wind out of my sails, and I cannot upbraid him.

"He continually asks for my help, and we have been trying together almost daily for five years to find an answer to his drinking problem, but it is worse now than ever. If we go away on a trip, he says he does not miss alcohol and goes without it a month or more at a time; but the minute we get back to the city, the very first day, in spite of all kinds of plans and protestations, he is at it again, sometimes coming home early and sometimes at five o'clock in the morning.

"He has been called lazy at times, but he often does more deep and clear thinking when he is sitting around than people like myself who always have to be busy puttering.

"In several notable instances he has tackled something hard and never given up until he has accomplished it. If his interest is aroused, there are no ends to which he won't go. And yet he is a drunkard and apparently cannot get over it.

"Can it be interest that is lacking? It would seem that he would be vitally interested in making us both happy by doing away with his own mortification and sense of unworthiness, the damage to his health, my tears and heartache. and, I'm ashamed to admit, my occasional flares of temper.

"I hate even to think of it, but if I went away for a short time and did not come back until he had behaved himself for a week at least, and then, if things did not continue as they should, stayed away longer, would that help? Would it finally arouse his interest?

"In writing this down, I can see that in spite of not having any children and in spite of worry and heartache much of the time, I really have been leading a richer, fuller life than most apparently more fortunate women.

"The problem is not about *my* life, of course, for probably the suffering is doing me good, but about his—the frightful harm this resolving and breaking down, resolving and breaking down again, must be doing to him. How can he ever accomplish anything with this frightful handicap? I worry more about the moral effect on him than I do the physical, although goodness knows the terrible stuff he drinks is enough to burn him up completely. Where can he ever go but down when he can't control this habit? And his aims have been so high!

"We understand each other as well as is possible for radically different temperaments. I admit I cannot understand the craving for liquor, for it has no appeal for me, although several times I have made myself drunk in order to try and find that appeal.

"I believe that people are good if you give them half a chance and that good is more powerful than evil. The world seems to me excruciatingly, almost painfully beautiful at times, and the goodness and kindness of people often exceed that which even I expect. Francis Bacon said that the human mind is easily fooled; that we believe what we want to believe and recognize only those facts which conform to that belief. Am I doing that identical thing? Are people bad, is love futile, and Bill doomed to worse than mediocrity? Am I a fool not to recognize it and grasp what pleasure and comfort I can?"

Later that day I wrote:

"I've just had a long talk with Larry Rankin [an old friend of Bill's] about Bill and about drinking in general, the outcome of which was rather discouraging. He believes the only thing that will cure Bill is the physical effect as the years go by, perhaps ten years more before it breaks him down so badly that he will stop. He also believes Bill has never absolutely made up his mind to stop, that I or someone else has done so for him.

Larry's view is that perhaps Bill *thinks* he has made up his mind, but that there are very few people who give up something they want for the sake of someone else.

"I'm afraid I have always been and still am too foolishly idealistic and sentimental. I had hoped Bill's love for me would cause him to stop drinking, for I know he loves me—but perhaps that is not enough. Is Larry right in saying that people seldom act against their own desires, to please another, and that Bill still doesn't want to stop for his own sake?

"After all these pages where am I? Have I made anything clearer? I don't know—but I do know that I am going to have faith in the ultimate success of our struggle, that I am going to appeal to the good in him and keep on everlastingly trying."

Soon after I wrote the above, I decided to see what effect leaving him would have. I didn't want to do it, even for a week. I'd rather have been unhappy with him than unhappy without him. But perhaps leaving him might help him. So I told him I was going and wouldn't be back until he was sober for one whole week. He was to report every day to my mother, and she would let me know.

So I took my portable typewriter and went to Washington and sat under the cherry blossoms and typed out a part of the diary of our motorcycle trip we had taken three years before.*

At the end of the week I phoned Mother, and she reported he had been sober ever since I left. So home I went. The whole episode was rather a farce, as he soon started drinking again. But perhaps it showed him I meant what I said.

In spite of the doubts I had indicated, I still felt sure he deeply wanted to stop. Besides often telling me so, he had written many heartbreaking letters expressing this desire; and three times he had written in our Bible, the most sacred place he knew, promises to stop forever. The last was dated September 3, 1930. After that he gave up in despair.

Once I found on the floor at home, beside Bill's inert body, a piece of paper on which he had written an analysis of his drinking in order to help him understand his problem:

"Why should I continue on this way? What is on each side of the balance? On one side of the scales are the love and devotion of my wife, whose whole life is given to the task of making me happy and successful in whatever I undertake. Her happiness is dependent on the outcome of her effort to help me. There is my mother, who is advancing in years, who wishes above all things my happiness and success. She may someday be

---

*Periodically through the years, I tried to put this diary into some sort of shape, but never finished it until 1973.

obliged to look to me for aid. There is Lois's mother, the dearest woman in the world, who may need my help and who is heartbroken over my failure in self-control. There is my sister with her two beautiful children, for whom I may do much. There are those who have lost everything in the stock market because of their confidence in me, which confidence I should justify. There is my pride—the desire to feel at the end that I have left the world better than I found it. These things are on one side of the balance.

"What is on the other? Not liquor, but rather my baser self. This thing, not evil in itself, is through its abuse the vehicle of my selfishness and sensuality. I am breaking the hearts of those near and dear to me. I am destroying as fine a mind and body as were ever given any man. And this for a fleeting sense of comfort and stimulation. Must this state of affairs continue? Must I live on, affording proof that the worse side of my nature has triumphed? Shall I go on breaking hearts over such a mess of pottage? I think not."

Upon reading the above I was so angry that I tore it up, then immediately felt sorry and Scotch-taped it together again.

Bill's concern about "those who have lost everything" referred to the stock-market crash of 1929. He, too, lost a lot of money; like everyone else at the time, he had bought on margin. We had to leave our fine apartment on Livingston Street and were lucky to be able to sublet it for part of the period of our lease, but at a reduced rate. Bill felt great remorse about those friends who had bought stock at his suggestion. Later he was able to make some recompense in most cases.

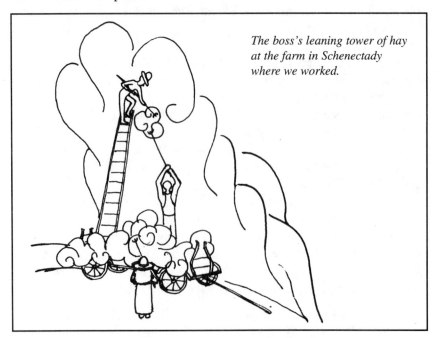

The boss's leaning tower of hay at the farm in Schenectady where we worked.

He had made some very good business connections in Canada, where the crash had not hit as hard as in the States. When R. O. Johnson of Greenshields and Company invited him to join its staff, we moved to Montreal. We lived a short time in a furnished apartment before renting an expensive suite in Glen Eagles, a new apartment house on Mount Royal, overlooking the city. Bill felt himself very fortunate when so many of his old Wall Street pals had lost everything in the crash.

Our stay in Montreal was a very pleasant respite. We joined the country club at Lachute, and starting at three o'clock, after the market closed, we often played golf during the long, sunlit afternoons. Before dinner at the club we would have a drink or two, which usually seemed to be all Bill needed; but occasionally, of course, he dropped into the old routine.

Harry Bates was a charming English playboy, a remittance man and a great buddy of Bill's in Montreal. Not only was he interested in the stock market, but he loved to drink. One night the three of us went to dinner at the Ritz Hotel. It was a gay, festive evening, and I enjoyed it; Harry was fun to be with. Although both the boys drank a lot, neither seemed too badly off until we got up to leave, when they were shaky on their pins. I found it wise to hold an arm of each as we left the elegant hotel.

Outdoors it was snowing and icy cold. As soon as the doorman had called a cab, we safely traversed "en masse" the short distance between the door and the cab. But just as we reached the curb, Bill on my right arm tottered and fell, followed immediately by Harry on my left. The doorman, acting as if nothing had happened, stepped over my "escorts" and ceremoniously handed me into the cab before assisting them to arise and enter it—all to my great embarrassment.

My mother came up to visit us. We had a happy time together, but upon her return to Brooklyn it wasn't too long before she became ill. She stayed in Ardsley with my sister Barbara, who could look after her well. After X-rays, it was found she had cancer of the bone. She had to go twice a week to New York City for radium treatments. In the meantime, Dad and Rogers fixed one floor at the Clinton Street home as an apartment where Mother could be cared for easily.

The Depression finally hit Montreal, and it seemed to coincide with an increase in Bill's drinking. So between the two problems he became excess baggage for Greenshields and was fired. What to do then? We had no money and many commitments.

We sublet our Glen Eagles apartment furnished for the five months until the termination of the lease. Bill, using his World War I life insurance as collateral, borrowed the money from Greenshields to get us out of Canada. Leaving the car with the Montreal Packard agency to be sold, we took the train to the Camp. We hated to let the family know of our ignominious step down from our previous affluence; but because of my Mother's illness I left Bill at the Camp and hastened to Brooklyn; he soon followed. Mother died on Christmas Day, 1930. Bill was drunk then and for days before and after.

We continued to live with Dad at Clinton Street. Bill finally got an investigating job with Standard Statistics while I enrolled successively in the practical and the advanced courses at the New York School of Interior Decorating.

When I finished, Bill took a week's vacation, and we renewed ourselves by hiking again on the Long Trail, this time between East Dorset and Bennington. The Long Trail was later made a part of the Appalachian Trail, a wilderness footpath completed in 1937, running along the tops of the East Coast ranges from Georgia to Maine.

Soon after our return to Clinton Street I applied for work in interior decorating at Macy's department store, but was told work in this department had to be led up to. As I had no experience in selling, they suggested I take a job demonstrating folding card tables and chairs. The Leg-o-Matic Company offered to pay my salary of nineteen dollars per week while Macy's gave me a one-percent commission on all sales. Thus started my department-store career, from which Bill later was continually trying to relieve me. "I want to get Lois out of that damned department store" was a constant theme after he had sobered up.

At the end of my job as demonstrator, I was made head of stock in Macy's novelty-furniture department with an increase in salary. The store was a good and fair place to work. I found the furniture-floor superintendent a kind and understanding man.

Macy's furniture floor was at that time a vast, open expanse running the long block from Sixth to Seventh Avenues, so that anyone, especially one as tall as Bill, could be seen at a great distance. On our fourteenth wedding anniversary, in January 1932, I saw a tall figure weaving up the long aisle. He held a parcel in one hand and a bouquet of flowers in the other. Waiting patiently while I finished with a customer, he then ceremoniously presented his gifts, to the interest of everybody around. The tissue-wrapped parcel contained a wristwatch and a check for $2,500, which he had earned by doing investigating for Joe Hirshhorn.

Our dinner celebration at a swanky restaurant was, of course, preceded by cocktails which, added to what he had already swallowed, made Bill uninterested in food. After a few sips of soup I had to take him home. The next day he asked me to give back the check.

I was shocked and disappointed but believed him when he said he needed it for an exciting new investment company that was being formed with him as manager. He had always been able to sell himself and his ideas. So even as late as 1932 in the downward plunge of his drinking career, he was able to pull himself together and impress a coterie of wealthy friends with his knowledge and ability. These men included the founders of the new company, Arthur Wheeler and Frank Winans, to whom my brother-in-law "Hobo" Swentzel had introduced Bill. But there was a proviso. They had heard about Bill's drinking, and the contract stated that if he drank during the life of the company, he would automatically be out.

This was a unique opportunity for Bill to get back into Wall Street. For a time, all went well. Then, as one opportunity seemed to attract another, the Pathé Company asked Bill to go to Bound Brook, New Jersey, with a group of engineers to investigate a new photographic process. Bill was glad to have this extra chance to retrieve his good reputation, and it did not interfere with his other project.

In the evenings at Bound Brook, the men sat around playing cards and drinking. As Bill was on the wagon and never liked cards, he became more and more bored. (When we were first married, I had tried to teach him bridge, but he didn't seem able to distinguish the jack from the king.) As the evening wore on, he became curious: What was in the big jug that was going around and around? Upon hearing it was Jersey lightning, he thought, "I've never had any. Wouldn't it be awful if I should go to my grave without ever having tasted Jersey lightning!" So that was it. Whenever the jug circled, he helped himself again and again, with the inevitable result.

But this time the result was far-reaching. He had broken his contract. This was a very serious thing to Bill. His New England conscience considered a contract a sacred thing, and he had broken it. His friends Arthur and Frank soon learned of his drinking, and they called to tell him that the agreement was canceled.

Virtually ended, too, was Bill's career on Wall Street. But more important still was the end of his confidence that he could overcome his drinking problem. His interest in stopping drinking for his own sake had been aroused, but he hadn't been able to do it.

I became more and more discouraged, and I feared I would have to look after him and support him all the rest of our lives.

Dr. L. V. Strong, one of the early osteopaths in Brooklyn and the father of Bill's brother-in-law, asked me to decorate his new office, and I jumped at the opportunity to earn an extra thirty-five dollars. I spent several industrious weekends moonlighting.

Bill began grabbing at straws. He thought Joe Hirshhorn and others he knew in Toronto might be interested in some mining stocks that he considered good buys. So up to Canada he sped. He was so drunk at the border port, however, that he was denied entrance.

My father loved Bill and tried to help him but did not fully realize the extent of Bill's drinking, because of his own preoccupation with his forthcoming marriage. In May 1933, three years after Mother's death, Dad married "Joan Jones," the ex-wife of their former minister, and moved to a New York suburb. He had become interested in Joan while Mother was sick. At that time Dad and Joan went together to church functions, which she had never attended with her minister husband. When I spoke to Dad about his hurting Mother, he said that he loved Mother more than anyone else in the world, that he always would and that she understood his attention to Joan. And I think she did.

My family was greatly distressed by his interest in another woman, because of his exceptionally happy marriage with Mother. So I was the only one of the family who accompanied him to the civil wedding ceremony. Dad's departure left free the second-floor apartment which had been fixed up for Mother at the time of her illness. Bill and I moved into that, and rented to friends the big upstairs front bedroom we had previously occupied.

When Bill wasn't drunk, he was so depressed by his condition that I felt I must do something drastic. I decided on a trip to the country, "to get him away from it all."

At Macy's I asked the floor superintendent, Guy Kolb, for a three-month leave of absence. He inquired why I needed the leave. When I told him my husband was ill, he said, "Well, what's the matter with him?"

I replied, "He can't work because of his illness."

"What kind of illness is it?"

"It's hard to define."

"I must know in order to consider the matter."

So I reluctantly spilled out the whole story. And he gave me the leave. A great guy, Guy Kolb! The other sales folk were astonished that I got it, because no one at Macy's rated a leave before completing five years of employment. I had worked less than two. The ignorant barge in where the wise fear to enter.

I took Bill to Dot's and Leonard's farm in Green River, Vermont. The Strongs and their children were abroad that summer; so we were there alone from June to September. Bill stayed sober and we had a wonderful time.

While there we read several books aloud to one another. A friend had given Bill Mary Baker Eddy's "Science and Health," which he read and reread, hoping thereby to strengthen his willpower.

We also did a lot of work on the place, repairing the water system, mending leaking pipes in the cellar and cleaning out the spring. Bill made a swimming pool down by the road by damming up the brook, so there was also a charming little waterfall. White iris grew on the bank. I helped with the digging and also made a wildflower garden under the spreading elm in the walled-in barnyard. On our hikes I found some arbutus in the distant woods and planted it in a similar location nearby. But arbutus does not transplant well, and it lasted only a few years.

When the Strong kids got back, they greatly enjoyed the pool and used it for several years. But as time went by, the spring floods ate into the dam and filled the pond with silt; the last time we saw it, it had become a mere puddle.

Upon my return to Macy's there was a new head of stock in novelty furniture; but although I was now only a salesclerk, Mr. Kolb arranged for me to receive the head-of-stock salary of twenty-two dollars and fifty cents per week plus one percent on sales.

The minute we hit the city, the carefree time was ended. Bill immediately started drinking and drank constantly so that he was soon again in terrible condition. I finally told my father about it, and he recommended that I send Bill to the Charles B. Towns Hospital on Central Park West in Manhattan. I did, and Bill was sober for a month or so afterward.

This was a happy interlude. We learned from Dr. William D. Silkworth, physician-in-chief of Towns, that alcoholism was a sickness and not a moral defect or a lack of willpower, and that Bill had a compulsion to drink combined with something similar to a physical allergy. We both believed he would never drink again, now that he understood about his illness.

But it wasn't very long before he was worse than ever. Newfound hope was utterly shattered. I was beside myself and could think of nothing to do but take him away to the country again.

This time I hadn't the nerve to ask for a leave, so I left Macy's for good in March 1934. Nothing went so well at the farm this time.

Bill loved to fish. The very first day he tried his hand at it, he ran across a man sitting on a log with a bottle at his lips. The man, of course, was generous and shared his bottle.

This unfortunate coincidence set Bill off again. He had to go to Brattleboro to get his teeth fixed. Without a car, the only way to get there was by mail stagecoach. Instead of paying the dentist, Bill bought a bottle, which he and the stage driver shared on the way home. This happened several weeks in a row, causing the stage to be late and annoying the other passengers. Once when Bill was the only passenger, the driver was so grateful to Bill for the liquor that he drove the coach up the long, steep, rough driveway from the highway to the house. The frost in the ground was thawing, and the stage was soon stuck in mud up to its hubs. While Bill and the driver dug to the best of their drunken ability, I ran for help to our nearest neighbor. It required all the strength of his team of big bays to pull the stage out.

On one of our walks I jumped over a stone wall, pulling a ligament in the same knee I had hurt in the motorcycle accident in 1926. Bill was an angel to me during the three weeks I was laid up. He waited on me hand and foot.

But I never will forget with what trepidation I lay helpless on a sofa and watched him, half tipsy, carry the kerosene lamp at a precarious angle up the steep stairs. What if he slipped! The whole house would burn like tinder.

After Bill's teeth were fixed, he seldom went to Brattleboro, which was the only place he knew he could get liquor. Then we had many fine walks, talks, and readings-aloud together. During this period Bill wrote several articles on finance and economics. But they were never sent to a publisher.

While working at Macy's, I had noticed that customers inevitably considered veneered furniture inferior to solid pieces. I had learned at the School of Interior Decorating that this was not necessarily true, that a laminated construction was often much stronger. I got tired of explaining this to my customers and felt the public should be educated on this point. So I started writing an article on veneered furniture and studied up on woods from various countries and the process of veneering. I worked on it while we were in Vermont. Soon after we returned home, I sent it to *House Beautiful*. It was refused. But later I mailed it to *House and Garden*. The check for seventy-five dollars from Condé Nast, publisher of the magazine, made me very proud,

After the Strongs arrived at the farm in June, we moved into an outdoor "habitat" we had constructed down in the meadow. Our tent rested on a mossy knoll. Bill built a fine stone fireplace or "arch," as he called it, for cooking and to keep ourselves warm. He had had practice building these arches as a boy. In the spring when the sap began to run in the maples in front of his grandfather's, he had tapped the trees; and after collecting the sap in buckets, he boiled it down over an arch. His sister, Dorothy, said he produced really good maple syrup and sugar.

At our habitat the laundry department was a canvas army pail. One day, upon our return from a walk, having left the wash soaking in soapsuds, we were surprised to find half-eaten shirts and underwear strewn all around the meadow. Apparently cows are like goats and relish soapy cloth. Bill had to build a fence to protect our place from the invading horde.

By July we had both gained a certain amount of equanimity and felt we must get back to the city to try to earn some money.

Not long after we reached Clinton Street, my husband, who had been my daily companion in Vermont, became a drunken sot who didn't dare leave the house for fear the Brooklyn hoods or the police would get him.

To prevent his jumping out an upstairs window, I dragged a mattress down to the basement to serve as a bed. Then I dashed for the doctor to prescribe a sedative for him. There was nothing to do but get him back to Towns Hospital immediately. Leonard Strong helped with the payments.

At Towns Dr. Silkworth told me he had expected Bill could be helped, because it was so apparent he wanted to stop drinking. But the doctor was now afraid there was little hope. In order to keep Bill alive or prevent his going mad, I would eventually have to "put him away."

This, because it was spoken by a professional, I believed for a minute. But the next minute I could not accept it. Many times I had given up hope. But inevitably, for some unknown reason, hope would always creep back. I guess I could not live without it.

Numbly I went about my duties. Not daring to let myself think or feel, 1 plowed ahead like an automaton.

Upon our return from Vermont I had begun looking for a job. Finally I found one, as salesclerk on the furniture floor of Frederick Loeser's department store in Brooklyn, at nineteen dollars a week plus four-percent commission on sales. Loeser's was near enough for me to walk to work. Although I was assistant buyer in infants' furniture for a while, it wasn't long before I got into the interior-decorating department as hostess for the eight charmingly decorated showrooms. I also advised customers on decoration in their own homes.

After leaving Towns in late September, Bill stayed sober until November 11, Armistice Day. As my work prevented me from celebrating with him, Bill went to Staten Island by himself to play golf. When I reached home that evening, he was not there. At five o'clock in the morning, after a sleepless night, I found him unconscious, propped up against the iron gate in the basement areaway, his head bleeding.

It seems the bus to the golf course had broken down. While waiting for another, he and his seatmate went into a pub. While Bill righteously sipped ginger ale, he carefully explained to his companion why he couldn't drink liquor. Soon the bartender came along and said, "It's Armistice Day! Have one on the house." With visions of the first Armistice Day in France, and without another thought, Bill gulped down the drink.

His companion was flabbergasted, saying, "You must be crazy."

"Yes," said Bill, "I am crazy."

After that day he hopelessly settled down to doing nothing but drinking and perhaps writing an occasional sarcastic letter to some VIP to whom he had taken a particular dislike. He wrote many such letters, most of them about the state of the nation. Politicians were among his pet targets. A few of these letters he mailed, but after finishing most of them along with his bottle, he lost interest in sending them. Many that started in good, clear handwriting got scrawlier and scratchier, then just stopped.

His only activity was to go out sometime during the day to buy more liquor, for I never bought it for him. I had to force a little food down him once in a while; he ate very little willingly at that time. This was his condition when his friend Ebby called.

One day in the late fall of 1934, I came home from Loeser's to find a sober Ebby earnestly talking with Bill in the kitchen. Bill had been drinking all day but was absorbed and interested in what Ebby told him. He excitedly related to me the story of Ebby's introduction to the Oxford Group. It seemed a miracle that Ebby was sober, but I passed off Bill's enthusiasm as just another false hope. He had been enthusiastic about plans to stop drinking so many times before that I didn't dare let myself believe.

And true enough, Bill continued his drinking for a number of days. But apparently he thought constantly of Ebby's change. About a week later when I returned home, he wasn't in his favorite chair in the kitchen, and I couldn't imagine where he was, because he had not left the house for a long time except to get liquor. Then the phone rang, and Bill, in a voice fraught with emotion, said he would be home soon to tell me about a wonderful thing that had happened to him.

His urge to hear more about Ebby's new source of strength had drawn him to Calvary Mission on Manhattan's East 23rd Street, where Ebby was staying. On the way from the subway to the mission, Bill had stopped at so many bars that he almost forgot his purpose. In the last bar he had offered a drink to a Finnish buddy who said he was a fisherman. This struck a chord in Bill's mind— "fishers of men" —and he remembered.

When Bill stumbled into the mission dragging Alec, the Finn, with him, Ebby immediately sensed that a cup of coffee and some baked beans were urgently called for. After this reviving snack there was an evangelistic service, which Bill and Alec—considerably sobered—attended. A number of the residents got up in front of the crowd and offered themselves to God. Bill was greatly moved and started to do the same. Afraid he was still too drunk to be rational, Ebby grabbed his coattails, but to no avail. Bill marched to the front of the room and spoke as the others had. He also recounted a little of his fruitless search for permanent sobriety. He could never remember just what he said, but Ebby told us later that he made a very reasonable and moving speech.

However, this still was not enough to stop Bill's drinking. As for me, I had never believed in emotional conversions, so I was not surprised when he did not stop drinking. But it was evidence of how much he wanted to stop and how very ill he was.

He drank for several days longer; then, recognizing that he could not think out just what had happened to Ebby unless he was sober, he started for Towns Hospital. On the way, like many alcoholics about to get dried out, he stopped for reinforcement. On his arrival at Towns, waving a bottle at Dr. Silkworth, he blustered, "Doc, I have found something."

"Indeed you have," the doctor replied. "You had better get upstairs to bed."

Lois on Jerry at Emerald Lake 1903.

The co-founder of Alcoholics Anonymous aged about four

In front of the Hotel Equinox in Manchester all set to go on a picnic: (from left to right) "Bolus," "Quinia" and "Bess," Alfred the driver, and the family with Lois perched in the rear of the buckboard and brother Rogers on "Jerry," probably 1903. (Below) Granddad sitting on the Camp steps.

(Top) Granddad in the canoe on
Emerald Lake.

(Center) Rog in the old Stevens-
Duryea, 1910.

(Bottom) Dad and Mother about
this same time.

(Top) Our new tent's homemade window with its mosquito netting and flap around four sides to keep the waterproof shade from blowing when pulled down. (Bottom left) Bill on one of his industrial investigations, Penic̶l̶ ̶ ̶d̶ Ford, 1929. (Bottom right) Digging out the Dodge on Ormond Beach, Florida, 1°

(Top) Henry and Clarace Williams, Oxford Groupers, who before AA in Akron opened their house to alcoholics and their families, among them Bob and Annie. (Bottom) The Williamses' living room where the Oxford Group meetings were held from 1935 to 1939.

(Top) The "Last Mile," the long entrance hall into the New York clubhouse, the first for AAs. (Bottom) Bob's and Annie's kitchen in Akron, where early AA members toasted each other with coffee, the universal AA beverage.

(Top left) The church directory in the Akron Mayflower Hotel where Bill chose the name of the Reverend Walter Tunks to help him find another alcoholic to work on. (Top right) The stoop of 182 Clinton Street. Bill and I lived here for many years before and after he sobered up. (Bottom) The fireplace in the Clinton Street living room before which Ebby told Bill his story and Bill in turn told his own story to new prospects.

(Top) "Stepping Stones" in Bedford Hills, New York, where Bill and I lived from 1941 to his death in 1971. (Bottom) Harriet, our devoted and much loved helper for many years at Stepping Stones.

As Bill became sober, he fell into a deep depression, lightened for a while by a visit from Ebby. At Bill's request Ebby repeated the Oxford Group formula which had released him from drinking. First Ebby surrendered his life to God, having recognized that he couldn't run it himself. Then he tried to be honest with himself as never before, making amends to the people he had damaged. He tried to give himself to others without asking for any return. Although he hadn't believed in prayer, he experimented and to his surprise found it worked. He was not on the wagon, he assured Bill; he was not fighting alcohol; the problem had been lifted from him. Then Ebby left.

Alone, Bill sank deeper than ever into the abyss. The last trace of his obstinacy was finally crushed out, and he said to himself, 'I'll do anything, anything for release." He cried aloud, "If there be a God, let Him show Himself."

The effect was electric. He later told how the room blazed with light, how he was filled with a joy beyond description. In his mind's eye he stood on a mountaintop, and a great wind, not of air but of Spirit, blew through him. He was free.

After a while the ecstasy subsided and a great peace filled him, comforting him like a living presence. "So this is the God of the preachers," he thought.

Then he began to be afraid that it was too good to be true, that he must be hallucinating. But the kind doctor, answering his call, reassured him. Dr. Silkworth said he had heard of such psychic occurrences but didn't understand them. No matter what the experience had been, the doctor told Bill, he'd better hang on to it, for it was so much better than what had held him a few hours before.

Bill had left a note for me at home. Upon finding it I was quite upset. Why hadn't he consulted me about going to the hospital? What good would it do anyway? He would get drunk again the minute he left. Who was going to pay the bill? The money I earned was just barely enough to keep us going—including Bill's liquor bills. We had been forced to ask for help in the payment of the previous hospital bills, but we couldn't do it again. Dad had no money. Where could I get it? We had occasionally pawned some silver; perhaps I could sell some wedding presents now. But what possible permanent good could it do for Bill to go the hospital again?

I soon found out. The minute I saw him at the hospital, I knew something overwhelming had happened. His eyes were filled with light. His whole being expressed hope and joy. From that moment on I shared his confidence in the future. I never doubted that at last he was free. I walked home on air.

8

Damn Your Old Meetings

Whaen Bill came home from Towns Hospital, he was full of plans to help other alcoholics. Since a miracle had happened to him and to Ebby, why couldn't it happen to others, to all the drunks in the world perhaps? I went along with the idea enthusiastically.

First he would make them feel the hopelessness of alcoholism, make them see it as a progressive disease of the mind, body, and soul, a disease for which there was no physical "cure," no future but death or insanity. He could cite medical authority for this. Then he would explain how he had been released from this dilemma.

It was an ecstatic time for us both. With Ebby and another alcoholic, Shep C., as our companions we constantly went to Oxford Group meetings at Calvary Episcopal Church on Fourth Avenue (now renamed Park Avenue South) at 21st Street in New York. Shep not only was a fellow grouper but also worked in Wall Street and summered in Manchester.

I shared Bill's gratitude for what the group had done for him and for so many other people, people I surmised must have had grievous problems of one sort or another. My only problem, Bill's drinking, was being solved, so I felt no personal need for their teachings. I was only too glad to do all I could to help them, but for nearly a year it never occurred to me to apply the program to myself. I had had sound spiritual training, having been brought up in a home where love of God and of my fellowman was the guiding motive. And during my life with Bill I had tried to live by that principle. I did not think I needed the Oxford Group.

Bill went back to Towns constantly to work on alcoholics there and often visited the Calvary Mission where Alec, the fisherman, had taken up residence. Alec, nicknamed "Buckets" because he was constantly swabbing down the mission decks, later came to live with us. We stood up for him as godparents when he was baptized into the Episcopal Church by the

Reverend Samuel M. Shoemaker, and we gave him the Bible I had received at my own baptism.

Alec stayed sober several months until, stirred by wanderlust, he left our home and asked me to keep the Bible and his baptism papers for him. After an absence of about two weeks he returned to the house sober but much the worse for wear. As he wanted to continue his travels, I gave him a little money, and off he went again. After another spell he once more turned up, but this time I hardly recognized the soot-covered, drunken figure that tottered in the doorway. He had taken a job on a coal barge but wouldn't be paid for some time. He wanted money. I told him to come back when he was sober, but he never did. To our sorrow we never saw Alec again and don't know what happened to him. I still have the Bible.

Alcoholics Anonymous (yet to be formed at that time) owes a great debt to the Oxford Group. We learned from them what to do, but perhaps even more important, what not to do. The Oxford Group was an international evangelical movement started by an American, Frank Buchman, a Lutheran minister. His good friend Sam Shoemaker, an Episcopal minister and pastor of New York's Calvary Church, was head of the Oxford Group in this country.

Frank (the use of first names was a custom in the group), believed that only by changing the individual could the world be changed for the better. He did something more about it than just preaching from his pulpit. He gathered a team of "disciples" around him and descended on Princeton to reform the students.

At the Princeton meetings the Buchman team stood up and "shared" their sins with the students, who in turn rose and shared theirs. This led to the exposure of so much "immorality" on the campus that the faculty ran Frank and his team off the grounds.

Frank then took his team to Oxford University in England, where they were better received than at Princeton. Later they left for South Africa, where they acquired the name "Oxford Group," which stuck to them until sometime during 1938, Oxford University demanded the name be changed. "Moral Rearmament" was chosen by the society, which by then had grown to be a real force for good throughout the world.

The Oxford Group precepts were in substance: surrender your life to God; take a moral inventory; confess your sins to God and another human being; make restitution; give of yourself to others with no demand for return; pray to God for help to carry out these principles.

There were also four "Absolutes": absolute honesty, absolute purity, absolute unselfishness and absolute love, moral standards by which every thought and action should be tested.

Frank held the theory that if the lives of heads of state and top men of industry were changed, the underlings would follow suit. Many high officials and leaders of commerce did join the movement and professed to be changed. No doubt some of them really were. Naturally money was needed to send missionaries all over the world. So people with money to give were also sought.

Before Ebby joined the Oxford Group, he had many serious alcoholic episodes. During the last one he drove his father's car through the wall of a house that suddenly loomed up in his path. Getting out of the car and finding himself in a kitchen, he nonchalantly asked his stunned hostess, "How about a cup of coffee?"

This was the last straw for the town of Manchester. He was about to be committed to an institution when the judge's son, Cebra G., and a friend, Rowland H., both alcoholics and OG members, convinced the judge that they could help Ebby through the Oxford Group. Cebra and Rowland brought him to New York and introduced him to their OG friends. Ebby was sober several months in 1934 under their care before he came to Clinton Street to help Bill.

More than a year before this, Rowland, a successful businessman, had been so concerned about his own drinking that he consulted the famous psychiatrist Dr. Carl Jung in Zurich, Switzerland. After about a year's treatment, upon leaving Dr. Jung, Rowland soon got drunk. Dismayed, he went back to the great doctor, who told him further treatment was useless. The only thing that could possibly free him was a "spiritual awakening." Rowland replied that he did believe in God and was an elder in the church. "That is not enough," Jung told him. He would need an overwhelming experience, great enough to change his motivation. When Rowland asked how such an experience could be found, Jung advised that he ally himself with some vital religious movement. So Rowland joined the Oxford Group and stayed sober. An influential and wealthy man, he remained an ardent Oxford Grouper until his death in 1945.

Cebra soon moved to Paris and later joined an AA group there. He has lived abroad most of the time since.

Many years afterward, in 1961, Bill wrote to Dr. Jung thanking him for his advice to Rowland and telling him of the chain reaction that had been the start of Alcoholics Anonymous—Rowland to Ebby to Bill to Dr. Bob. Bill received a most interesting answer from the good man.

The Oxford Group, as we knew it back in the early months of 1935, worked in teams of six to a dozen, sitting quietly together like a Quaker meeting and listening for the guidance of God for each one. Bill belonged to a team for a while, but I didn't. The rest of the team would get guidance for him to work with such and such a person in order to "bring him to God." Bill usually had different guidance and felt no identity with the person they selected. He became a bit annoyed at being told what to do. He knew he could be far more useful working with alcoholics, with whom he could identify. He had been helped because Ebby was a fellow alcoholic and understood his problem. Therefore Bill began to invite all the alcoholics he ran into to meet with him at Stewart's Cafeteria after the Oxford Group meeting or to come to him at our home in Brooklyn.

The Oxford Group meetings on Sunday afternoons were usually led by Sam Shoemaker or one of his two assistants, and various members of the congregation were asked to speak. One Sunday Bill had been chosen to "share" or "witness," as it was often called. He recounted his alcoholic story, ending with his dramatic spiritual awakening. When he had finished, a big, florid-faced man jumped up and said he would like to talk to Bill later.

He turned out to be Fred B., a professor of chemistry at a famous college. He told Bill that he, too, had an alcoholic problem, so bad that one of the thirty teachers under him had to cover up for him constantly or he would have been fired. He needed Bill's help. From then on we saw much of Freddie, as he lived not far from us. He was an erudite, dignified, lovable person, about whom there are many stories.

Freddie didn't sober up completely for some time. One day, Green (the handyman we had inherited from my father) found Freddie lying drunk in the vestibule. As Green was about to throw him out, a voice whined, "It's only me, Freddie. Please don't kick me out." Could this be the pompous, self-assured, learned professor we had met at Calvary!

Freddie's wife, Florence, divorced him several years after he became sober. He had grown used to her money, so he looked around for another well-to-do wife. On a trip to Milwaukee to speak at a meeting, he met two sisters. One was tall; one was fat; he heard that one was very wealthy. Not knowing which, he invited them both to visit him. Deciding it was the tall one, he married her but soon found he was wrong. He divorced her, then tried to win the fat one but couldn't make it. In spite of his sometimes ridiculous behavior, we all loved Freddie.

Besides working with alcoholics, Bill had been looking around for a job on Wall Street. In May 1935 a friend, Howard Tompkins of Baer and Company, became interested in a contest for the control of the National Rubber Machine Company in Akron, Ohio, and he got Bill the job of collecting as many proxies as possible. Bill went to Akron with several other men. But the fight seemed hopeless, and the others returned to New York, leaving Bill alone at the Mayflower Hotel with only ten dollars in his pocket.

Discouraged but determined to see the job through, he walked back and forth in the hotel lobby, feeling more and more deserted and lonely. The voices in the bar sounded friendly and jolly, and he was tempted to join them. Then he remembered he was an alcoholic. Although he had not permanently sobered up anyone in New York, simply trying to help others had kept him from even thinking of drinking. He realized he must immediately find another alcoholic to work on.

At the other end of the lobby from the bar was a church directory. Picking a name at random, he called the Reverend Walter Tunks and explained his need. At first the minister was floored by the idea of one alcoholic's wanting to talk to another alcoholic, but he soon caught on, especially when Bill mentioned the Oxford Group. He gave Bill the names of people who might know of someone wanting help.

Bill had no luck with the list until he came to the last name, Mrs. Henrietta Seiberling. Hesitating at first to call a person with a name so well-known in Akron, he mustered his courage, and a charming Southern voice responded.

Henrietta was the daughter-in-law of Frank Seiberling, the tire manufacturer, and she lived in the gatehouse of the Seiberling estate. She understood immediately and invited Bill right out. Henrietta told Bill she knew just the person for him to talk to, Dr. Robert H. S— —, and thereupon called Annie, the doctor's wife. Annie said she was sorry; they couldn't make it. Bob had just come in and placed a potted plant on the table for Mother's Day (the next day). She might have added that Bob was so potted he had fallen under the table.

However, Bob and Annie were able to get to Henrietta's the following day. Bill and Bob met on Mother's Day, May 12, 1935.

Bob had been trying for some time to stop drinking. He and Annie had joined the Oxford Group a year or so before, when Harvey Firestone had brought an OG team over from England to help one of his family. The

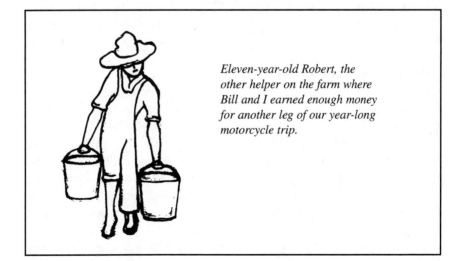

Eleven-year-old Robert, the other helper on the farm where Bill and I earned enough money for another leg of our year-long motorcycle trip.

group had aided Bob and Annie but Bob had not become sober.

Bob and Bill were drawn to each other immediately. They identified; they understood each other. It was marvelous for Bob to talk with a man who had known the same yearnings and disappointments and yet had found his way, through God's grace, to a life of service and happiness.

As for Bill, he had at last discovered someone like himself. Bob, too, wanted with his very soul to stay sober. He lapped up what Bill said and vowed to do his best. Bill was strengthened by his fellow alcoholic's enthusiasm. He needed Bob as much as Bob needed him.

In talking with earlier prospects, Bill had tried to induce them to have a spiritual experience like his own. Now he took Dr. Silkworth's advice and talked with Bob primarily about the hopeless medical prognosis of alcoholism. Bob already understood the great opportunity for regeneration through practicing the principles of the Oxford Group. He stopped drinking.

In June there was a medical convention coming up. Bob had always attended it, and Bill agreed he should go. Upon Bob's return from Atlantic City, he was drunk, Bill and Annie tapered him off as quickly as they could, because he had to perform surgery the next morning.

After operating expertly, he disappeared, and Bill and Annie were worried. But he turned up bright-eyed late that evening. He had been making restitution to those he had harmed with his drinking. Bob never had another drink, and that day, June 10, 1935, marked the beginning of Alcoholics Anonymous, though the Fellowship—with only two members—then had no name.

Annie and Bob asked Bill to stay with them, and he lived there the rest of his three-month sojourn in Akron.

I was working as assistant buyer of infants' furniture for Loeser's when I received an invitation from Annie and Bob to visit them. Only too tickled to do so, I traveled there by bus in June to spend my week's vacation with them.

I loved Annie and Bob from the moment I saw them. They were so warm, so gracious, so *good*. Bob was a tall, lanky Vermonter like Bill and, like him, yearned to be of use to others. In other respects they were very different.

As Annie, a most loving and understanding person, had weak eyes, she used to sit in a dark corner of the living room, smoking endless cigarettes. Soon Annie was showing great wisdom in giving help and advice to those who sought it. In the years to come, that little, dark corner of 855 Ardmore Avenue became a haven for those in trouble, both alcoholics and their families.

Bob and Annie had two children. Robert Jr., then in his late teens, was as crazy about cars as Bob was. Sue, a few years younger, was just beginning to be interested in boys. Sue and I seemed to be drawn to each other from the start.

A most erratic alcoholic, Ed R., and his wife, Ruth, were staying temporarily at Annie's and Bob's while I was there. At one time Bill had to take a carving knife away from Ed, who, in a drunken rage, was flourishing it around the heads of Annie and Ruth. At another time Ed phoned Bill and Bob from Cleveland to say he was about to jump off a pier and drown himself in Lake Erie. Having thoughtfully explained the exact spot he had chosen for his suicide, he was awaiting them patiently when they arrived to "rescue" him.

Bill was excited about all the new friends he was making in the Oxford Group in Akron, about his work with alcoholics and about the proxy fight. To his surprise the fight had been refinanced from New York. His life was very full.

Back from my one-week vacation, I missed Bill more than ever. My job in infants' furniture became very frustrating, but I was soon transferred to interior decorating, where I had wanted to be all along. At home, life alone was pretty dull. I went to an occasional Oxford Group meeting at Bill's urging and spent a few weekends with relatives or friends. Many of the latter were people we worked with in the Oxford Group. We knew them intimately for a while and then lost contact with them.

In Akron City Hospital, where Bob was on the staff, he and Bill had found another alcoholic who wanted to get well. Bill D., a lawyer, had been in the hospital many times; but upon leaving he had never reached home without getting drunk on the way. This time "the man on the bed," as Bill called him, got home sober (and stayed sober until his death in September 1954). Now there were three! And before Bill left, they had interested a fourth, Ernie G., who later married Sue, Bob and Annie's daughter. The Akron Group was on its way.

I thought Bill would never come home from Akron. He was so interested in everything he was doing that at one time he even considered our moving there.

I nagged and nagged him to return. He finally wrote me a long explanatory letter. It was not just that he wanted to win the proxy contest; he also had a responsibility to get the old management ousted, he believed. He wanted to prove to himself that he could succeed at something, now that he was sober. He felt he had always failed at whatever he had undertaken during his drinking years. Now he must win. When I realized this, I became more patient.

Finally, after three months in Akron, he was able to get a showdown between the two sides, and reorganization took place. Then he was no longer interested in the National Rubber Machine Company or in being its president, as had been suggested. So he rushed home.

The next few months were a happy time for Bill. He had the companionship of his alcoholic friends, the spiritual inspiration of the Oxford Group and the satisfaction of being useful to those he worked with.

For my part, I would not let myself perceive that I was not as happy as I should have been after all my dreams of Bill's sobriety had come true. Although my joy and faith in his rebirth continued, I missed our companionship. We were seldom alone together now. There was no time for outdoor weekends. Bill was busy working with his alcoholics, attending to a small business he and Hank P. had started in New Jersey, and doing occasional investigating for some investment firm. I felt left out and unneeded.

But we did go to the Oxford Group meetings regularly. I went along with Bill for his sake, because that was what a devoted wife should do, not because I needed the meetings. I felt I already had the knowledge and discipline these kind folks were seeking.

My daydreams as a young girl were of changing bad people into good ones. My mother seemed to have this gift; everyone who had intimate contact with her was the better for it, I felt. My dreams took various forms. In one of the more obvious I caught a burglar stuffing our silver into a bag. Greeting him in a friendly fashion, I tried to reason with him. It wasn't my words, my "sweet reasonableness," that made him put back the silver, so much as the power of my personality. I inspired him to want to be good.

Such frightening egotism as these daydreams portrayed! Bill's power drives were nothing to my subtle self-assurance, which, however, I thought was not too evident to observers, as I was diffident and shy in groups.

With this background was it any wonder that I thought I could inspire Bill to stop drinking and that I kept trying for seventeen years? Even after Bill's spiritual awakening, it didn't occur to me that *I* needed to change. The idea must have been working in my subconscious, however, for a trivial incident woke me up with a start, and I realized my own need for spiritual growth.

One Sunday Bill casually said to me, "We'll have to hurry or we'll be late for the Oxford Group meeting."

I had a shoe in my hand, and before I knew what was happening, I had thrown it at him and said, "Damn your old meetings!"

This unexpected display of anger surprised me even more than it did him. I might have had an excuse for losing my temper during his drinking years. But why now, when everything was fine, had I reacted so violently to his very natural remark? I began thinking about it on the way to the meeting. A friend there helped me to realize that, although I had been in the group for nearly two years trying to help others, I had never put my reliance wholly on God but had been trying to do it all by myself. That day I began to look at myself analytically for the first time. Until then I had taken myself for granted. Because I loved Bill and wanted to help him, I had felt I must be in the right.

It has taken me a long time to understand the situation, but bit by bit over the years I have come to recognize what our relationship had been before and what it later became.

Gradually the true picture became clear. When, soon after we were married, it developed that Bill drank to excess, the discovery did not dismay me too much. I had faith in my own power to change him. Living with me would be such an inspiration, I thought, that he would not need the balm of alcohol. But as time went on and his drinking got worse instead of better, neither my willpower nor my "inspiring personality" seemed to be accomplishing its objective. Then I prayed to God to help me. I communed with God but did not submit my will to Him.

I had such belief in my own will that I kept saying to myself just before an operation, "I am the captain of my soul, the master of my destiny." I believed that even under an anesthetic I could bring myself through an operation, although a little aid from God, my lieutenant, might be helpful.

After Bill sobered up, it was a great blow for me to realize that he did not need me in the way he had before. My primary aim in life, helping Bill achieve sobriety, had been canceled out, and I had not yet found anything to take its place. Slowly I recognized that because I had not been able to "cure" Bill of his alcoholism, I resented the fact that someone else had done so, and I was jealous of his newfound friends. Little by little I saw that my ego had been nourished during his drinking years by the important roles I had to fill: mother, nurse, breadwinner, decision maker. As we had no children, the mother role was very necessary to me. Also my ego was bolstered by my ability to support us both, however meagerly, and to make the family decisions that Bill was incapable of making. I had felt myself very much needed.

I also saw that I had been self-righteous and smug, thinking I was doing for Bill all that any wife could do. I have come to believe that self-righteousness is one of the worst sins. Yes, sins. It is impregnable. No shaft of light can pierce its armor. It keeps its victims apart and aloof from others.

When Bill stopped drinking, no doubt I continued trying to run things, and it took me a long time to adjust to the role of partner.

God, through the Oxford Group, had accomplished in a twinkling what I had failed to do in seventeen years. One minute I would get down on my knees and thank God (by then He had been promoted to captain and I demoted to His lieutenant), and the next moment I would throw things about and cuss the Oxford Group.

I have come to see that even well-intentioned good deeds often fail of their desired purpose when they are done from our own power alone; that the only real good is accomplished by finding God's plan and then using all of whatever ability He has given us to carry out that plan.

Ever since the shoe-throwing incident, I have taken a daily inventory and tried to be honest with myself, to analyze my thoughts and feelings as objectively as possible. It is so easy to fool oneself. The habit of rationalizing motives is hard to overcome, and I'm sure I still do it without realizing it. But over the years I have begun to understand myself, just a little.

9

The Group Conscience

H ank P., a dynamic, redheaded salesman just out of Towns Hospital, was the first of the men Bill worked with in New York who stayed sober any appreciable time—four years. Because of drinking he had been fired from a fine executive job with Standard Oil of New Jersey.

Hank was full of ideas. He had a plan to organize gasoline dealers so they would have a united buying front. He got himself a small office in Newark and a secretary by the name of Ruth Hock. Hank visited all the dealers in northern New Jersey and chose those he considered would live up to the organization's name, Honor Dealers. In the fall of 1936 he and Bill formed a small company, Sharing, Inc., to raise money for this project.

We often visited Hank, his wife Kathleen and their two boys in their home in Teaneck, which soon became the meeting place for local alcoholics and their families. Our unknown bunch of drunks was growing in New Jersey, too.

Fitz M., or to be exact, John Henry Fitzhugh M., came out of Towns soon after Hank. In no time he, too, became an intimate friend. Fitz's personality was the opposite of Hank's. He was a charming, aesthetic, impractical, lovable dreamer. For several years Bill and I practically commuted to his home in Cumberstone, Maryland, and Fitz came as often to others.

Fitz, like Bill and me, and most of us in the Oxford Group, held a daily "quiet time" to find guidance. Fitz's and Elizabeth's whole household, including three children—Cary, Hugh and Mary Potter—the black cook, Willie, and any and all guests, gathered together before breakfast. The sharing was inspiring, often touched with humor.

Fitz's sister, Agnes, administrator at the Corcoran Art School in Washington, D.C., was present at that morning session whenever she spent a weekend in her small apartment over Fitz's garage. She was so grateful for her brother's rebirth that later, when the AA book was stranded at the warehouse for lack of money to pay the printer, Agnes lent the Works Publishing Company $1,000 from her small savings. She became our friend for life.

One of the men with whom Bill worked at Towns Hospital was Silas B., who had been a reporter on the Kansas City *Star*. After he and his wife Beth moved to a house made of logs near Long Island Sound at Old Greenwich, Connecticut, he wrote several successful books.

One day Beth called Bill to come quickly, because Silas was having an attack of some kind. He had been drinking heavily for a couple of weeks after nearly a year of sobriety.

Bill got Silas, practically unconscious, into a cab for the twenty-mile ride to Towns. As they approached the hospital, Silas's heart began to fibrillate, beating so fast and irregularly that Bill was scared he wouldn't make it. At the hospital Dr. Silkworth had the patient carried very carefully to a bed while he told Bill what a sick man Silas was. Bill felt guilty, thinking he should have called a doctor at Old Greenwich instead of taking Silas for the extended taxi ride to Towns. He prayed long and earnestly at the foot of the patient's bed and then went out to talk to Dr. Silkworth, who was very gloomy about the chance of Silas's survival.

It wasn't more than half an hour before there was a pleasant voice at their elbows asking, "Why am I here?"

Dr. Silkworth, dumbfounded, yelled, "Get right back into bed!" But Silas had recovered, and he lived many happy years longer without liquor. Dr. Silkworth thereafter believed that Bill's prayer at the foot of Silas's bed had performed a miracle and that there was very much more behind the work of this band of unknown drunks than just one person's helping another. Prayer had a miraculous power of its own, a power far greater than any human power.

The weekly meetings at our home were growing in attendance. Fitz would often come from Maryland; Hank and Kathleen, from New Jersey. Shep joined us a few times; Freddie (the chemistry professor) attended, of course. There were always two or three who came several times and then stopped. Ebby and Alec, before they lived with us, would bring other alcoholics from the Calvary Mission. Brooke B. was among these, and he stayed sober as long as we knew him. Bill R., a new prospect, brought his nonalcoholic wife Kathleen with him. Ernest M., his buddy Herb D., and Herb's wife Margaret came to Brooklyn from New Jersey before meetings were started in their state. Then, of course, the boys living at our house attended. I'm sure there were many others I can't remember.

It was great to watch the change in these folks as they came to realize that there was a way out of their despair, that others had gone through the same sort of suffering. From feeling as if they were dragging anchor through life, they suddenly sailed free before the wind.

Though this new Fellowship had been strongly influenced by the Oxford Group at the start, incidents occurring early indicated that the two movements were not on the same course, I can see now.

Bill and Sam Shoemaker of the Oxford Group were very good friends, but one of Sam's assistants did not approve of Bill's working only with alcoholics and holding meetings in our home, away from the church influence. In an informal talk the assistant gave at a Sunday Oxford Group gathering, he made a reference to special meetings "held surreptitiously behind Mrs. Jones's barn." The atmosphere of the group from then on became slightly chilly toward us.

Then, near the close of 1935, the powers-that-be behind the Calvary Mission forbade the alcoholic boys living there to come to the Clinton Street meetings, saying that Bill and I were "not maximum." This not only hurt us but left us disappointed in the group's leadership.

Sam Shoemaker ultimately became a great admirer of Bill's work and apologized for the lack of understanding by members of his staff and others in the OG. For reasons of his own Sam became disenchanted with the Oxford Group and resigned. Later, in 1955 and 1960, he made grand talks before thousands of AAs at the two International Conventions celebrating the twentieth and twenty-fifth anniversaries of their Fellowship. Sam was a great man, an understanding, tolerant, inspiring human being, with a personality that drew people to him.

In spite of the rebuff, Bill and I were not immediately discouraged with the Oxford Group as a whole. Occasionally we went to OG weekend house parties. A house party was a cross between a convention and a retreat. People came from far and near to be with one another, to worship, to meditate, to ask God's guidance, and to gain strength from doing so together. Usually two or three well-known persons would lead the meetings, inspiring the rest of us to do as they had done.

Bill went to his first house party in December 1935 in Richmond, Virginia, taking with him the last cash we had—twenty-five dollars. By the time he was ready to start for home, the money was gone. While he was descending in the hotel elevator, not knowing how he was going to get to Brooklyn, a woman member handed him a ten-dollar bill, saying she was guided to give it to him.

Many such miracles, or coincidences, or evidences of man's humanity to man occurred in the group, and much inspiration was gained from the gatherings. I went with Bill to three house parties: to Stockbridge, Massachusetts, in June 1936; to the Poconos, in Pennsylvania, in December of the same year; and to West Point, in New York, in January 1937. An Oxford Group woman drove Willard, Russ, and me to West Point. Bill met us there.

But in the summer of 1937 Bill and I stopped going to OG meetings.

In Akron, T. Henry Williams and his wife Clarace, ardent Oxford Group members but both nonalcoholic, had opened their home one day a week for OG meetings. (T. Henry had lost his job as chief engineer in the National Rubber Machine Company at the time of the reorganizational trouble that had taken Bill to Akron in the spring of 1935.) Bob and Annie S. and the alcoholics they collected all considered themselves part of this group.

The Akron alcoholics continued to call themselves Oxford Group after the New York bunch adopted the name Alcoholics Anonymous in 1939, when the book of that title was published. By that time, AA groups having little OG affiliation had been started in Philadelphia, Cleveland, Washington, Chicago, Detroit, Los Angeles, Richmond, and other places.

So the Akron AAs felt it was time they, too, should stand on their own feet as alcoholics and not be allied with the Oxford Group. To many in Akron it was a heartbreaking severance. They had all learned to love T. Henry and Clarace, who had done so much for them, providing a charming meeting place, supplying delicious refreshments, and giving them much helpful advice and love. T. Henry and Clarace remained our friends, however, and the Oxford Group's part in AA's beginnings can never be forgotten.

Throughout these early years Bill and I also had the everyday responsibilities of keeping a household going, and it was not always easy. Finally acquiescing to Bill's wishes that I "get out of that damned department store," I quit work in Loeser's in March 1936. I was anxious to test myself in the decorating business on my own, and I already had a couple of customers. While at Loeser's I had started with one, who was redecorating her whole house. The other, a teacher of speech, had just moved into a new apartment.

I had fun doing the work and felt no reluctance in sending my bill to the Loeser customer, since the financial arrangements had been made at the store. But with the teacher it was a different matter. I had become friendly with her and could not seem to ask for money for my services, only for reimbursement for what I spent on materials. When she insisted I send my bill, I suggested she pay me in speech lessons. Then I never went for the lessons.

Earlier, in my first decorating job, furnishing Dr. Strong's office, I had wanted to appear professional so had presented a bill, but I greatly understated the value of my services.

I think this reluctance to take money from a friend harks back to my upbringing, which has proved wise, I believe, in other respects. As children my brothers and sisters and I were never paid for any work we did for Mother and Dad or for anybody else. We were taught we should help where we could, not for payment, but for the love of our parents and friends and for the reward of feeling useful to others. This ideal, I believe, accounts for my strange attitude about taking money from a friend. However, it did not deter me from doing so from an impersonal organizaton, such as the YWCA or a store. There I could even ask for a raise.

So I brought little money into the household after leaving Loeser's. Bill got several small stock investigating jobs. One, found for him by Evans Dick, an Oxford Group member, was to collect proxies again. This time the proxies were on behalf of an investment trust in Harrisburg, Pennsylvania; it held stock in Loft's candy stores and Pepsi-Cola. Other jobs in Chicago and Detroit brought in some money.

When I think back on those days, I wonder *what* we lived on. The Carlin sisters, whom I had met at Macy's, had a room on our top floor from 1933 to 1935 and paid a small rent. My diary for 1936 has scant notations, mostly stating that Bill went to or returned from such and such a place. Others include: "Ebby paid me two dollars for his board"; six entries about ordering another ton of coal; "While Bill and I were away in Maryland keeping house for Fitz's family during Elizabeth's operation, Joe and Ebby looked after 182"; "George H., sent by Dr. Silkworth, came to live with us"; "Bill C. came for one night. . . ."

Bill C. stayed nearly a year. He was a brilliant, Canadian-born lawyer, who worked for a well-known law firm during the day and played bridge for money at night. Hence we seldom saw him and did not know him as well as we did most of our other guests. For him gambling seemed to be an even greater obsession than drinking.

One day in the summer of 1936 my Bill came home from a visit with Fitz and family before I did. Immediately upon opening the front door, he smelled gas. Dashing upstairs, he found Bill C.'s body lying on the bed with a tube from the gas jet in his mouth. The deed had apparently been done several days earlier.

By the time I reached home the next day, Bill had attended to every detail. It was several months before we realized that Bill C. had been selling our dress clothes, which hung in a closet near the hall bedroom he occupied. Among the missing articles were Bill's dress suit, his evening jacket, my black velvet evening wrap, lined with white velvet, and several evening dresses. Suitcases had also disappeared. All these were relics of our well-to-do days.

In contrast to the grim event, occasional amusing things happened at 182. I remember one slightly intoxicated man who was sent over by Dr. Silkworth, spent the night with us and was terribly nauseated in the morning. We didn't realize what ailed him until I found an empty, Christmas-wrapped whiskey bottle in the kitchen. Before his arrival it had been full of Vermont maple syrup. Thinking it was whiskey, he must have swallowed it in one long, swift swig in order to have gotten the sickly-sweet stuff down.

After finishing my two interior decorating jobs, I didn't try to get another, but I was kept very busy. I did volunteer work at my old stand, the YWCA, besides helping with the growing family of potential AAs and commuting back and forth to our friends in Maryland. Elizabeth was sick a lot of the time, and I was called on again and again to lend a hand. I had to give adorable, two-year-old Mary Potter her insulin injections for diabetes, and I remember with what trepidation I practiced on a lemon first.

My attendance at the Y often suffered from the demands of my AA family, and I would miss meetings of the Adult Education or Public Affairs Committees, on which I worked for several years. However, the classes I taught there in interior decoration and arts and crafts were of a short, introductory nature, and I was usually able to find a substitute.

Bill's mother, following the death of her husband in June 1936, came east to visit Bill and Dorothy. This gave me a chance to really get to know her, and we became close friends.

She was a very brilliant and forceful woman, with perhaps more love for ideas than for people. After she married Dr. Charles Strobel, a cancer specialist at Memorial Hospital in New York, they both semiretired and traveled a lot. One season during a stay in Vienna, she studied psychology under Dr. Alfred Adler, the former associate of Freud. Another season they lived in that houseboat at Fort Myers, Florida, where we visited them during our motorcycle trip. When they moved to San Diego, California, and opened joint offices, he was the consultant for medical and surgical cases, and she attended those requiring osteopathy. But she found he was getting most of the patients. So she gave up her office and put to use the knowledge of psychology she had gained from Adler by leading a group of young people interested in learning more about their own behavior.

Following her visit in the East, she returned to San Diego on a freighter via the Panama Canal. Then she became absorbed in the study of the stock market. With great perseverance, she learned everything she could about it, while keeping up a lively correspondence with Bill, who teased her for being a "second Hetty Green." Showing a lot of perspicacity, she made a stack of money, most of which disappeared in real estate losses. She died in May 1960 at the age of ninety.

My dad didn't live as long. He died at eighty-one in September 1936 after a short illness. The later years had been rough for him financially. The mortgage company took over the Clinton Street house and gave him a mere $200 for the deed. He had sold the Camp and its surrounding property to Robert Shaw in August 1935, receiving only $6,000 for it all.

Although we Burnham children were all married by that time, we felt very deeply about losing the place that had meant so much to us as youngsters.

But perhaps the story of the lake isn't too sad after all. Several years after Robert Shaw's death, the state of Vermont bought the property and made it into a public park and camping area. Kept in good condition, the park gives much pleasure to a lot of people.

In the fall of 1936 Bill came home all excited because he had been offered a job by Charlie Towns as lay therapist at his hospital. I didn't analyze just why, but the idea didn't appeal to me. When Bill told the alcoholics about it at a meeting that night, they pulled him up short.

"Bill, you can't do this to us," they said. "We know you are hard up, but don't you see that for you, our leader, to take money for passing on our magnificent message, while the rest of us try to do the same thing without pay, would soon discourage us all? We'd either stop trying to help other alcoholics or else attempt to get some money out of it. Why should we do for nothing what you'd be getting paid for? We'd all be drunk in no time."

Bill immediately saw the truth in what the members said. This was the first instance of the group conscience being put to work and proving wiser than any one member, even the leader.

In January 1937 Bill got a job with Quaw and Foley, stockbrokers, and did a lot of investigating for them in cities in the East and Midwest. At one time they almost succeeded in getting him placed on the board of the Fisk Tire Company in Boston, and he was made a director of the Pierce Governor Company at Anderson, Indiana. I had to handle our alcoholic household alone while he was away, which seemed to me more than half the time.

For a short period, however, I did have some rather doubtful help. Florence R., the alcoholic wife of a business friend of Bill's, stayed with us for a while when she was fresh out of Bellevue Hospital. She soon left to look after Ruth Hock's young son while Ruth was at work in Hank's Newark office. Then Florence helped Fitz M. start the Washington Group. It was she who later objected to the title "One Hundred Men" when it was proposed for the AA book. Her story appeared in its first edition. After having made an unfortunate second marriage, she started drinking again and disappeared. Her body was found in the Washington morgue.

The business depression returned in 1937, and toward the end of the year Quaw and Foley had to let Bill go. He went to Detroit and Cleveland looking for new job ideas and, of course, stopped off at Akron on the way.

He and Bob assessed the current status of the movement. They were surprised to find that, although many of those they had worked with had fallen by the way, forty members enjoyed an average of two years' solid sobriety. This was flabbergasting, awe-inspiring. They really had hit on a program for helping alcoholics. Now they saw it could develop into something tremendous—if it was not diluted or garbled by word of mouth as one person passed it on to another.

Suppose a book was published to explain the program and give stories of how individuals had attained sobriety. Wouldn't that offer many more alcoholics an opportunity to follow suit, and wouldn't it also save the program from distortion? Bob and Bill and their forty cohorts could never hope to reach the number of prospects that a book could.

And then the movement might need hospitals. Most hospitals did not accept alcoholics, and when they did, they only calmed patients down with sedatives. They had nothing to help alcoholics stay well.

As Bill and Bob talked together and grew more and more enthusiastic, Bill began to take fire. With the promoter's imagination, he suggested that if they had their own hospitals, they might make enough profit to send missionaries far and near to carry the message. In his enthusiasm he temporarily forgot how the group had reacted when Charlie Towns offered him a job as lay therapist.

All these dreams of expansion would, of course, require money, perhaps a lot. Where and how could they get it? They must put on a campaign to raise money. Rich people certainly would be glad to give to such a noble cause.

Bob suggested they call the group together immediately and get the members' opinions on all these ideas. To Bill's surprise and disappointment the group as a whole endorsed only the book project, and some of them did not even approve of that.

At their suggestion Bill came right back to New York to try to raise money and start to write the book. The members of the Clinton Street group were more enthusiastic than those in Akron. Hank jumped into the money-raising project with both feet.

After drawing up a list of rich men who might be interested in donating money, Bill and Hank wrote or called on them all and on completing the efforts, were shocked to find they could neither procure one single dollar nor arouse the slightest interest.

One day in the fall of 1937 Bill went to see his brother-in-law. Leonard was not only our doctor but also our great friend. Although not an alcoholic he became a great friend to AA, too. Bill told Leonard about the hard luck they had been having in raising money, adding that he wished he had an entree to John D. Rockefeller Jr., who, Bill surmised, would be interested in helping alcoholics stop drinking, since he had backed the Prohibition amendment so vigorously.

After a short pause Leonard said, "Wait a minute. I think I have something. A girl I used to go out with in high school had an uncle, Willard Richardson, who was the head of all the Rockefellers' church charities."

(The Reverend Willard S. Richardson was an ordained Baptist minister but had no regular pulpit and was usually called Mr. Richardson. Later, when he had become a good friend, he was more often referred to as Dick Richardson.) "I knew him well," Leonard said. "Suppose I call him. Perhaps he'll remember me."

Sure enough he did. When Leonard told him about Bill's work and the need for money, Mr. Richardson asked them to come right over. He was most enthusiastic about the project and set up a meeting in December 1937 at 30 Rockefeller Plaza with some of Mr. Rockefeller's other advisers, to hear more about it. Dr. Silkworth and a number of the recovered alcoholics were invited to attend.

Elated, Bill immediately called Bob. He was eager to come from Akron and bring Paul S., who had been in the group a year or so.

Mr. Albert Scott, chairman of the trustees for Riverside Church, where the Rockefeller family worshipped, led the meeting. When he heard the stories of the members, he said, "Why, this is first-century Christianity!"

However, the idea of raising money for hospitals and the book did not go over so well. Mr. Scott asked, "But won't money spoil this thing?" Mr. Rockefeller's friends did concede, however, that Mr. Rockefeller should hear of this exciting new movement and that a certain amount of money was undoubtedly needed to get it under way. Mr. Frank Amos, who had done some investigations for Mr. Rockefeller, offered to go to Akron to assess the group there and make a detailed report for Mr. Rockefeller.

When Dick Richardson presented Frank's glowing account and his own comments of approval to Mr. Rockefeller, the latter was greatly impressed, except for Frank's suggestion that he donate $50,000. Like Mr. Scott, he felt too much money would spoil the motives behind the group's good works. He did offer, however, to place $5,000 in the treasury of the Riverside Church to help out Bill and Bob personally. Most of this donation went to pay off Bob's and Annie's mortgage on their home, which had been in danger of foreclosure.

Mr. Rockefeller's reaction was a disappointment to the small group of alcoholics; but as it turned out, it was one of the greatest blessings for the budding society to be known as Alcoholics Anonymous. Money would undoubtedly have finished AA before it really got started.

However, Mr. Rockefeller's friends did not entirely agree with him and sought other means to help. They suggested a tax-free foundation, so that wealthy persons could contribute to it and deduct their gifts on their tax returns. As a result the Alcoholic Foundation was formed, comprising five trustees. Three were nonalcoholics: Mr. Richardson, Mr. Amos, and Dr. Strong, who was named secretary. The two alcoholics were Bob S. and a New York member. Bill thought he himself ought not to be on the board of trustees. It was stipulated that the nonalcoholic trustees should number one more than the alcoholics, because alcoholics might get drunk. If they were in the majority, suppose they all got drunk at once! Surely chaos would result. And the alcoholic New York member of the board soon proved the wisdom of this decision by doing as feared. He had to be replaced by a more stable member.

Still there was no money coming in. A friend of Dick Richardson's, Carlton Sherwood, a successful money raiser for charities, offered to do his bit, but all for naught. Not a penny was raised.

This was the situation in the spring of 1938 when Bill started to write the book that would be titled "Alcoholics Anonymous" and would thereby give the nameless movement a name.

10

The Big Book

Bill began to write the book in May 1938 while the money campaign was still on. He dictated to Ruth Hock at the small Honor Dealers office at 17 William Street in Newark, New Jersey. The first two chapters — his own story and "There Is a Solution" — although still in the rough, were mimeographed to be used as ammunition for members to fire at hoped-for donors to the new Alcoholic Foundation.

Frank Amos introduced Bill to his friend Gene Exman, the religious editor of Harper Brothers (now Harper and Row, publishers). Gene was enthusiastic about the book. When Bill told him it would probably take nine or ten months to finish, Gene said he thought Harper would agree to a $1,500 advance during the writing period, to be deducted from future royalties.

This was extremely good news. But on the way home Bill began to think of the difficulties that might arise if a commercial publisher owned the book. Who could answer the flood of inquiries that would undoubtedly come in to Harper? If the group itself printed and distributed the book, the members had the know-how to answer inquiries helpfully and constructively. Surely the Fellowship should have control over its own book.

When Bill reported Harper's offer to the trustees, they were very pleased but couldn't understand Bill's doubts and his conclusion that it might be better for the members to publish the book themselves. The trustees felt sure that no author had ever had success in publishing his own works.

Hank, on the other hand, was very enthusiastic about the group publication idea and suggested that they forget all about the trustees and form their own publishing company. But Bill was troubled by the trustees' objections, so he went back to Gene Exman of Harper and told him about the controversy. Gene immediately saw that the group would benefit by controlling its own book, and he generously advised Bill to have the members print it themselves.

This professional opinion made little impression on the trustees but was just the push that Hank and Bill needed. Most of the New York members agreed with the group publication idea; so did Bob in Akron, but the rest of the Akron group thought it a dangerous undertaking.

Bill and Hank laid plans, however. They looked into the matter of printers, costs, and what profits could be expected. To their surprise they found that each copy of a 400-page book selling for three and a half dollars could be printed at a cost of about thirty-five cents (a far cry from today's inflated costs).

Even the possibilities of making a good profit on each book did not impress the trustees. Bill hated to go against the advice of these good friends, but he felt surer and surer that it was right for the group to own its literature.

Hank worked out a prospectus for the new publishing company. As this book would probably be the first of many works, he called it the Works Publishing Company, with 600 shares at twenty-five dollars' par value. Before Bill knew what was happening, Hank had bought a pad of stock certificates at a stationery store and typed "Works Publishing Company" at the top. At the bottom was Henry's full name followed by "President," which he certainly was not.

As the stock was just a gimmick to get the members of the Fellowship to help in the publishing of their own book, and as Bill was sure they would all be paid back with interest when the book began to sell by the thousands, he made only slight objections to Hank's irregularities in issuing these certificates.

But even with Hank's and Bill's selling expertise, the stock did not move.

Then a really constructive idea struck Hank. Why not get a magazine like the *Reader's Digest* to carry a piece about the Fellowship and mention the book? Wouldn't the interest it aroused cause the book to sell widely?

Bill and Hank immediately sped to Pleasantville in Westchester County, New York. The managing editor at the *Reader's Digest* seemed quite interested and told them that he felt sure the magazine would want to print a piece about the book, but that they should return in the spring when the book was finished.

This was the best news yet, and the stock in Works Publishing began to sell. The group pitched in when they got this added assurance that they would get their money back.

It wasn't long before 200 shares had been purchased by the members and their friends, such as Dr. Silkworth and Dr. Harry Tiebout, a noted Connecticut psychiatrist.

Charlie Towns lent Bill and Hank $2,500 to live on while working on the book, and it was then that Agnes, Fitz's sister, offered them the $1,000. These loans, we hoped, would tide us over until the coming deluge of money after the book was put on the market.

Bill left the selling of book certificates to Hank and returned to his writing. He commuted every day from 182 Clinton Street to Newark, where he dictated to Ruth Hock. (The Honor Dealers plan was by then nearly defunct.) Ruth was paid, when paid at all, with book stock.

As Bill finished each chapter, he read it to the group that met at Clinton Street. After these members had discussed it, going over every detail and making suggestions, Bill sent it to Akron for the opinions of members there.

The pros and cons were mostly about the tone of the book. Some wanted it slanted more toward the Christian religion; others, less. Many alcoholics were agnostics or atheists. Then there were those of the Jewish faith and, around the world, of other religions. Shouldn't the book be written so it would appeal to them also? Finally it was agreed that the book should present a universal spiritual program, not a specific religious one, since all drunks were not Christian.

By this time Bill was ready to start the fifth chapter, "How It Works." He was not feeling well, but the writing had to go on, so he took pad and pencil to bed with him. How could he bring the program alive so that those at a distance, reading the book, could apply it to themselves and perhaps get well? He had to be very explicit. The six Oxford Group principles that the Fellowship had been using were not definite enough. He must broaden and deepen their implications. He relaxed and asked for guidance.

When he finished writing and reread what he had put down, he was quite pleased. Twelve principles had developed—the Twelve Steps.

But when he showed them to the group, the old discussion was resumed. There was "too much God," it was said; and "For pete's sake, take out that bit in Step Seven about getting down on your knees." They thrashed it out this way and that with Bill as umpire. Finally they hit upon the phrases "God as we understood Him" and "a Power greater than ourselves." These expressions were ten-strikes; they could be used by anyone anywhere.

During this time a number of the members with one, two, or three years of sobriety were writing their personal stories of drinking and recovery. In Akron the group was larger and one of them, a newspaperman named Jim, helped with the writing; so there were more Akron stories and they were better written than those from New York.

By then I had had my own awakening and realized how much the understanding and loving cooperation of the wife could help the alcoholic in his newfound sobriety. Earlier Bill and I had been puzzled and disappointed that not all the families continued as happy as it seemed they

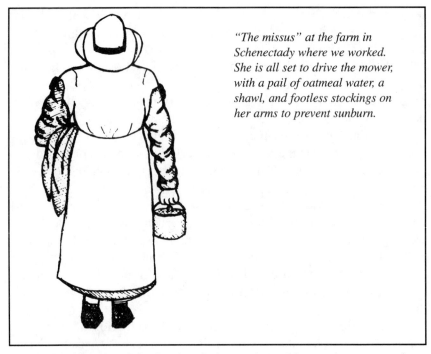

"The missus" at the farm in Schenectady where we worked. She is all set to drive the mower, with a pail of oatmeal water, a shawl, and footless stockings on her arms to prevent sunburn.

should be, after the pink-cloud period experienced by many new members had waned. We had begun to realize how distorted the relationships in families of alcoholics could often be, how important it was for families to understand about alcoholism and to rearrange their own thinking.

Therefore I had expected Bill to ask me to write the chapter "To Wives" and perhaps the following one, "The Family Afterward." When I shyly suggested this, he said no; he thought the book, except for the stories, should all be written in the same style. I have never known why he didn't want me to write about the wives, and it hurt me at first; but our lives were so full that I didn't have time to think about it much.

Then the question of the title arose. By that time 100 or so members had an appreciable length of sobriety, so the name "One Hundred Men" seemed appropriate until one woman, Florence, joined the group and objected. "The Way Out" was very popular for a while, but Bill thought it trite and had Fitz, who was often in Washington, look it up in the Library of Congress. There were already twelve books registered under that name.

At one time Bill was tempted to call the book "The W— —Movement" (using his last name) and to sign it as author. This natural but egotistical impulse was soon overcome by more mature reasoning.

Thinking up titles for the book was a great game, and dozens were suggested, among them "Dry Frontiers" and "The Empty Glass." The New York group had labeled itself simply a nameless bunch of drunks, and this led one of the men, a former writer for the *New Yorker* Magazine, to dream up the title "Alcoholics Anonymous." Bill immediately saw this was just right and so persuaded the others.

When the manuscript was finished, he wanted to be sure that it would appeal to doctors, psychiatrists, ministers, judges, and the like. These were the channels through which many alcoholics could be reached. Besides, these people might have good suggestions for improving the book. So 400 copies were made by the Multilith process (a kind of offset), and sent out marked "Loan Copy" to protect the copyright.

These typed sheets of paper, with covers of red or blue cardboard, did do some good. Just before the book went to press, a young man in California, who had heard about AA through Dr. Silkworth and had received a copy, wrote Bill to say that he had stayed sober alone for some time after reading the manuscript. Bill was so excited about this, the story of the first AA "loner," that he wired and received permission to include the letter in the book.

Some manuscript readers sent in very helpful ideas, such as: "Make it more personal by using the pronoun 'we' instead of 'you'"; "Change the musts for getting sober into suggestions; no one likes musts"; "Change the past tense to present."

Bill, Hank, and Ruth tussled greatly to make these changes and then sent the manuscript to be sharpened by a writer on *Collier's* Magazine, Tom U., whom Hank knew. Dr. Silkworth wrote an introduction, and then the book was ready for printing. The boys drove the precious document to Cornwall Press in Cornwall, New York, on the Hudson River. There they had the nerve to order 5,000 copies. The printing was finished in the spring of 1939.

In the meantime Bill and Hank returned to the *Reader's Digest*. Ushered into the office of the man they had talked with earlier, they announced, "We're ready to shoot."

"Shoot what?" returned the editor. "Oh yes, I remember now. I forgot to let you know the staff decided not to carry an article about your book."

Sad and weary, the boys reported this discouraging news to the group. Here they were with the book they had struggled over so hard, printed at last, ready to sober up "all the drunks in the world," and they couldn't get it to a single drunk. It was stuck in the warehouse, because they had no money to pay the printer.

The only prospect they now had of getting their specific know-how before the public was a radio interview conducted by Gabriel Heatter. Morgan R., a brand-new member who knew this popular radio commentator, arranged to be questioned by him on the air.

Morgan, handsome and charming, was just out of Rockland State Hospital, and the group felt uneasy about the possibility of his getting drunk before the broadcast, ten days hence. An AA member of the Downtown Athletic Club offered a solution. They locked Morgan up in the member's room at the club and guarded him night and day.

Meantime Hank had another brilliant idea. There was just $500 left in the bank. Why not use this to notify doctors about the forthcoming broadcast? Upon hearing it, no doubt thousands would send in orders for the book. So 20,000 return postcards were typed and mailed.

Many AAs had their ears glued to the radio, and all went well with the broadcast.

Hank and Bill waited breathlessly for three days after the great event before going to the post office. Armed with suitcases, they unlocked the box. They couldn't believe their eyes—only twelve cards. Five hundred bucks had gone down the drain.

During the summer there were two excellent book reviews. One, appearing in religious publications, was written by the Reverend Harry Emerson Fosdick, the popular minister of the Riverside Church, which the Rockefellers attended. The other review was in the *New York Times*. Bill and Hank previously had placed a $200 ad for the book in the *Times*.

Still the books didn't move. Something had to be done. Through Charlie Towns, Bill met Morris Markey, a writer who promised to do an article for a September issue of *Liberty* Magazine. This was fine, but September was a long way off. So Bill asked Bert, an AA who had a fine tailoring business on Fifth Avenue, if any of his customers might be interested in lending the Works Publishing Company $1,000. Bert finally got a Mr. Cockran, a Prohibitionist, to lend him the money personally. Bill received this gratefully from Bert but made sure it put the Works Publishing Company under no moral obligation to the Prohibitionists.

Thus the printer was kept quiet until September. After the appearance of the article, "Alcoholics and God," in the September 30 issue, *Liberty* was swamped with mail. It forwarded 800 inquiries, including 350 book orders, to the small Works Publishing Company office. By then Hank had a job in western New Jersey, at some distance from Newark; so it was up to Ruth Hock and Bill to personally answer every single one of the letters, assuring the writer that there was indeed new hope for alcoholics and their families.

11

The Clinton Street Boys

Once there was a funny man
Who lived at 182.
He had so many drunks around
Who didn't know what to do.
He nursed some, he razzed some,
He taxied some to Bellevue.
But the funniest thing about him was,
He really "fixed" a few.

The pulse of life was beating so fast for Bill and me at this time, impelling us forward and onward, that we seldom had time to look back. So there are many unconcluded stories in these pages. Bill had given up preaching to alcoholics, but we still took them into our home, "institutionalizing" them to a certain extent. Undoubtedly we did too much for them, because very few of the prospects that we housed at 182 Clinton Street became sober, responsible people for the rest of their lives. Russ is the only one I can think of who did.

One of the saddest days in Bill's life and mine was the day Ebby got drunk after two years of sobriety. It seemed as if the bottom had fallen out of everything. Our first reaction was to wonder: since Ebby had faltered, could *any* alcoholic live a sober life to the end? But then we thought of Ebby's recent behavior. He had begun to feel sorry for himself because he hadn't a girl or a job. Although he went to Oxford Group meetings regularly, he was not enthusiastic about digging up new alcoholic prospects to work on. A slip in thinking can lead to drinking.

Although it was heartbreaking to realize Ebby had slipped after having sparked so many others through Bill, it didn't mar my confidence in Bill. Ebby's drinking seemed to make Bill more careful to stick closely to his high principles and to work harder helping others.

From then on Ebby had a most erratic career: periods of sobriety mixed with long periods of maudlin drunkenness. It was hard to know how to handle him when he came begging for money, for we all felt so deeply in his debt that we hated to refuse him.

One time he lay in our Clinton Street vestibule cursing me and calling me ugly names the entire night because I wouldn't let him in. Bill was away; so in the morning I got someone to take Ebby to Bellevue Hospital.

Ebby stayed sober for about seven years in Dallas, Texas, where several AAs had offered their help. He found a girl who, he felt, couldn't remain dry without him, and the AAs got him a job. Altogether it was a fine period for Ebby. But when his girl left, he began drinking again. The Texans were most patient and kind, but he could not stay sober. He drifted back to New York, where he might have become a heavy burden for Bill if Bill's gratitude had not been so great.

Later, when we lived at Stepping Stones, Bedford Hills, New York, Ebby stayed sober for a year with us. Finally Margaret M. and her invalid husband offered to take him under their wing, along with several other alcoholics they were drying out on their farm at Ballston Spa, New York. During the latter part of his stay, he got sick. Margaret, who was a trained nurse, looked after him patiently while also attending to her ill husband and to the other alcoholics. I believe Ebby stayed sober most of six years, during which Bill collected a fund to pay his expenses. Ebby died sober in 1966.

After those first two years in the Oxford Group, why did Ebby get drunk? It was he who gave Bill the philosophy that kept him sober. Why didn't it keep Ebby sober? He was sincere, I'm sure. Perhaps it was a difference in the degree of wanting sobriety. Bill wanted it with his whole soul. Ebby may have wanted it simply to keep out of trouble. Or maybe he *couldn't* want it with his whole soul, because he was too ill. Beyond that crucial visit with Bill, Ebby seemed to do very little about helping others. He never appeared really a member of AA. After his first slip many harmful thoughts seemed to take possession of him, and he appeared jealous of Bill and critical, even when sober, of both the Oxford Group and AA.

Ebby loved the ladies and considered himself a great connoisseur of women. He never missed a good-looking ankle. This sometimes embarrassed both the women and their husbands.

Bill's gratitude toward Ebby was so deep that, ironically, this very feeling and the protectiveness it engendered may have made it harder for Ebby to stay sober. Bill never got over this gratitude, but maybe his later policy that "gratitude should go forward [to newcomers], rather than backward" was at least partially a result of his own experience.

I feel disloyal in writing these notes about Ebby, but it is important that future generations of AAs know why Ebby was never considered the founder of AA. Bill always thought of Ebby as someone special—not just one of our Clinton Street boys.

Once when I was sick, my sister Kitty came to nurse me, and one of the boys milling around in the living room said, "One woman can look after five men, but five men can't look after one woman." I don't remember exactly who those five men were, but here are brief sketches of some of the boys who stayed with us for short, long, or broken periods.

Russ was a good-looking, extremely intelligent man, who had conducted his own band while a student at Brown University. After he lost a good position at Time-Life, nothing but a few odd jobs interfered with his drinking. It took him some time to quit entirely, but today he has been sober thirty-odd years.

Wes W., whose humor took the edge off his Napoleonic complex, was a roly-poly advertising man with whom I had several adventures, amusing now but trying at the time. Although he first came to meetings in 1935, he took up residence in our basement in February 1937. We put a cot in the old dining room down there, and he cooked for himself in the old kitchen. One Sunday morning when I asked him up for a pancake breakfast, he was late; but the other boys had left him a normal share of pancakes. After bolting these down, he immediately started out the door without a word. When I asked where he was going, he said, "To Childs for pancakes."

As Bill was away a lot, I made a rule: no one who was drinking would be allowed into the house. So one night half-drunk Wes, nearly as wide as he was tall, slid down the coal chute into the cellar. Why his great bulk did not stick in the chute, I'll never know. Later he did get stuck in the old-fashioned, soapstone washtub in the kitchen, where he was taking a bath. He yelled and screamed so loud that I dashed down to see what was the matter. There he was, folded like an accordion, with his chin on his knees and a faucet over each shoulder, yelling for me to get him out. I brought him a towel, and then as he ducked under the faucets, I yanked his arms, and he came out easily enough.

One time after an argument with another hopeful, Wes grabbed a carving knife and chased his antagonist all over the house.

Another time, when he had been on a binge for several days, he wanted to sober up in order to keep an appointment about a job in the morning. He asked me to call a doctor to give him something to settle his nerves. It was late at night; no doctor wanted to come out to sober up a drunk. So Wes and I started out on foot to find one. Our neighborhood was nicknamed "Murderers' Row" because there were so many doctors on every block.

I helped Wes up and down front steps, held his arm steady as he lit cigarette after cigarette, and rang a dozen doorbells, all with no success. One doctor, in a nightshirt, yelled out of the window that he'd call the police if we didn't get off his steps immediately. But we kept on. Finally spotting a policeman, I asked him where we could find a doctor, explaining that my friend had been drinking too much, had a very important appointment in the morning, and needed a doctor's help to sober up. The cop replied, "Very commendable, very commendable," and told us about a physician at the nearby Hotel St. George. When we called the doctor on the house phone, however, he would have none of us.

Wes, who had become shakier and shakier, said, "This is it. I have to have a drink." So I took him around the corner to Childs and held a whiskey to his lips.

When I said, "Now let's go home," Wes returned, "But a bird can't fly on one wing." *That* was it for me. I left him sitting on the stool in Childs. Of course he never went for the job interview the next day.

Since I often had to cope with the boys on my own, another sort of trouble might have seemed likely, but I encountered it only once. My theory that advances from men were caused by the woman's attitude held water through all my experience with alcoholics—with one exception. The exception was a dearly loved friend of Bill's and mine. This man must have misinterpreted my expressions of gratitude for his sobriety. One night while Bill was away, the man, to my dismay, walked into my bedroom. However, he did not make too much fuss at being rebuffed, as there were others living in the house who could have been alerted.

One of the men whom Dr. Silkworth sent over to see Bill was Chris, a rugged wire-rope salesman who wanted to recover from his alcoholism. Recognizing Chris's skepticism, Bill first talked pragmatically about the program before cautiously leading up to his own discovery that only a Power greater than himself could remove his obsession with drinking and restore him to sanity. But this tough customer was skeptical about everything, and when Chris left after about two hours, we both felt Bill had made no headway.

A half hour later, however, the bell rang. When I opened the door, there stood this hard-boiled guy with tears streaming down his cheeks, repeating over and over, "I have found it, I have found it."

He told us what had happened. After he left the house, the thought had come to him: "If Bill has discovered a Power greater than himself, so can I." Dizzy with joy at this realization, he had clung to a lamppost, and crying like a baby, he had prayed, perhaps for the first time in his life.

Chris became a stalwart member of AA. He stayed sober many years. After he married a second time and moved to a farm in southern New Jersey, we didn't see much of him. Occupied with his two young daughters, Lois and Christina, and his farm, he rarely went to meetings and found little opportunity to work with other alcoholics. One day, out of the blue, we

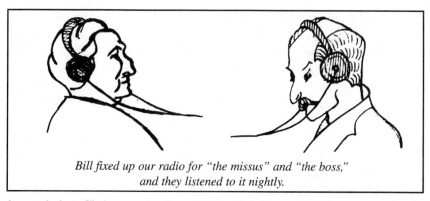

*Bill fixed up our radio for "the missus" and "the boss,"
and they listened to it nightly.*

learned that Chris was in Towns Hospital. It was another great shock, because Bill and I had both felt very close to Chris. He never got back into AA. I guess his pride was too great.

Often alcoholics like Chris came to Clinton Street to talk with Bill; sometimes it was Bill who went to them. One such occasion strangely recalled our shell-hunting expedition to Sanibel Island years before. Henry Ford heard about AA in some way and wrote the Alcoholic Foundation asking "the head man" to come to Detroit to "fix my friend." On Sanibel Bill hadn't wanted to meet "the daddy of all flivvers." Bill felt this time was different. He was not intruding; he was needed. He went to Detroit and saw Henry Ford. The friend, who eloquently conducted a radio program sponsored by Ford, was often so drunk that the broadcast had to be called off. At other times the podium was pulled over near the entrance, where an assistant would steady the speaker till ready and then give him a slight shove so he could grab hold of the podium. He could talk when he couldn't walk. Bill had a chance to explain alcoholism to the man's wife, but the radio man himself refused to see Bill and made only one or two more broadcasts before Ford had to take him off the air.

Among the people we worked with were Jack and Jean W., who lived nearby. Jack, a homely, likeable little scamp, was always getting into trouble and maneuvering himself out of it. He never stayed long in any place he didn't like, no matter how strong the bars nor how secure the lock. Manipulating two pairs of apron strings, his mother's and his wife's, he was forever pulling first one pair and then the other. Jean, his wife, would put him in the hospital, and Mary, his mother, would immediately get him out and take him home with her to baby him. Mary was a great gal but had absolutely no idea of what alcoholism was.

George H., who lived with us, and Jack were good friends. One day George, although drinking himself, recognized that Jack was drinking so much he should go to the hospital. George determined to take him to Bellevue. At the admission desk George, fairly sober, was telling the clerk how intoxicated his friend was. Jack, who had barely been able to stumble into the hospital, was yet able to sober up momentarily when strategy called for it. Behind George's back, Jack kept pointing at George, tapping his own forehead and shaking his head. The clerk got the message, put George in the lockup ward and let Jack go. George, later an airplane mechanic, was killed during World War II. Jack never entirely sobered up but stayed around AA for a long time until his death.

In 1940 when Jack was at High Watch, a retreat for alcoholics, his wife, although not trained in cooking nor particularly interested in it, was commandeered to prepare the food for the fifteen or so boarders and guests.

High Watch Farm, situated in the hills near Kent, Connecticut, belonged to an inspired philanthropist. She wanted to be called Sister Francis and thought that by opening the doors of her charming old farmhouse to any wayfarer, she could help those in need and spread her belief in what was known as the New Thought Movement.

Nona and Walter W., both early AAs, were friends of Sister Francis. She invited Nona to this peaceful spot to recover from a period of heavy drinking. Thus began AA's contact with Sister Francis and Joy Farm, as High Watch was then called. Many alcoholics went there for help. A corporation was formed in April 1940 by a few interested members, and an AA member was hired as manager, not to do AA work, but to run the farm. This was the first of a great number of rehabilitation homes for alcoholics initiated by individual AAs, as private citizens.

Another home like ours, also constantly full of stray drunks, was that of Bob and Mag V. and their four children. It was a rambling house called Bog Hollow, in Monsey, New York. In Mag's grandmother's time two huge rooms had been added, one above the other, each heated only by an open fireplace. We called them "Upper and Lower Siberia," and they housed many alcoholic graduates of nearby Rockland State Hospital.

Bob V., a brilliant, capable executive in a pharmaceutical house, had become enthusiastic about AA in 1937. He stayed sober a good part of the time afterward, but when he made business trips overseas, he invariably got drunk. In spite of this he started AA groups in several South American countries.

Mag was loved by everyone. Always good-natured, she took Bob's often autocratic behavior in a most philosophic manner. Mag's and Bob's experiences with their "boarders" were similar to ours at Clinton Street. Very few of those they took in recovered permanently.

One person from Rockland, who lived at Bog Hollow for some time and helped with the cooking and cleaning, did stay sober until his death in the 1960s. He was Tom M., a retired fireman. When the AA clubhouse on 24th Street in New York was opened in 1940, Tom became its caretaker.

Hard-boiled, yet kindly and honest, he made a good watchdog.

Another longtime guest at Bog Hollow was Jim W., the perfect confidence man. Alcohol was just a shield for James Russell Lowell W. The people he hoodwinked could be counted in the hundreds. To him the truth was that which served him best. He fooled all of us except Mag, who recognized from the first that Jim was totally phony.

He was a handsome, well-mannered, apparently cultured scion of an old Massachusetts family. He must have gone to medical school, at least for a while, because even doctors believed his claim that he had lost his doctor's license because of drinking. He could get anything he wanted from a hospital, even drugs from locked medicine cabinets. One Christmas he gave us all fine gifts. Bill's was a nice, warm navy pea jacket. We learned much later that Jim had "borrowed" all the gifts from the hospital. His exploits grew to such dimensions that they were on all our tongues. Mag's spinster cousin was bewitched by him and gave him anything he asked for, including her car.

A few years later Bob was transferred to Washington, D.C., and Jim went along. Jim found some kind of mechanical job with the government, something like putting up lights in a new parking lot. World War II was on by this time, and an edict went forth that all employees had to be fingerprinted. Opportunely Jim managed to have his right hand smashed between the bumpers of two cars. At Bob's and Mag's, where we were visiting, Jim appeared with his hand all swathed in gauze and splints. He told us maggots had been inserted beneath the bandages to eat up the infected flesh. He couldn't be fingerprinted.

Another time Jim convinced doctors at Bethesda Naval Hospital that he was dying. Bill was called down from New York, and a lawyer in AA, Ned P., was asked to make out Jim's will.* Bequests totaling $116,500 were to go to various members of his family, to Bob and Mag, to Mag's cousin, and to Bill. True to form, Jim didn't die, and there was not a penny in the banks he had designated. But what was his purpose? Perhaps to get drugs at the hospital.

Sensing he had run his course in AA and must seek fresher fields, Jim disappeared completely—with the cousin's car. He was never heard from again. Was he, as he claimed, a former physician? One incident showed that he did have some medical skill.

When Marty M., an early AA who had come to meetings at Clinton Street, had a slip, Bill found her where she was hiding and took her to Bog Hollow. There she suffered what seemed to be a gallstone attack. Ever on the alert, Jim borrowed an instrument from Rockland to remove the stones. After some trouble in persuading Marty that she could swallow the tube,

---

*Note: In the spring of 1975, soon after Mag died, Jim's will was given to me as a great curiosity by her son and daughters.

he gently pushed it down her throat and apparently snaked up small, gravel-like stones. Marty soon recovered.

Although not the first woman to enter AA, Marty has had by far the longest sobriety among AA women. When she first heard of AA, she was a patient in Blythewood Sanitarium in Greenwich, Connecticut. Dr. Harry Tiebout, her psychiatrist, handed her a copy of the AA book, with which he was greatly impressed. It was one of those prepublication copies sent to selected doctors and ministers. It is reported that when Marty threw the book out of the window, Dr. Tiebout insisted she get it back, read it, and go to the meeting in Brooklyn.

I well remember the day she came. She was afraid of what she would find at the meeting, so she preferred to stay upstairs with me. I finally persuaded her the AAs wanted and needed her. We went down together.

Back in Greenwich Marty reported her Brooklyn trip to another alcoholic at the sanitarium with the still famous remark: "Grennie, we are no longer alone." In a short time meetings were held in the sanitarium.

For most of the years since then Marty has devoted herself to educational work in the field of alcoholism. Her buddy, Greenville C., also stayed dry. After teaching flying in World War II, he retired to Nantucket Island, where he lived quietly until his recent death.

Although most of the Clinton Street boys did not stay sober, they nevertheless gave a lot, unknowingly, toward the development of AA. They taught Bill, Bob, and other early members—and me, too—what worked and what did not. A rehabilitative or rejuvenating period in a "caring" atmosphere is beneficial for any recovering alcoholic; but at Clinton Street, Bog Hollow, Ardmore Avenue in Akron, and similar homes, we tried to offer more than that in our eagerness to be helpful. We often made the mistake of overprotecting our new prospects, thus encouraging dependence on other people rather than on the AA program.

Such early AAs as Hank and Chris, who stayed sober four or five years, did a tremendous amount of actual work for AA, then fell to pieces completely, demonstrated for future AAs the great danger in giving free rein to unhealthy emotions like pride, jealousy, and resentment, and in drawing away from the Fellowship.

These slips of our close and trusted companions might have discouraged others about the future of AA, but Bill and I had such strong faith in the success of AA "for as long as God shall need it" that it never occurred to us to worry about the Fellowship: We worried only about the dear friends who had slipped. But we had nothing to go on except our faith.

P.S. *Several readers of this manuscript have suggested that the author of the jingle at the head of this chapter be identified. But ... can't you guess? It sure wasn't William Shakespeare or Ogden Nash.*

12

Living Around

After my father remarried and left Clinton Street, we paid the mortgage company a tiny rental to stay on there. The owners were glad to have the house lived in until, when values rose, they could sell it at a good price. This time came in 1939; toward the end of April we had to move out. It was necessary not only to pack up our own possessions but also to get rid of those accumulated by my parents from 1888 on. The Salvation Army and Goodwill Industries got carloads.

It took me a month to sort things out, distribute some to our friends and relatives, and pack what we wanted to put in storage. Having no money for even a small apartment, we had no idea when or where we would ever again have a home of our own.

I am compulsively orderly in small matters. So every tightly packed bureau drawer or bookshelf was labeled and its contents listed in a notebook. These lists would come in handy when we needed to get something out of storage, such as blankets or silver, and particularly when we finally unpacked at our new home, wherever it might be.

It was sad to leave Clinton Street, but our AA friends helped us out. Many invited us to stay with them until we were able to afford a place of our own. The local group, meeting at the home of Hank and Kathleen, voted to provide a "Bill and Lois Improvement Fund" (they didn't state just what was to be improved—perhaps our dispositions!) and passed the hat at meetings to raise money to help meet our living expenses for a year. I believe we were richer by twenty dollars a month because of their generosity.

We felt it unwise to accept Ed E.'s offer of his Connecticut farmhouse, "Dun Nibblin," for the summer, because we were not sure that he had "dun nibblin'." But we gratefully accepted the kind proposal of Chris's family that we use their bungalow at Green Pond in northern New Jersey until June. Harold S. drove us there, bag and baggage.

It was delightful to be in the country, especially when spring was transforming the world. Delicate new leaves slowly embroidered the stark silhouettes of the trees, each variety making a different lace pattern against the sky—Irish, Brussels, Duchess, Italian Point, and others. The new, rolled-up grape leaves, with their pink linings, looked like little rosebuds.

Sounds were as thrilling as sights. Awakened by the unmistakable honking of geese, we dashed out to watch the orderly triangle flying north to nest, a faint trace of their honking lingering after they had faded into the distance. To Bill the beating of wings heard as a flight of ducks rose from the water seemed to crescendo like the start of a great motor.

A nearby cottager, who had just arrived for a weekend, apparently was hunting for an old friend. As we passed by, she asked us, "Have you seen a wren around here?" Although enchanted by the great variety of birds, we had not seen a single wren.

We had no car, so we had to walk about four miles to Newfoundland for provisions and to take the train to New York. Bill had many things to attend to about his book and the Alcoholic Foundation, so he went to New York frequently. We therefore rented Jack C.'s big, sporty Lincoln Zephyr at one cent a mile. I'll never forget one rainy afternoon when, on my way to pick up Bill at the station, I had a blowout while still in the wilds of Green Pond. Alone, I spent nearly two hours changing that heavy tire in the muddy road. As there was no way to let Bill know I would be late, he was terribly worried when I finally reached him.

Many AAs visited us at Green Pond. When we were alone on the days when Bill didn't have to go to New York, we did many fun things: rowing on the lake, hiking, even trying out our old bath-towel-sail idea. It worked much better on Chris's canoe than it had on the Hudson River rowboat.

Roaming through the area, we found many lovely wildflowers such as arbutus and pink lady slippers. After a good hike we would often duck in the pond and then sunbathe on a large, flat rock.

But before we knew it, the end of May had come, and it was time for Chris's family to take over their cottage. Then we started our visiting merry-go-round, hopping from here to there among AA friends and our relatives. During the years 1939 and 1940 we changed our abode fifty-one times, not counting weekend stops!

When I read over my diaries, it seems impossible that any two people could pack as much activity into their lives as we did in those early days of AA. And I felt, as I still do, that I belonged to AA. While jotting down the group's activities, I would write that "we" did this or that, for hadn't I discovered how much I needed the AA program, and didn't I attend most of the meetings with Bill? Not yet had I recognized the need for two separate Fellowships.

By this time at least a dozen AA groups had evolved in the New York metropolitan area, and those of us who were mobile went to as many meetings as possible, no matter how far away. In 1939, soon after we left Clinton Street, Hank and Kathleen started holding Sunday meetings at their new home in Montclair, New Jersey, and Bert T. let us continue our Tuesday meetings at his elegant Fifth Avenue tailor shop. While Marty and Grenny were patients at Blythewood Sanitarium in Greenwich, Connecticut, the two of them, together with Bill, persuaded Mrs. Wylie, the owner, to let them hold meetings there. Then a friend of Leonard and Helga H. lent us an apartment for a few months at 72nd Street and Riverside Drive in Manhattan. Leonard was a nonalcoholic who served many faithful years as a member of the board of trustees of AA. His lovely wife, however, soon died of alcoholism.

Harold and Emily S. constantly opened their Flatbush home to the group. Bert T. suggested that his tailoring loft on the West Side was more practical for AA gatherings than his Fifth Avenue shop, so when the 72nd Street apartment was no longer available, we switched to his loft.

In August 1939 Mag and Bob, at Bog Hollow, took over the Sunday meetings. As I mentioned earlier, Bob started meetings among the patients at nearby Rockland State Hospital. The doctors there felt the AA get-togethers were so important for their alcoholic patients that they sent a busload weekly the forty miles to the Tuesday meetings in New York as well. At first these were held at Steinway Hall, since AA was then prosperous enough to be able to rent a room there. When AA acquired its own quarters in early 1940, the Tuesday meetings were transferred to that location. The unique building set back from the street at 334½ West 24th Street was the first clubhouse for AAs anywhere.

In October 1939 Gordon M. and others found a room to rent for AA meetings in the South Orange Community House, the first New Jersey meeting that was not held in homes.

One of our personal way stations was Morgan R.'s apartment on 51st Street, Manhattan. The Foundation had formed a revolving advisory committee, which met there weekly. Each session was preceded by a spaghetti-and-meatball supper, and the preparation of this fell to my lot.

Another way station was a vacant apartment loaned to us for a week. Once when I returned there late, Bill greeted me holding a spoon in one hand and a can of cold tomato soup in the other. What a way to live, I thought. But I quickly pushed the unhappy feeling away. Like others, I often fooled myself into believing what I wanted to believe, just as I had when I convinced myself I was totally happy after Bill sobered up. Suppressing my true feelings then about the lack of our companionship, which was so important to me, had resulted in that shoe-throwing episode.

Now the same sort of thing happened again. I hadn't let myself realize how deeply I longed for a home of our own, nor how tired I was of living around in other people's houses. One day in February 1940, as Bill and I were going through Grand Central Station, I suddenly sat down on the stairs and exploded, "Will we ever have our own home?" I wept oceans right there in public.

Bill understood perfectly; he, too, wanted a real home. At that point we started looking for a place to live. Wherever we stayed—Brooklyn, Westchester, Connecticut, New Jersey, or the big city—we took some time out to consult real estate agents or scour the countryside looking for a house. The hunting was mostly a gesture, for we did not yet have the wherewithal for such a move. But hope persisted. I couldn't erase my vision of Bill with a spoon in one hand and a can of cold soup in the other.

That winter other concerns were on Bill's mind. He had been seeing much of Mr. Rockefeller's friends, some of whom were trustees of the Alcoholic Foundation; but there had been no personal word from the big boss himself since the spring of 1938. Then one day in early 1940, Dick Richardson told Bill that Mr. Rockefeller was planning a dinner for many of his wealthy friends, so they could hear the AA story. The members were ecstatic at this news. What a bonanza! The dinner was held on February 8th at the Union Club. Bill and Bob and the other AAs told their stories and listened to Dr. Foster Kennedy, an eminent neurologist, praise their Fellowship. Then they began counting up on their cuffs how great could be the haul from those present, many of whom were well-known tycoons.

John D. Jr. was ill, so he had sent his son Nelson to host the dinner. When

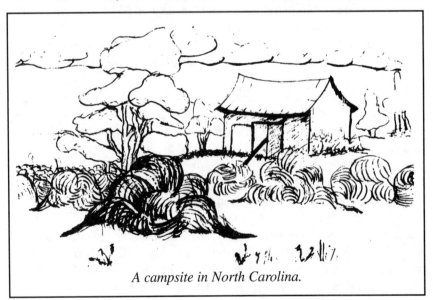

A campsite in North Carolina.

Nelson finally got up to talk, there was a great hush of expectancy. He told how impressed his father was with this unique movement, which resembled early Christianity. What it needed, he said, was encouragement and understanding—but not money. Money might spoil the spirit of unselfish giving of oneself that was the very core of the AA program. He said his father was donating a small amount, $1,000, to help them get started. The AA boys' hearts sank. When the meeting closed, they despondently watched an estimated one hundred million dollars walk out of the door.

Afterward Mr. Rockefeller wrote a letter commending AA to each of the friends who had attended. A few of them sent in small amounts to the Foundation for several years; as a result, Bill got thirty dollars a week for a short time, every penny of which was eventually paid back.

However, the publicity about the dinner was a great boon to AA. Soon Bill and Bob and the others saw that its near failure as a money-raising venture was a blessing in disguise, for now each AA could feel an individual responsibility for carrying forward the work of the Fellowship. Large quantities of money could have caused disagreements and bad feeling that might have disrupted the Society. Thus the tradition of self-support evolved out of what had seemed a great disappointment.

About a month after the dinner the Alcoholic Foundation moved its headquarters from Newark to New York City, at 30 Vesey Street, Room 703. The move was a main point of disagreement between Bill and Hank. Hank wanted the office left in New Jersey, where he lived and could carry on what business remained of his Honor Dealers.

Also Hank had not wanted to give his stock back to Works Publishing Company. But Bill had persuaded him that for the good of AA they both should do so, with the stipulation that a ten-percent royalty on the book sales be given to Bob and Annie for their lifetimes.

There was a third, more personal reason for Hank's growing grudge against Bill. For some time Hank's marriage had not been going well. He had many arguments with Kathleen, and they were planning to get a divorce. Now he wanted to marry Ruth Hock, formerly his own secretary and then the secretary for the Alcoholic Foundation. But Ruth was not interested in his proposal. The work of Alcoholics Anonymous fascinated her, and she went with the Foundation to New York.

Hank's thinking became more and more erratic. Soon he was drunk and blaming Bill for Ruth's refusal. This was a very sad thing for Bill, since Hank had been a great help for four years in planning, writing, and selling the book and in forming the early New Jersey AA groups.

Kathleen was eager to be free of Hank, because she was tired of his threatening behavior. Dr. Silkworth had warned Bill that Hank was vicious when drunk and could be a real threat to Bill or anyone else who got in his way. I was to be a witness at the divorce; but Bill felt that because of Hank's murderous mood, it would be too dangerous for me to be present. So we dashed to Monsey in New York State to avoid my being subpoenaed in New Jersey.

Later Hank got back on the program for a short period and rewed Kathleen after a couple of unsuccessful marriages. But his drinking finally grew worse, and in a few years it ended in his death.

From June 1939, when we left Green Pond, until July 1940 Bill and I steadily rode the visiting merry-go-round. We settled down for three months when a friend of Ora T. sublet to us her furnished apartment at 42 Barrow Street in Greenwich Village. The rent was reasonable, and we could just scrape up the total. It was a godsend.

Bill had been thinking that AA was well established and didn't need him any longer, and he ought to put his own house in order by getting a job. So he began hunting around. Joe T. introduced him to an executive of the Torpedo Motor Boat Company, where he applied for a job as financial analyst—unsuccessfully. Chris, who was making money selling wire rope for Paulson and Weber, convinced Bill that he should join that firm. All summer Bill heroically tried selling wire rope, although he had no interest in the product and few entrées into maritime and other industries where it was used.

For a time I, too, had been thinking that I should try to find some way to bring in money. Our life was so hectic that a regular job would be almost impossible to hold down. While working at Loeser's, I had sold my article on veneers to *House and Garden*. Why not try writing, which I could fit in between our many activities? So I squeezed in as much time as possible writing an imaginary tale for the magazine *Romantic Stories*. I sent it off in September, but it was soon returned.

Several jingles I wrote were returned also. Discouraged by these failures, I concentrated on typing up my "Hoboes' Diary," the account of our 1925 motorcycle trip.

Ebby, who was sober at this time and attending meetings, was also job-minded and got work at the New York World's Fair. He could sometimes give us passes to one or two of the shows. It was great fun to be able to take friends from out of town to the fair occasionally.

Bill was getting tired of selling wire rope, and when Ned F., an AA lawyer from Washington, D.C., suggested he should be selling something inspirational like democracy, Bill flew higher than a kite. We even took three or four lessons together in a Dale Carnegie course on public speaking. Herbert W., an AA who managed the course, had recommended it as being useful in "selling democracy." Bill came down to earth only when he began to figure the hows and wheres.

The year before, the New York AAs had assured Bill that they *did* need him as their guide and leader. Finally he gave in to their persuasions and told Paulson and Weber that he felt unsuited to sell wire rope.

But he made one more try for an outside job. Don V., who had a good mortgage business, asked Bill, as an industrial analyst, to investigate two companies. After Bill reported on these companies, he called it a day and gave his full time to the future of the AA Fellowship.

He had been thinking for some time that a national magazine article about AA would be highly beneficial to the Society and to the sale of the book. So in October 1940 Bill went to Philadelphia to see Curtis Bok, one of the owners of the *Saturday Evening Post*. And before we knew it, Jack Alexander, a *Post* feature writer, was in New York scanning AA from all angles. Jack was at first very skeptical and expected to write a derisive article. But as he met the members and heard their stories, he grew more and more interested in the AA philosophy. After a visit to Akron he became an excited enthusiast.

He wasn't the only excited one around. "We AAs" could hardly wait for his piece to be published. Ruth Hock and I worked out a plan to use volunteers to help answer all the inquiries that would flood in. I was to handle these AAs and their families, serve as liaison between them and the Foundation office, and use as headquarters, the 24th Street Clubhouse. That was very handy since Bill and I were then living at the Clubhouse. We had just moved, our next-to-last, though we did not know it at the time.

After the end of the sublease at Barrow Street we had jumped back on the visiting merry-go-round for a month or so until there was a chance to fix up a tiny room for ourselves in the Clubhouse. We painted the walls and curtained two orange crates to use as dressers. From an old friend we bought a bed without a footboard, so Bill could hang his feet out. We had to crawl over the bed to reach our clothes, which hung on hooks on the wall. About ten feet square, the room had a window; but for air it was easier to open the door to the fire escape. A lot of space was taken up by an old, broken dumbwaiter to the kitchen below; it had been used by the previous tenants, the Illustrators Club of New York.

The room had little privacy and few conveniences, but living at the clubhouse had advantages in addition to my work there. Even after our last move we kept the room for the nights we spent in town.

At the clubhouse that winter Bill first met Father Edward Dowling, a Jesuit priest who, upon hearing of AA, came all the way from St. Louis to New York to meet Bill. He remained one of Bill's closest friends, and Bill often spoke of him as his spiritual sponsor.

Father Ed did much to increase AA's growth. In the beginning many Catholic leaders were dubious about AA because of its nonreligious, although spiritual, attitude. Father Ed not only wrote a splendid review of the book but recommended in many Jesuit communications, that AA be encouraged in every possible way.

We were hoping for similar encouragement from the *Saturday Evening Post* article, and our hopes were fully realized. On February 25, 1941, the issue dated March 1 hit the newsstands. For five or six weeks, Bobby and I and the helpful corps at the club spent our days answering telephone calls, writing letters, keeping records, and talking with newcomers, their families, and their friends. AA meetings were held at the club every night for the newcomers.

Upstairs at the club, there was a weekly meeting for the relatives of alcoholics already in AA. But when Bobby and I talked to inquiring families of alcoholics, we simply encouraged them to go to open AA meetings. It did not occur to us then that the upstairs family meetings might also be enormously helpful to these desperate relatives, even though the alcoholics they loved were not yet in AA. Al-Anon Family Groups were still in embryo.

After the *Post* story the number of members at local AA meetings began to swell. Even as early as March 4, 150 were present at the club meeting, and by March 31 the South Orange group had more than doubled its membership. It was the same everywhere. Groups outgrew their meeting places and had to be divided. Older members worked frantically with newcomers. These newcomers in turn, after a month or so of sobriety, were sent on Twelfth Step calls to help still newer-comers. It is estimated that 6,000 AAs owe the start of their sobriety to the *Post* article, and nobody knows how many more thousands were sparked by them.

What a hectic but fruitful time it was!

13

Bil-Lo's Break

Two wonderful things happened in early 1941: Bill and I got a home of our own, and I was taken on a six-week cruise to South America.

We had been hearing about a house in Bedford Hills, New York, that a friend of an AA wanted to sell us. The idea of our buying property in Westchester County was so fantastic, so remote that we paid little attention when Joan C., the AA, and her philanthropic friend, Helen Griffith, told us about the latter's house, which they thought was just suited to us. Even when Helen said she would make the price within our means, we hardly heeded.

But one day while we were visiting some AA friends in Chappaqua, Ruth and Wilbur S., we realized we were not far from the famous house. Our friends drove us up to look at it, just out of curiosity.

It was a sunny March day with patches of snow on the ground. The interesting, brown-shingled, hip-roofed dwelling stood among trees on a hill, overlooking a valley. We were charmed by its secluded location and wanted to see the interior. A window was unlocked, and we clambered in. Bill was crazy about the large living room with its huge stone fireplace. I, too, liked it all but had always pictured a little white cottage beside a brook. This house seemed too big and formal to me, and there was no brook, although the surrounding woods were lovely.

Actually it wasn't very big, having only seven rooms: living room, three bedrooms and a kitchen downstairs, and a long, bookshelved library and one bedroom upstairs. And it wasn't really formal, for the rough stone fireplace implied cheer and friendship and hominess.

So after Don V. offered to help finance the house and its 1.7 acres, we accepted, as of May 1,1941, the plan Joan and Helen had worked out. The contract called for forty dollars' a month amortization on a $6,500 selling price, with nothing down and no interest the first year. Joan, in real estate in New Jersey, had investigated our circumstances and reckoned that, since the twenty-dollar monthly storage charge on our furniture would be eliminated when we moved, we could easily raise another twenty dollars, all that would be needed, except money to pay the back storage bill and the moving expense. That's where Don's help came in. How could we lose with such a generous arrangement? We soon made another visit to take measurements and figure out the placement of our furniture.

Naturally we now had to have a car, and Bill made a deal with Ed E. for his old Stutz. (Dame Rumor had it that no sooner did the thirty dollars hit Ed's palm than he dashed for a drink.)

Because of the April 20 sailing date for my cruise to South America, Helen let us move early into "Bil-Lo's Break," as we first called the house. Before I left, I tried to get our furniture and utensils in place in bedroom and kitchen, so Bill would have comfortable places to sleep and eat. Boxes of books and barrels of china still cluttered the living room, however.

Fan Williamson, Chris's mother, who took me on the cruise, was kind and charming, but Bill always affectionately called her "Ironsides." She was the sister of Moore of the Moore-McCormack Steamship Line. Fan and I had become good friends after she and Chris had lent us their cottage at Green Pond. She was very grateful for her son's sobriety.

We were the only passengers on the freighter, and the captain was an old friend of Fan's. He had a canvas swimming pool put up on deck. We had our meals at his table with the officers and played bridge with him at night. At the various ports, while freight was loaded or unloaded, he guided us on tours of the cities. In Rio de Janeiro he took us for a breathtaking ride in a cable car slung from a mountain peak across the bay to Mount Corcovado, where a huge statue of the Christus stands. The view was superb. In the evening we danced at a couple of nightclubs. Unaccompanied young women solemnly strutted around and around the dance floor, apparently to attract partners. The heavy, monotonous beat of the Brazilian rhythm throbbed through my head for days afterward.

It was a great trip and a wonderful experience, but I kept wondering what was happening at "Bil-Lo's Break." How was Bill getting on in the house alone? What spring flowers were out, and were there any birds around? After all these years we now had a home of our own in the country, and I wasn't there to watch the drama of spring.

When I did get home, I learned that Bill had had a miserable time. He had tried to make order out of chaos. The fireplace was the only source of heat in the house, and a bad cold had settled in his chest. I had been enjoying myself on a marvelous cruise while he was working hard, ill and lonely. I felt guilty, particularly when he told me about the following episode.

His cough was getting worse and worse, so he went to the drugstore for medicine. Like many alcoholics he figured that if the recommended dose was helpful, two or even three times that amount would do more good, so he sipped and sipped from the medicine bottle. When it was about half empty, ideas popped into his head. "Lois is away. I'm alone. Very few people know where I am. Whiskey is what I need to stave off this cold. It would cure me in no time, and no one would know the difference."

Quickly he recognized the crazy thinking. He hadn't thought this way for years and then only twice, not long after he stopped drinking. What had caused this distorted notion? He read the label on the medicine bottle and found there was a high percentage of alcohol in the cough mixture. That was it. Even the small amount of alcohol his system had absorbed was enough to change his thinking. This was a great lesson to us all.

The first of Bill's other two temptations to drink, as I told earlier, was just before he met Bob in Akron, when his business had run into a dead end and his friends had left.

The other incident happened while we had four or five alcoholics living with us at Clinton Street. I was beginning to feel rebellious, since Bill didn't seem to need me anymore. But one of those boys did. I needed to be needed. So I spent much time trying to help him out of his difficulties. I told Bill about my interest in helping this man, and Bill was most understanding and loving for a long time. But one day a jealous streak struck him, and he ran out of the house to get drunk. Fortunately, either out of habit or by divine guidance, Bill made his way to Hank's house. There he calmed down. He came home sheepishly, without having gone near a bar. I think this was the only time I ever worried about his getting drunk.

It was so cold on Christmas Day in the sunny South that we piled on all our clothes. Wearing layers of sweaters and a leather vest, Bill heated stones in the open fire. wrapped them in newspaper and placed them in our tent.

How wonderful it was to have a home of our own! At that time in our lives a home was first of all a refuge from wandering. Then it fulfilled the need to use many of our dormant aptitudes. And it gave us a chance to enjoy such interests as music, reading, and gardening. All of these perfectly normal activities had been mostly denied us for a long time. It gave us, particularly, an opportunity to be alone together and to plan for the future, both for the improvement of the place and for the growth of AA. Characteristically, neither Bill nor I had any doubts about the future of AA.

Much needed to be done in the house. There was no furnace, and the upstairs rooms were unpainted. In late spring Bill saw a coal-burning furnace on the sidewalk in front of the Bedford Hills bar, which was changing over to oil. Bill gave the bar owner ten dollars for it, and an alcoholic plumber helped him with the installation. The bar furnace served us adequately, if sootily, until the royalties from the book began to come in and we, in turn, were able to change to oil.

It is strange how liquor, irrespective of AA, has been associated with the house. Helen Griffith, the former owner, had to pay for its construction twice because of alcohol. Originally, after the foundation had been laid, a builder friend was supposed to finish the job while she was abroad. When she returned, not a stick or a stone had been added. Her "friend" had completely disappeared with the $5,000 she had paid him. She later learned he was an alcoholic.

Of course we had no money to hire painters or floor scrapers or to buy draperies. As I had always liked to work with my hands, I tackled the various jobs. Bill had to commute to the office three or four times a week. At home he was often busy writing papers and figuring out policies for AA. He helped around the place whenever he was free.

Did you ever paint a ceiling? If you did, your neck was probably stiff for days afterward, as mine was after I painted the ceiling of the upstairs library, forty-three feet long.

The living-room floor had to be scraped down and stained to make a background for the Oriental scatter rugs I had inherited. My knees had calluses on them before I got it done.

The wall around the six French doors onto the porch looked bare and unfinished so I painted swags of draperies across the top and down the side walls—really quite effective. As the windows of the house framed pictures of the lovely outdoors, I didn't want to obstruct the view with curtains. A few remnants and seconds that I picked up at sales were sufficient to make valances and decorative shades, which emphasized the windows. By laboriously prying out all the tacks from an old Victorian chair, I learned how to reupholster it. For many other pieces of furniture I made slipcovers. In the kitchen I carefully laid squares of linoleum in an interesting pattern.

Bill had to fix the waterworks. A pump, in its tiny house down the hill, pushed water from the spring all the way up to a tank under the porch and then through the pipes in the house. But it had a hard time getting the water upstairs, where our bedroom was. So Bill purchased from Sears Roebuck an open tank for cattle and put it up in the attic. Because of the weight of the water, he felt it wise to reinforce the attic supports in that area. This tank was filled periodically by the pump, and then gravity supplied the house with water. Bill worked out a Rube Goldberg system for knowing when the tank was empty and when the pump had filled it: a float in the tank turned on a red light in the kitchen when the water reached a low level; when the pump had filled the tank, a bell rang and kept ringing until the pump was turned off.

This worked well until one day when Bill was afraid there wouldn't be enough water in the tank for company on the weekend. He turned on the pump "only for a short time." But friends unexpectedly invited us out for the evening, and we forget all about the pump.

On our return we could hear the alarm bell ringing before we entered. Our hearts sank. Inside, water was cascading down the stairs. My carefully laid linoleum in the kitchen had all risen up. Even to this day the library ceiling has not recovered and shows stains no matter how often it is painted.

A long, rough right-of-way led from the main thoroughfare past a group of neighbors' homes and our garage and then wound up the steep hill to the back steps of our house. Bill worked hard and long on this right-of-way, improving it for our neighbors as well as for us.

To get from the house to the garage, we used a shortcut of rugged stone steps down the steep hill. Because of the constant climbing up and down, we changed the name of the house from "Bil-Lo's Break" to "Stepping Stones." This also implied a connection with the Twelve Steps.

When we were able to buy a little more land, Bill laid out a better road that avoided the steep hill, and he and another AA built a garage nearby. Later, on a knoll beyond the house, they also built a studio where Bill could write and meditate.

One afternoon when he was away, I returned from a call on some neighbors, and, wondering why the porch was so dark, I discovered the entire outside of the screen was covered with fluttering, mahogany-colored moths. Why? I couldn't imagine until I noticed a larger, more brilliant moth on the inside. Then I recollected. Several months earlier I had found a caterpillar and, as I had often done when a child, put it with leaves of the plant it was eating into a jelly glass covered with mosquito netting, to watch it make its cocoon and later emerge as a butterfly or moth. When this moth had broken from her cocoon, she had escaped to the screen and sent out her signals to the males that she was ready.

137

Early the next morning the female was still on the screen, but most of the males were dead on the ground outside, their wings separated from their dried-up bodies. However, a new army of suitors, darkened the screen that evening. The performance was repeated once more, but by then I felt I was being cruel. When I let the female out, away she flew with her gallants chasing her.

I collected fifty or so beautiful wings of the defunct males. Today, more than thirty-five years later, many of the wings, mahogany-colored with a green eye at the tip, are still intact. I have since learned she was a cecropia moth that can attract males from as far away as three miles.

Wherever we went, we brought home plants or seeds to beautify the house and garden. We labored on a vegetable plot but found the moles, rabbits, woodchucks, and deer enjoyed most of it. It was fun to see the animals around, especially deer under the apple tree in the morning, but not so much fun to find the tomato plants eaten away, the lettuce and spinach nibbled off and, just as the kernels of corn became tender, the ears stripped by woodchucks.

Bill came to the rescue. He buried a wire fence deep in the ground and strung electrified wire along the top. The deer could have jumped over this; but the constant click-clack of the battery scared them, and they never did.

In April 1942 Bill applied to the War Department for an appointment in the Army but was refused because of minor physical defects, his tennis elbow for one. So we continued to plant and putter to improve our home, in between receiving AA guests and making trips to group meetings, many near home and some far away. Bill was also working on the future structure of AA service.

Among our guests at Stepping Stones were our beloved Bob and Annie, who used to visit us every year. They got so fond of the area they thought they would like to live nearby. Together we looked around for a home for them, but we never found just the right place, and they gave up the idea.

Another of our visitors was Gladys S. from Madras, India. We were terribly excited about her advent. She had read about AA in *Liberty* Magazine and had come all the way to New York to seek sobriety.

Gladys looked very regal in her sari and spoke beautiful English, learned in London. Since she had limited funds for a three-month stay, reluctantly given her by her mother for her "cure," she rented a dismal hotel room in the New York theater district. When Bill went to see her, she salaamed three times before him. The "Princess," as some AAs called her, had ordered up tea and a dozen sandwiches. Having expected dainty tea morsels, she was shocked at their uncouthness—great thick slabs with the stuffing hanging out—and there were twelve of them.

She developed a crush on Bill and would swish up to Bedford Hills bringing love poems and armfuls of flowers. She stayed sober a year or so until her death in an accident after her return to India.

Another visitor was Sibley D. Marty M. had found her in Bellevue Hospital and helped her into AA. An extremely talented violinist, Sibley had suffered a paralytic stroke and was most depressed. Her teacher, Leopold Auer, whose pupils also included Mischa Elman and Fritz Kreisler, is reported to have said she could become the top woman violinist of all time.

Bill would often bring Sibley to Stepping Stones for a few days, and we tried to encourage her to teach violin playing, but she felt it would be too frustrating. For several years she had long periods of sobriety. When a Stradivarius lent to her by a violin maker was stolen, Bill helped the police find it. But Sibley began to drink heavily again and was taken back to Bellevue and thence to an institution on Long Island. Although I wrote to the institution, Sibley was never heard from again.

Helen, Bill's half-sister, had been working in Montreal. She came to live at Stepping Stones and it was a joy to have her with us. Soon, she got the first paid job in the subscription department of the *Grapevine*, AA's monthly magazine. She became so enthusiastic about AA that eventually she married into the Fellowship.

By the time of her arrival Ebby was living with us. Bill had scooped him up drunk in New York and brought him to Stepping Stones. His year of sobriety here gave us so much hope for him that Bill and I went off for a vacation on Nantucket and left Helen and Ebby at home. We had reckoned without the impact of his fiftieth birthday. Apparently the idea of reaching such an advanced age without being married was so devastating that he couldn't take it and accordingly got drunk.

Soon after Ebby's departure Howard arrived. Bill found Howard, his second cousin, dead drunk in a New York hotel and brought him home. Becoming a good AA and doing much constructive work on the house, Howard stayed for five years, before getting married and moving away.

During this period Bill and I and some of our neighboring AA friends became interested in extrasensory perception and used to meet every Saturday night to experiment. Much enlightenment was gained by all. Bill, as usual when his interest was aroused, became absorbed in the subject and could talk of nothing else—except, of course, AA.

14

Teacher Turns Pupil

Throughout the 1940s there was a great deal to talk about in AA. In 1941, because of the *Saturday Evening Post* article, a second printing of the book became necessary. Soon the debts were all paid, and the Fellowship was self-supporting through the sale of books and pamphlets and through the voluntary contributions from the groups that Bill had suggested as the chief basis for financing. Ruth Hock left the AA office to marry a member from Ohio in 1942. Bobby B. took her place, the first alcoholic secretary at the Foundation.

Groups were started mainly in two ways. Before the Alcoholic Foundation (later called the General Service Board) was formed or the Big Book was available, personal contact was needed to start a new group, but afterward many groups came into being through use of AA literature. The West Coast groups and those abroad mostly began in this way.

But the individual personal contact continued and probably always will continue to be the most dramatic and effective way.

There were several AAs who carried the message to a great number of alcoholics. Irving M., from the lower East Side of New York, sold venetian blinds in the South from door to door to the well-to-do, whom he called "the silk-stocking trade." Any number of groups were started through his enthusiasm. Larry J., a newspaperman from Cleveland, also worked in the South and did much for AA in Texas through his articles in the Houston *Press*. An entirely different type of AA ambassador was Captain Jack S., who started many groups in overseas ports when he went ashore from his tanker.

Johnny P. of Detroit was another who traveled a lot and, like Johnny Appleseed before him, scattered seeds. Wherever he went in the Midwest, he inspired alcoholics to band together and start meetings.

A prisoner released from San Quentin got AA on the outside and in 1942 went back to form a group within the walls, the first prison group. Letting

*Vista up Clinton Street,
Brooklyn, from the stoop of
number 182.*

him do this was an act of faith in AA by the prison authorities, as San
Quentin was a maximum-security establishment for criminals.

Other prisons were soon permitting AA members to help alcoholic
inmates and to form groups within their walls. Most of the "inside" members were sincere and proved so after their release. There were also those
who just went along for the ride, but even many of these came back to AA
later. Regular AA groups soon saw the need to establish institution committees, periodically visiting hospitals and prisons in their neighborhoods.

Over the following years, as groups sprang up in far-flung places, AA
legends grew around them. This yarn picked up in the boondocks was
popular in AA, whether true or not. A drunk in the Utah desert ordered a
Big Book from the Foundation. When he got sober, he thought of his
friend the town drunk at Moab. The town drunk sobered up, as did several others. Becoming public-spirited, the newborn AAs took pictures of
scenery to impress a railroad that contemplated building a spur through
Moab. The films showed white flecks and markings on canyon walls.
Some members sent for a Geiger counter. There was uranium in them thar
hills. The AAs all cashed in and revived the defunct mining town. Now
rich and influential, they took the place over, one becoming mayor,
another chief of police and so forth.

In the large cities new groups constantly forming needed information
centers or intergroups to assist them. The foundation office encouraged
these local centers to get underway. Among the first intergroups estab-

lished, the association for the New York metropolitan area continues to this day its custom of holding a dinner each fall to celebrate the start of Bill's sobriety. At one of these Norman Vincent Peale, popular minister of the Marble Collegiate Church in New York and a compelling radio preacher, was the guest speaker. He said he thought AA was "the greatest spiritual force in the world today."

Bill and I visited many groups on various occasions. In late 1943 and early 1944 we took an extended trip to the West and South. We had never seen the Grand Canyon, so after visiting the Chicago, Omaha and Denver groups, we took this opportunity to do so. Both of us were terribly impressed by the canyon, but our physical reactions were very different. From the brim, Bill got the squeams looking down the mile or so to the bottom, whereas I could gaze down with perfect equanimity. Because it was wartime, the ordinary tours to the bottom were not given, and the precipitous, corkscrewing path had not been cleared of rolling pebbles. But Bill and I wanted to go, so we hired a guide with army mules. On top of one of these huge animals, I was scared out of my wits every step of the winding eight miles down, especially when the mule stopped at an outside curve and shifted its feet to make the tight angle. Bill felt perfectly at ease on the animal's back.

After a picnic lunch in the tropical green beside the Colorado River, we ascended. By then I had myself better in hand and even ventured to look around occasionally. I hadn't dared do that riding down.

From the canyon we took the train to Los Angeles, and Bill's mother met us there. She was greatly impressed by the large AA meeting in Hollywood, where more than a thousand were present. During our stay in San Francisco we visited San Quentin Prison, but I wasn't allowed to attend the AA meeting held there. Later at Folsom Prison near Sacramento, 137 convicts signed an illuminated appreciation of AA and gave it to Bill. After visits to Portland and Seattle we took Bill's mother back to her home in San Diego.

I spoke briefly at most of the AA meetings during this trip, but at Seattle I tried to make constructive talks at the gatherings of the families of AAs.

At a monastery-like retreat in the desert at Trabuco where we rested for several days, Dave D. from Palo Alto, California, introduced us to Gerald Heard, a nonalcoholic, who was a great philosopher, writer, and student of both Eastern and Western religions. He became a lifelong personal friend and admirer of AA, and soon introduced us to the famous writer Aldous Huxley, who became another lifelong friend and admirer of AA. It was Aldous who wrote that Bill was "the greatest social architect of the century."

In Tucson, Arizona, and Houston, Texas, there were good meetings; but in New Orleans at a dinner for sixty members, the AA chairman arrived slightly squiffed. A woman, Esther E., had started the group in Dallas, Texas, so there were proportionately more women there than in any other place we visited. The Little Rock, Arkansas, group was so anonymous that the leader, Bud G., spoke from behind a curtain to the audience of 1,200. But Bill spoke from the open platform.

Oil wells were the predominate feature in Oklahoma City. Even the poorest of shacks, surrounded by goats, chickens, and tin cans, had wells of "liquid gold" in the front yards. The AA meeting in that city was fine and well-attended.

It was lucky that the purpose of this trip was not to get away from the cold, for we saw snow on the palm trees in Los Angeles, frost on the cacti in Arizona, and ice glistening on the Spanish moss in Houston.

Our next stop was home, where we watched the arrival of spring in the woods around our own house.

As summer approached, the first issue of the *AA Grapevine*, June 1944, was published. So much was happening in AA all over the country that a few members thought a periodical with news of the various activities would be welcomed by AAs everywhere. But the *Grapevine* was at first an eight-page newspaper supposedly just for members in the New York area and for those serving in the armed forces all around the world. For that year's December *Grapevine*, I wrote a short account of my experiences as the wife of an alcoholic, through the drinking years and the early years of AA.

The *Grapevine* soon established itself as a real "meeting in print" (to use Bill's description) and reported such news as the celebration in Cleveland of AA's tenth anniversary, June 10, 1945, attended by 2,500 members including two from Canada and one from Mexico. After the groups approved the idea, the *Grapevine* became AA's national publication with the December 1945 issue. A private operation at first, it was later taken over by the Alcoholic Foundation, which formed a separate corporation to manage and publish it. Bill worked hard on this structure, as he did on the whole AA fabric.

By this time public interest in AA had been aroused. Articles about it appeared in magazines and newspapers, and ministers praised it from their pulpits. The 1945 movie version of "The Lost Weekend," a novel by Charles Jackson, although not about AA, presented an accurate picture of an alcoholic, which helped to educate the public.

The need for such education became more and more obvious. One of the early members of AA was a man who lived in Maryland. He often got drunk, and when upbraided by another AA, he explained why. He had a health-insurance policy which, unlike other health insurance or any thinking outside AA at that time, recognized alcoholism as an illness. So in order to get money to support his family, our friend had to be drunk at checkup time.

Facilities for detoxification were rare everywhere. Doctors considered alcoholic patients a nuisance, unreliable in paying, and morally weak. Few physicians took them seriously or had the patience to treat them. Most hospitals refused to admit them. Towns Hospital, a private facility for addicts (of alcohol and other drugs), where Bill had gone and Dr. Silkworth was in charge, was small and expensive. New York City's Bellevue admitted alcoholics but kept them only a few days under sedation in the psychiatric ward, or sent them to Rockland State Hospital as mental patients.

So in order to get alcoholics hospitalized, their illness was often disguised as something else. Sister Mary Ignatia, of the Sisters of Charity of St. Augustine, was administrator of St. Thomas Hospital in Akron. The guile (now famous in AA) that she and Dr. Bob had to employ in smuggling alcoholic patients into the hospital is an outstanding example. Beginning in 1939, they made an unbeatable team, tagging an alcoholic with any ailment—heart disease, kidney trouble, or anything else of which he may have had some symptoms. When Sister Ignatia was transferred to St. Vincent's Hospital in Cleveland, the recovered alcoholics themselves saw to it that there was a ward for alcoholics. Bob and Sister Ignatia treated as many as 5,000 alcoholics during a ten-year period.

In 1945 New York AAs were fortunately able to get Knickerbocker Hospital to set aside a small ward for alcoholics. This was presided over by a trained nurse who was in AA, Teddy R., and attended by Dr. Silkworth.

Even to this day there are not enough hospital beds for alcoholics, although the situation is much better than at the start of AA. Throughout the country AA members themselves have established many rehabilitation homes where alcoholics get expert medical treatment as well as an introduction to AA. These homes are operated privately, of course, not by AA itself.

Some professors at Yale University, Dr. E.M. Jellinek among them, had become particularly interested in the study of alcoholism, and inaugurated the Yale Summer School of Alcohol Studies in 1943. Social workers and teachers attended it, as well as many AAs and other alcoholics who desired to learn more about themselves and to help others. Bill was invited to tell about AA on the closing day of the six-week course.

For many years thereafter, even after 1962 when the summer school was transferred to Rutgers University in New Jersey, Bill and I always attended the closing sessions. I usually spoke briefly about my reactions and the need for families not only to understand as much as possible about alcoholism, but also to live by the AA principles of recovery.

The burgeoning of new treatment and understanding of alcoholism in the early 1940s was welcomed by AAs, of course. But it began to present dilemmas for the Fellowship.

Bill recognized that, although the individual AA had the Twelve Steps to guide him, the groups needed some sort of framework within which they could operate. The ordinary rules and regulations that held other societies together would not apply. AAs would not accept them. In addition to the question of relationship with outside agencies, there were problems of unity, ultimate authority, membership, singleness of purpose, effect of one group's actions on another, money in all its aspects, public relations, and anonymity.

As Bill, guided by his long experience, helped groups work out their problems, he saw certain principles evolving. He began to assemble them into what became the Twelve Traditions.

A national committee for education on alcoholism, formed in 1944, provided two examples of the events which led to the Traditions, specifically those of anonymity and nonaffiliation. Its founder and director, Marty, was a solid AA and a good friend of ours. Since the purpose of the committee was to educate the public about alcoholism, Bill and Bob thought it would be all right for Marty, when she told her own story, to mention that she had reached sobriety through AA.

At an earlier time Bill had done the same. Newspapers had shown his picture and stated that he had founded AA. At first he had not resisted the publicity too firmly, but when other members began to tell about their connection with AA in the public media, he realized what a serious mistake it was. A well-to-do member broadcast over his own radio station that he had joined AA. Next day, drunk on the air, he laughed it to scorn. A famous baseball player joined AA and then told the press about it, so that his membership was widely publicized. Recognizing that all AAs should be anonymous at the public level, Bill pleaded with the press to preserve individual anonymity, warning that otherwise the whole Society might collapse. The press thereafter was unusually understanding about AA and carefully guarded members' anonymity on most occasions.

Ever since the name Alcoholics Anonymous had been adopted, anonymity had meant different things to different AAs. A few members didn't believe in it at all; people in the limelight sometimes felt they were aiding AA by associating their well-known names with the Fellowship; others were very fussy about keeping their anonymity, even at AA meetings. But to most, anonymity was a social and business protection outside meetings. As time went on, however, some began finding in their anonymity more and higher spiritual values.

A second problem was involved in Marty's mentioning her AA experience: the public became confused about the distinction between AA and the health committee she headed. When the committee solicited funds, some people sent money to AA, stating mistakenly that it was in response to AA's appeal. AA has never solicited funds from the public and declines all donations except those from its own members.

Experiences such as these showed Bill, Bob, Marty, and the others how important it was to keep AA separate from any other society. Thus the Tradition of nonaffiliation evolved.

Through constant correspondence Bill noticed that when AA principles were applied, group problems could be solved as they arose or could be prevented from coming into being. He also recognized that certain actions almost invariably led to trouble.

For instance, a well-to-do AA died and left $10,000 to the foundation in her will. At first this seemed like a godsend. Then Bill remembered how the accumulation of too much money in group treasuries had caused argument and disruption. Once or twice a member or two had even gotten drunk as a result. Bill talked with Bob and many other members about it, then took the matter to the trustees. They passed a resolution that AA should be self-supporting and should accept no large gifts, even from members. So the bequest was turned down, and the case added material for the proposed AA Traditions.

Bill often went to Akron to consult with Bob, whose practical viewpoint and deep spiritual insight were always beneficial. Bob agreed with Bill's analysis of the principles that evolved from the groups' experiences. Finally, after much consultation with members around the country, Bill set down on paper the resulting guides, AA's Twelve Traditions. They were first published in the April 1946 AA *Grapevine* as "Twelve Points to Assure Our Future," in what is now known as "the long form."

Bill called the Traditions for AA Group Unity the Second Legacy, the First Legacy being the Twelve Steps for Individual Recovery. Both were to become the foundation for Al-Anon Family Groups, too. The Traditions safeguard the Fellowships and the group unity needed to give individuals opportunity for recovery through the Steps.

The growth in every aspect of AA during the 1940s was miraculous. In a 1949 letter Bill wrote, "I have become a pupil of the AA movement rather than the teacher I once thought I was."

15

Later Years Together

In the summer of 1946 we drove our new De Soto to many of the beauty spots of the West and North. The trip included a visit to Bill's dad and his wife, Christine, in Marblehead, British Columbia. It was not all vacation, however, as things at the AA office in New York began to pile up. Bill received several frantic wires, so he had to take time to write a bulletin about anonymity to be sent to all the groups.

We also stopped in Hollywood to see how a script was progressing for a movie about AA to be produced by Hal Wallis. The writer had been to Stepping Stones to talk with Bill about it. But the script was never filmed, because the Alcoholic Foundation indefinitely postponed any offer of AA's collaboration in the production of a commercial AA picture.

Bob S. (known to most AA members as Dr. Bob) had to have a serious operation in 1947, and Bill went to Akron to see him several times. Fortunately Bob recovered satisfactorily and continued his many AA activities.

Our next extended trip to the groups was in 1948. We went by train through Canada to the West Coast, stopping at Toronto, Winnipeg and Calgary, where there were excellent meetings.

We were on a boat steaming up Kootenay Lake, headed for a second visit to Bill's dad, when he wired us that snowslides had made the road impassable from the landing to his home at Marblehead, and that we should return to Nelson. It was already dark when the boat reached the landing, but we wanted to see the folks and were willing to take the chance. So, with the aid of one dim flashlight, we waded, burrowed and slid our way for three miles through sixteen slippery, shifting snowslides, which at any moment might continue their journey to the lake below. Dad and Christine were surprised at our midnight arrival and greeted us with warm embraces, hot tea, and cozy blankets to replace our drenched city clothes.

After a lovely visit we took the train to Vancouver and Victoria, hence south and east, visiting groups along the way. We were cheered by how much they had grown in both maturity and size.

Annie and Bob met us in Los Angeles, where about 6,000 at the Shrine Auditorium listened to Bob and Bill. Back in 1943 only 1,000 had attended a similar meeting.

It was also encouraging to find more interest shown by the families of AAs. In some places family groups had already been formed. I usually told my story at the many teas and luncheons to which I was invited.

It was great to get home. But home did not mean rest or leisure, as there were always things to do and many people to see. We loved to have our friends visit us, and we asked many to do so. For obvious reasons our phone was not listed, so other AA friends—some we already knew and some we were glad to meet—would drop in to see us unexpectedly, especially on weekends.

This was fun. But there were papers to be written and policies to be thought out, so Bill and I found a nearby hideaway where we could escape for weekends. We also drove up to Vermont or took a vacation as often as possible.

In the Laurentian Mountains of Quebec we picked a small inn on a small lake, where we thought we could be by ourselves. The minute our car reached the inn's parking lot, a pleasant voice called out, "Oh, a Westchester license plate." The voice belonged to a gal who later became a very enthusiastic AA and a good friend of ours.

But that was just the prelude. While we were eating dinner, the cook peeked through the small window in the door of his kitchen and recognized Bill. The cook was an AA and had a picture of Bill. He immediately told the inn manager, another AA. Thereupon we were deluged. A plane of AAs from Montreal was flown up, and we had good meetings and interesting conversations, but little time for renewal on solitary (two as one) hikes in the quiet beauty of the Laurentians.

Another episode was similar but not as drastic in its consequences. On one of our trips to Bermuda we were walking along a dirt road when a car passed us. It slowed, stopped, and backed up, and an occupant called, "Are you Bill W. ?" (Bill's tall figure and rugged profile often gave him away.) After a short conversation these AA friends considerately drove on, and we didn't hear from them again while on the island.

Travel, for the pleasure of seeing the world and its wonderfully varied people, always meant a great deal to both of us. I suppose we remained "two motorcycle hoboes" at heart, so we did as much traveling in our later years as possible.

We took car trips to such interesting places as Charleston, South Carolina, Williamsburg, Virginia, the beautiful Southern gardens, the Gaspé

Peninsula, and Nova Scotia. We made a nostalgic retracing by car of our 1919 hike across Maine, New Hampshire, and Vermont.

We sailed on a freighter through the Panama Canal and roughed it for a week or so on the small island of Taboga off the Pacific coast of Panama before taking the train back along the canal to the Caribbean coast and another freighter home.

We stayed for several weeks in a glassed-in cabin on a St. Thomas beach, and we also visited the other U.S. Virgin Islands, St. John and St. Croix. After we flew to Mexico and saw the pyramids and other interesting sights near Mexico City, Bill's mother met us. We hired a car and the three of us drove south down the mountains to Oaxaca. There we stayed two weeks, enjoying the local life and viewing the Zapotec ruins at Monte Alban and Mitla.

That trip was so absorbing that the next year, after stopping off in Florida for an Audubon tour through the Everglades, Bill and I again went to Mexico, this time to see the Mayan ruins of Chichén Itzá and Uxmal in Yucatán.

Another year we had over a month's vacation in Spain, Portugal, and the Canaries. We took short trips to towns near Madrid, including Segovia and Toledo, before touring with a party south to Granada, then west to Galratta. There we crossed on a ferry from one Pillar of Hercules to the other and landed at Tangiers. What a different but fascinating world! After leaving the tour at Lisbon, we hired a car and drove for five days through Portugal up to Oporto and back to Lisbon. From there we flew to the Canary Islands for a few days before flying home.

And the next year we were lazy and took a Caribbean cruise, but there was plenty of exercise after all when we stopped at the various islands.

One time we boarded a steamer to cross Lake Superior to Isle Royale near the Canadian border. This was a truly wild spot. On a hike in the woods we saw one of the comparatively few moose left on the island. We were told they were dying out, not from being shot, but because the winter weather had become less severe. During cold winters when the channel between the island and Canada is frozen over, the wolves come across and kill the old, young, and weak moose, leaving the herd vigorous and strong. But when there is no ice bridge and the wolves cannot cross to the island, the moose actually eat all the forage on the island, eating themselves out of house and home. The strong die as well as the weak.

Some of our vacations ranged farther. Hawaii was great. We enjoyed our stay of three or four days on each of the islands of Hawaii, Maui, and Kauai more than we did our visit to Oahu, the island where Honolulu is situated; but that was great, too.

Bill had always wanted to visit the Scilly Isles, so we flew to London and took a train to Land's End and a helicopter to the Scillies in late

March one year. My, but it was cold, in spite of the fact that the islands are the fresh-flower suppliers for London markets. There were acres of daffodils, tulips, and narcissus. Fruit trees were in bloom. It was lovely. But each night, although the housemaid placed a couple of ceramic hot-water bottles under the piles of quilts on our beds, we shivered. The damp cold, although never reaching the freezing point, penetrated to our very bones. Silly isles indeed!

Those two trips were among our last. Our 1967 stay in the Scilly Isles was in the nature of catching up, for we had been to England seventeen years earlier without visiting its southernmost tip.

Our earlier flight across the Atlantic was part of our AA travels. Throughout the 1940s groups had been growing in many overseas countries, and they wanted us to visit them. So in the spring of 1950 the AA office laid out a ten-week plan for Bill and me to tour the groups in eight countries: Norway, Sweden, Denmark, Holland, France, England, Ireland, and Scotland.

The minute we arrived at the becurtained and beflowered Oslo airport, we recognized a bunch of AAs by their eager expressions.

We found the meetings in Norway and Sweden quite different from ours. Although serious about their recovery, the Norwegian members sat at tables drinking coffee and munching snacks all through their three-hour meetings. AA talks were distributed in between recitations, violin and voice solos, and unison singing from their *"Sang Bok,"* which contained AA words set to familiar tunes. In Norway we were always eating smorgasbord and never seemed to catch on to the Norwegian mealtime rhythm.

The recovery programs in the three Scandinavian countries then were subsidized to some degree by their governments. AA was pronounced "Ah Ah" in Norway, and the Fellowship was called *Lankarna* in Sweden and *Ring i Ring* in Denmark. There were 1,100 AA members in Norway, fewer in Sweden, and just a handful in Denmark.

As we were going to a meeting in Stockholm, we were given a handbill which was translated for us. Among other announcements, it stated: "Mr. Bill visits Stockholm. Care for hopeless alcoholics. Three drinkers made a secret movement." At the meeting we were surprised to hear a psychiatrist guest emphasize the spiritual aspect in recovery. Bill tried to be diplomatic and at the same time to present some true idea of AA. He urged the alcoholics to help one another.

At Amsterdam Henk Krauweel, a nonalcoholic social worker, was trying to start AA in Holland. He had come to the U.S. to learn about it and had stayed with us. But AA in his country continued to have a struggle to rise above the social-service grounding.

No Frenchman at that time had joined AA, but a handful of American

AAs residing temporarily in Paris held weekly meetings there, one of which we attended.

The reserved Britishers were most anonymous and also stayed clear of almost any mention of a Higher Power. Nonetheless there was a large and enthusiastic crowd at the meeting at Caxton Hall.

The British sense of humor pulls them through whenever things are a bit sticky. One day we visited an AA meeting at "The Hall," Dr. Lincoln Williams's high-class sanitarium near Harrow. At one time the estate had belonged to Blackwell of Cross and Blackwell, the exporters of food stuffs. Next door lived Sir William Gilbert of Gilbert and Sullivan. Blackwell's dog was forever digging up Gilbert's garden, until finally Gilbert wrote Blackwell: "If you don't keep your pickles out of my preserves, I shall be Cross."

AA started in Ireland before it did in England. At a gathering in Dublin there were 300, including a man from Scotland, who took this opportunity to get drunk and heckle the proceedings.

Sackville, the Dublin secretary, had had an inquiry from a woman named Mary, and we went to see her at Blarney Castle. Later in Limerick, more than a hundred miles away, the doors flew open in the middle of Bill's talk at the AA meeting. Mary and her father escorted a tottering drunk, her mother, to a seat next to me. Mary and her father sat like statues; her mother blabbered protestations and finally got up and left. As Mary and her father still sat like statues, I followed the drunken one

Christmas card of Clinton Street living room sent in 1938.

downstairs and into the bar, where I listened to her whining complaints until the meeting was over and she was thoroughly potted. As Bill and I watched the chauffeur drive the three of them away, Mama slowly slid off the seat onto the floor. Mary and Papa continued to stare straight ahead. We never did hear the end of that episode.

The Scot who had been drunk at the meeting in Dublin turned up sober in Belfast (where the violent unrest had not yet begun).

A few of the AAs in Scotland wore kilts, making the meetings colorful, but there weren't as many members as there were in England and Ireland. In Edinburgh the wives met separately, and I told them my story. In the other English-speaking countries I also took the opportunity to tell wives how I had learned I had to live by the AA principles.

Of course we did a lot of sightseeing as well. In Norway we flew over the fjords and snowcapped mountains. From Sweden to Denmark we traveled over the water on a train which was ferried across the Kattegat to Helsingør (Elsinore), where the events inspiring Shakespeare's "Hamlet" are supposed to have taken place.

In Amsterdam we floated under 600 bridges and visited quaint villages behind seventy-foot-high sand dunes protecting them from the sea.

In spite of a touch of the flu in Paris we were able to enjoy many of its beauties—the Louvre, the Eiffel Tower, Montmartre—and to visit such fascinating places as Versailles and Fontainebleau.

During our many trips around the English countryside, its order and finish greatly appealed to me. The mystery of Stonehenge was an emotional peak. Winchester Cathedral brought back memories of Bill's first visit there during World War I. Hearing a debate in Parliament and visiting a night court strengthened Bill's already great admiration for British law.

We gained a sense of history by viewing in Dublin the ancient Book of Kells, four New Testament Epistles illuminated in the eighth century by Irish monks. At Blarney Castle we touched the stone but didn't kiss it, because it was covered with lipstick.

The Giant's Causeway isn't a causeway at all, but a rocky area on the shore of Northern Ireland, shattered by a glacier into tightly packed, six-sided pillars of rock.

Before we left the States, Harden C. had told us about his ancestors somewhere in Scotland. According to a family legend his great-grandfather, the Laird of Harden, had married Scotland's homeliest maiden, Muckle-Mouth Meg, in order to keep from going to jail for stealing her father's sheep.

During a drive in Scotland with Philip R., at whose home we had been staying, he pointed out a ruined castle and said to our astonishment, "That is where Muckle-Mouth Meg, the homeliest maiden in Scotland, lived."

And he continued with the rest of the story Harden had told us. The same legend became the basis of a poem by Robert Browning.

In between all these interesting experiences, Bill was continually thinking about AA's future. He learned much from the groups overseas on these visits, as he had during our travels around the United States and Canada.

We reached home in July 1950 just in time for the First AA International Convention, in Cleveland, where the Twelve Traditions were adopted— AA's Second Legacy. This was the last time Bob was to speak at a large AA gathering, and his brief recorded speech is one of AA's treasured possessions. In his talk, he reiterated the essence of his famous formula "Keep it simple," one of his great contributions.

AA's Third Legacy from its cofounders—Service—was already taking shape. The need for the AA General Service Conference, with delegates elected from the groups, first became clear to Bill while he was working on the Traditions. But the trustees did not approve and made every effort to prevent its formation. In 1948 four of them offered their resignations because of it. However, the rest of the board would not accept the resignations.

I suppose the reason for the trustees' disapproval was natural enough. At the time of the establishment of the board, Bill, Bob and other AAs had wanted a majority of nonalcoholic trustees on the board to insure its continuity in case the alkies got drunk. Although a new confidence in themselves was evolving among the AAs, the nonalcoholic trustees still held to their paternal attitude and didn't judge it prudent that the board should be placed under the yearly supervision of a body of alcoholics, no matter how long they had been sober or how mature they had become.

From the beginning of the Alcoholic Foundation, Bill had difficulty in persuading its members to agree with him. Undiscouraged, he continued to work on the conference plan. It was on his mind during our 1950 trip overseas, and he sent the trustees many of his thoughts on the matter. Eventually he won them over.

Bob had favored the conference idea all along, and his serious illness made its adoption seem even more urgent. His life of devotion and hard work for AA ended in November 1950 after a cancer operation.

In the December 1950 *Grapevine*, an article explained the conference plan to the membership, presenting it as a recommendation from both cofounders. And the next spring saw the first meeting of AA's General Service Conference.

Today, from the vantage point of twenty-seven years later, it is quite apparent that the Conference, for which Bill worked so long and arduously, has served a very useful purpose. It has done much to maintain the unity of AA. It helps to spread the knowledge of AA throughout the country. It brings the members to their General Service Office and GSO to them, and it keeps that office on its toes, to be sure it is doing the very best for AA as a whole. But in April 1951 it was still an experiment, and a five-year trial period was agreed upon.

After the Traditions were adopted by AA, a book on both the Steps and the Traditions was in demand, and Bill undertook to write it at Stepping Stones. His recently finished studio ("Wit's End," he called it) provided the seclusion he needed. Tom P., our devoted AA neighbor, helped with the editing. The book *"Twelve Steps and Twelve Traditions"* was first published as a series in the AA *Grapevine* during 1952 and 1953.

In January 1954 I had a heart attack. The day before, for over an hour, I had shoveled snow out of our long driveway. The next day, our wedding anniversary, I had gone into New York to do some shopping before celebrating with Bill, who was spending a few days at the Bedford Hotel in the city. The pains started during shopping, and I dropped into a movie house, thinking I'd be all right after a rest there. Instead the pains got worse, and I found a cab to take me to the Bedford. I could hardly stand up while waiting for the elevator to Bill's room. When he had put me to bed, he called Leonard Strong, who came immediately and got me into New York Hospital under the care of one of the best heart specialists in the country.

In his anniversary note to me, written before the attack, Bill said, "Come any peril, we know that we are safe in each other's arms because we are in God's."

Recuperating at home, I followed the doctor's instructions about keeping quiet for a year, to everyone's surprise, since I was always so active. The enforced rest gave me time to watch two orioles building their nest in an ash tree on our lawn and to read many delightful books. I never had a recurrence of my heart attack, nor any further trouble with my heart.

A stay in Vermont was always a healing and rejuvenating period for both Bill and me, and we tried to get there every year. This time we stayed nearly a month.

We often walked through the woods along a back road above East Dorset. At a certain season we had noticed many red lizards four to six inches long crossing the road all in the same direction. For a space about fifty feet long there were two dozen at least. At a later time the lizards all crossed in the opposite direction. Ordinarily, however, there was not one to be seen on the road. We figured that all their clocks were set at Lizard Mean Time, and when the alarm went off, they headed for the nearby swamp to breed. Later, on schedule, they returned to their woodsy habitat.

On another back road across the valley, after a sudden heavy downpour, we marveled at the immediate appearance of frogs in every puddle, no matter how small. Where had they come from? Had it rained frogs? Or had they perhaps gone to sleep in a hideaway to forget their thirst until the next rain?

Before the year was out, Carry, our pleasantly plump and wily houseworker at Stepping Stones, had become sick, and her niece, Harriet, had taken her place. I later learned that when we were away, Harriet had often done the work without any pay while Carry sat back and directed. Harriet, who is with me still as I write, turned out to be a blessing. Her loyalty, devotion, and responsibility are outstanding, and it was a lucky day indeed when she came to us. She is my memory and my checker-upper. I trust, need, and love her.

That same year Yale University offered Bill a Doctorate of Laws, and he was tempted to accept it. Almost all the trustees of the Alcoholic Foundation (in 1954 renamed the General Service Board of Alcoholics Anonymous) thought he should except Archie Roosevelt. Archie said his father, Theodore, realized that he had certain liabilities as a power driver; so in restraint of this tendency, TR resolved that he would never accept a personal honor of this sort. Bill was convinced. He declined Yale's offer.

I believe time has proved Bill right. He had feared that by refusing he might be throwing away a means of increasing, if only temporarily, the spreading of AA. This fear was unfounded, it seems to me. I doubt very much that his acceptance of the honor would have done more than impress a few prospective AAs momentarily. His example of declining personal honors for AA work has done far more for the integrity of the Fellowship.

When Cliff W. of California proposed to Bill that the General Service Office publish Bill's correspondence with Yale in pamphlet form, Bill said, "Cliff, you shouldn't tempt me to exploit my humility that way."

After the First AA International Convention at Cleveland, such a gathering was held every five years, successively at St. Louis; Long Beach, California; Toronto; Miami; and Denver.

At St. Louis in 1955 Bill turned over leadership of AA to the Conference, the voice of the entire membership. His mother was present and was very much moved by the proceedings. For once the annual Conference met in July, at the same time and place as the Convention, rather than in April in New York. The five-year trial period was over, and the Conference was firmly in place as an embodiment of AA's Third Legacy, Service.

By the time the Long Beach International came along in 1960, the Fellowship of Al-Anon had been established for nine years, and the Al-Anon members present enthusiastically voted to start our own annual World Service Conference of Delegates in New York the following spring.

With twenty-five years of group experiences to draw upon, Bill was now going more deeply into the whole question of service structure. His ideas, of course, were unique for any society. He had studied and analyzed the structures of various types of organization: the United States government, the churches, and the Washingtonian movement (Washington Temperance Society), among others. He believed the AA Society should be democratic, like the government, but not authoritative. He felt the adoration for their founders in certain religions was something AA should avoid at all costs. Every founder was human and had frailties, which could be disillusioning to members if the founder had been set on a pedestal; and in the case of AA adulation might be devastating to the founders personally, as well as to the whole Fellowship.

Bill found particular interest in the study of the Washingtonians, a society formed back in 1840 to help alcoholics recover through spiritual means and mutual help. Why did this movement, so similar to AA in many aspects, first flourish and then fail dismally? He figured that it was the dominance of money and the members' definite stand on political matters, including laws to promote temperance, that had wrecked their society. He became determined that disagreements about either money or outside issues should not do the same for AA. Bill seemed to have a prescience about what was right for AA.

He worked out what has proved to be a practical set of service principles for this unique society, and presented it in detail in the booklet "Twelve Concepts for World Service," first published in 1962. Like the Steps and the Traditions, the Concepts have proved to be models for Al-Anon as well as AA.

The next AA International, held in Toronto in 1965, was most warm, friendly, and impressive, in the spirit of the Canadian members themselves. They are among AA's and Al-Anon's most dedicated and useful members. Appropriately the theme of the Convention was responsibility, expressed in this declaration: "I am responsible. Whenever anyone, anywhere, reaches out for help, I want the hand of AA always to be there. And for that: I am responsible."

An important question of responsibility within AA itself was approaching a crucial point. When the Alcoholic Foundation was first started, as I mentioned earlier, it was composed of both nonalcoholics and AA members, and the majority were nonalcoholics. This was for the protection of the Fellowship, since the AA members had only recently sobered up and become responsible members of society. However, as time went on and both the Fellowship and its members had matured, Bill felt very strongly that AA members should play the dominant role in their own affairs. Protection was all right for the early days, but now they should stand on their own feet.

Bill had a long and unhappy discussion with the trustees on this matter. Even some of the AAs on the board themselves accepted the paternal attitude of the nonalcoholics. In 1966, however, Bill finally persuaded them, and the ratio on the board between drunks and nondrunks was changed. Today its normal complement is fourteen AA members and seven nonalcoholics.

After this had been accomplished, Bill felt he had done all he could to help build a framework within which AA could function into the future at its best.

He then became interested in the physical side of alcoholism, particularly how useful the vitamin B_3 could be in the treatment of the illness. Drs. Abram Hoffer and Humphrey Ormond (whom he had met through Aldous Huxley) had drawn his attention to this treatment. Bill wrote a brochure on how helpful B_3 (niacin) could be for alcoholics, and sent it out to AA doctors. He continued this work until his death.

In 1968 Bill and I had been married fifty years, and we rather expected to be given a celebration; hence we had planned nothing ourselves. We were a bit disappointed to find not even a suspicion of any activity. However, Nell Wing, Bill's longtime secretary and our cherished friend, had been invited up for the weekend, and she took us out for dinner but insisted that we go early, as she had made reservations for twelve noon. We thought this a bit odd, more like brunch than Sunday dinner and suspected we were to meet others there. Although, the three of us had a pleasant time, no one else joined us.

On returning home, we were surprised to find our parking lot filled with cars, some with licenses from distant states. Waiting inside for us were Helen and Owen from Arizona, Dot and Leonard and Rog and Laura from Vermont, Lyman and Florence from New Jersey, and nephews, nieces and cousins from Connecticut and New York. Harriet had organized a huge two-family party. The dinner with Nell was just a ruse to get us away from home while the guests arrived and Harriet prepared a buffet dinner. It was truly a great affair, and our egos were more than satisfied.

Bill was ill during most of 1970. His emphysema was particularly bad after we reached Miami in July for the Fifth AA International Convention. He was able to appear only at the Sunday spiritual meeting—and in a wheelchair, from which he rose to make a brief but moving talk to the more than 10,000 AAs and Al-Anons present. Afterwards, our dear AA friend Dr. Ed B. and his wife, Ethel, kept us in their home in Miami for a whole month so Bill could recuperate under Ed's care.

Soon after our return to Bedford Hills, however, Bill's health deteriorated. He began to need a constant supply of ranked oxygen to aid his breathing. Several emergency trips to the hospital were necessary when he developed pneumonia.

At first I did all the nursing. Then a friend came in to stay with Bill at night. But the work soon became too heavy for both of us, and night and day nurses were called in.

In the meantime Dr. Ed's hospital in Miami had procured a new breathing tank similar to those divers use in being depressurized. Ed felt this would be a great help to Bill, and he asked one of our well-to-do AAs to charter a small plane to transport Bill to Miami. Bill's doctors here at home were not too enthusiastic about this but felt it might at least give Bill a temporary lift.

On January 24, 1971, our 53rd wedding anniversary, Ed arrived on a plane with two pilots at the Westchester airport, where Bill (on a stretcher), Nell, and I disembarked from an ambulance.

Bill's doctor had suggested that the plane fly high so the pressure on his lungs would be less, but the plane could not carry enough fuel to do this and had to fly low and more slowly. Although Bill was given oxygen constantly, the trip was long and arduous for him. But when I saw him in the hospital after supper, he seemed fairly comfortable.

I was awakened about six the next morning by Ed, with tears streaming down his face. Bill had passed away during the night. He had sunk into a coma soon after I left him. The doctors revived him once or twice but couldn't do so again, although they worked all night until his breathing finally stopped.

Ed and I fell into each other's arms.

16

Worldwide Love

How can I express my feelings?

Bill's death had been expected by the doctors at several periods during his illness, and I had known it was a probability; but we had both been so hopeful about this new treatment of Ed's.

The missing him would come later. But the hurt of not being at his side at this supreme moment was immediate. Why was I not called? Bill and I had shared so many of life's adventures; now, when the door opened for him into the greatest of mystical experiences, I was not there.

I try to be practical about it. It was to save me that the doctors hadn't called me. Perhaps they were being kind to me. The pain might have been worse if I had been there. Bill might have been in a coma and not known me. But even so I wanted to be there, and the hurt of not being at his side is still with me.

The devotion and caring I have received from others have supported me. The love and sympathy in the thousands of letters I received from great and small all over the world have held up my hands.

There were memorial services for Bill in many cities overseas: Antwerp, Bombay, Dublin, Glasgow, Hälsingborg, Johannesburg, Melbourne, Oslo. There were services in Sri Lanka and Trinidad, plus many more in Latin America, Canada, and the United States. A service at the Cathedral of St. John the Divine in New York was attended by an overflow crowd, as was that in London at St. Martin's-in-the-Field. Danny, the son of our devoted house-helper Harriet, was in the United States Marines stationed in Tokyo, Japan, at the time of Bill's death and attended memorial ceremonies there. After the services, when he told some of the AA members that he knew Bill personally, they couldn't believe him until they saw the tears in his eyes.

With the appearance of Bill's obituary and picture on the front page of the *New York Times*, his anonymity was broken for good. But I continue to try to keep my anonymity, for the sake of the example it sets other Al-Anons.

It is perhaps little known that during Bill's AA life he refused several other awards in addition to the Yale LL.D. degree, in order to encourage the spirit of anonymity in those following his leadership, as well as to reinforce his own humility.

In 1949 the Steubenville College of Ohio offered the Poderello Award to both Bob and Bill. When they declined the honor, the college gave it to AA as a whole. Early in 1951 Bill declined to be listed in "Who's Who." Later that same year he was offered the Lasker Award. Bob had passed away by that time. In Bill's letter of thanks he suggested it be given instead to the AA Fellowship, and it was.

In 1959 *Time* Magazine proposed to write a cover story about him, which, like other personal publicity, was refused.

The state of Vermont, the birthplace of both AA founders, wanted to honor Bill and posthumously Bob in 1960, but Bill again asked that the recognition be given to AA.

In 1976, to do what I was sure Bill would want me to do, I declined for him posthumously a Doctorate of Humanities offered by his own alma mater, Norwich University.

Thank God for Al-Anon and AA. I still have a purpose in life even with Bill gone. He and I had planned "someday soon" to take a trip around the world to visit AA and Al-Anon in places we hadn't visited in 1950 and in those many countries where groups had sprung up during the ensuing twenty years.

Why wouldn't this be a good thing for me to do now, taking an Al-Anon member with me? I had money enough. The royalties on the books Bill wrote for AA—his and my only income—had mounted and were continuing to arrive regularly. (Bill never would accept royalties on AA books sold overseas.)

So that's what I did, with Evelyn C., one of the early volunteers at the Al-Anon Clearing House and then a staff worker at our World Service Office (WSO) for many years. The New York AA and Al-Anon offices contacted the various groups around the globe, and these groups arranged meetings and offered hospitality.

A sight-seeing trip was planned in Africa to see the wild animal reserves near Nairobi and the Victoria Falls between Zambia and Rhodesia. At the Ark, a barracks-like viewing inn for tourists, it was fascinating to observe five bull elephants at the water hole and salt lick, so near you could almost touch them. When animals approached at night, we were awakened by a buzzer. We missed the leopard but saw a rare white rhinoceros in the Ark's spotlight.

Seeing Victoria Falls was a highlight experience for me, dimmed only by not having Bill along. He would have been so greatly moved. In eight consecutive ravines the mile-wide Zambezi River plunges into a deep, narrow crevice in the earth's crust with such force that the spray can be seen in the sky for miles around and forms a tropical rain forest on the downriver bank. The natives call the falls "The Smoke That Thunders."

At Johannesburg, Andries and Glen, two AAs whom we had met at the First AA World Service Meeting in New York in 1969, were among the delegation that greeted us. At an informal meeting in the evening we were given a copy of *Twelve Steps and Twelve Traditions*, its first paperback edition in the whole world, they proudly said. Glen and Andries told us that in New York they were afraid to meet Bill, afraid it would be disappointing, but when they did see and talk with him, the opposite was the case.

Sue, Andries's wife, took us to an Al-Anon meeting where Evelyn and I were plied with questions even after the AAs joined us for coffee.

The South African members couldn't get a hall big enough for the AA open meeting. The large government hall would not allow blacks and "colored" (the local term for persons of mixed or Indian descent) to enter, and the AAs would not hold this meeting without these fellow members. Therefore, at a small private hall, people were standing in the street and sitting in the windows. AA and Al-Anon meetings are among the few places in South Africa where the races can assemble together.

We took a six-day trek in a tour company's zebra-striped bus to Durban, a seaport on the east coast, driving through the scenic Drakensberg (Dragon) Mountains. We stopped in several reserves to see the animals—lion, hippopotami, every kind of deer and antelope, ostriches, thousands of zebras and monkeys—and parrots and many other beautiful birds. We mistook a group of giraffe in the distance for high-rise buildings. A lioness strolled nonchalantly twenty feet ahead of us as we drove slowly down a trail.

One of our most moving experiences was an Al-Anon meeting in Helen's and Harold's home in Sydenham, a suburb of Durban, where the government segregates the blacks and colored. Many of the latter are Aryans from India. We were shocked to realize that these educated and cultured people were treated as second-class citizens. The members were so warm and grateful that when we clasped hands—black, brown and white—and sang "God be with you till we meet again," tears wet all our cheeks.

At Port Elizabeth, after a joint meeting at the clubhouse where the Fellowships of AA, Al-Anon, and Alateen have their own meeting rooms, Deirdre, an AA who sponsors an Alateen group, and some of her youngsters took us to the Oceania Arena. Helping to train dolphins is Deirdre's hobby.

At the AA and Al-Anon meetings at Capetown we felt perfectly at home. The city has a magnificent location at the foot of Table Mountain. We were thrilled to gaze from the historic Cape of Good Hope across the waters of both the Indian and the Atlantic Oceans.

Capetown Group No. 2 evolved in a unique way. In Sparks, Maryland, U.S.A., Tom B.'s wife had long tried to get him into AA. He promised he would write the AA office but kept putting it off. Finally she pressed him so urgently one day that he had to pick up his pencil and write, but instead of addressing his letter to the General Service Office in New York, he thought up some place where there probably was no AA, hoping thus to appease his wife but get nowhere AA-wise. He addressed his letter, "Alcoholics Anonymous, Capetown, South Africa." To his great surprise he received an immediate reply, telling him of the members' experiences and suggesting he write GSO in New York.

Tom was so taken aback that he did just that. But all through his long AA life he continued to correspond frequently with "his" group in Capetown. And since he made many tapes of AA talks all over the country, he sent a copy of each to Capetown. He started a group in Sparks, Maryland, and called it Capetown Group No. 2.

We flew from Capetown back to Johannesburg and from there to Perth, Australia, for a joint AA and Al-Anon meeting in a monastery. After an overnight stay, we flew on to Melbourne. We were delayed in reaching there by a terrific storm. So much rain fell that parked cars were lifted up and floated down the street.

Al-Anon in Australia was in the throes of starting a central office and an

Bill and I walking towards Stepping Stones, our home for many years, sent as Christmas card 1949 to 1969.

annual Conference of Delegates. I got sick there, and the Al-Anon and AA members were most attentive. This, however, prevented me from going to meetings and delayed our flight to Christchurch on the South Island of New Zealand. But what a welcome we received from Alateens, Al-Anons, and AAs when we did arrive there.

New Zealand is intriguing, and I would like to go back sometime to see the fjords, lakes, and snowcapped mountains in the south. Soon we were flown to Rotorua, a geyser and thermal area on the North Island. Ian McE., a very early AA, was ill; but his wife, Heather, a longtime Al-Anon, and Edith, the Wellington AA and Al-Anon secretary, in her wheelchair, were among those who gathered there to visit with Evelyn and me. We went to a Maori concert and viewed remarkable sights such as Trout Springs, where we could catch fish in the icy cold water on one side and cook them in the near boiling water on the other.

A number of us took a bus to Auckland, stopping en route to visit a huge cavern filled with myriads of "stars." The thousands of glowworms hanging on invisible threads were duplicated in their reflections in the water below.

Among the splendid meetings in Auckland was a gathering of fifty Al-Anons, where Thelma asked members to read selected passages from our book *One Day at a Time in Al-Anon* and then make comments.

From Auckland we flew back to Australia for a stay in Sydney. Nearly a thousand AAs and Al-Anons were at the Town Hall meeting one night. We dined at the famous rotating restaurant on top of one of the city's tallest buildings. From that height the new opera house looked like a huge bird about to take flight across the harbor.

As we flew north to Hong Kong, the colors of the endless, unoccupied Australian outback repeated the red and green of the polished stones we had just been given as souvenirs.

Cosmopolitan Hong Kong was fascinating. Persons of every nationality walked the streets, and merchandise of every variety lined the shops. At one of the meetings on Hong Kong Island we met a reporter who had written one of the first articles about AA in Akron thirty-five years before. After drinking heavily all those years, he had only recently come into AA. Besides visiting the AAs and Al-Anons there, we toured the mainland to a spot where we could see into Communist China.

I had always greatly admired Japanese art and had looked forward to our visit in Japan. However, the nation was in such a hurry to industrialize that a trail of debris was left behind everywhere. Many spots remained excruciatingly beautiful, but the Japanese' constant and elaborate distortion of nature somehow bothered me. The trees bordering Tokyo's main streets were all kept trimmed to exactly the same shape, with no individuality or life of their own. And the parks were filled with shrubbery which might as well have been artificial, it was so cleverly pruned into artistic or humorous shapes. But I shall never forget the many beauty spots.

Danshu-Kai, a Japanese program to rehabilitate alcoholics, includes some of AA's ideas. Although it is definitely not AA, it seemed to be making some strides in fighting the alcohol problem. There is also a society for alcoholics' families, called the White Chrysanthemum. Evelyn and I spoke through a translator at a joint meeting of these societies, but felt we had made little impression. A Japanese nurse, Harumi Katon, who had come to New York the year before to learn about Al-Anon and AA, took us to a government hospital for the mentally ill where she worked. Our talks there to a handful of alcoholics seemed to be better understood.

Regular AA and Al-Anon meetings are held in Tokyo by American AAs and their families living there. Evelyn and I went to one meeting and later met some of the wives at lunch with Harumi. The latter had proved invaluable in the translation of some of our pamphlets into Japanese and had also helped in production.

Honolulu, our last stop, made a fitting climax to our trip. We were given so many leis that Evelyn said we looked like walking flowerpots.

Seeing and feeling the loving devotion and oneness of AA and Al-Anon around the world did much to submerge in an overwhelming sea of gratitude my sense of personal loss. This warm contact continues to be an inspiration to me.

My next two trips were informative and fun. On both my companion was Nell, Bill's secretary for seventeen years and now head of AA's archives. In August 1972 we went on a cruise to view an eclipse of the sun from an area miles out in the Atlantic Ocean where it could be seen to best advantage. The scientists aboard lectured and showed slides and movies en route. The eclipse itself was both exciting and eerie. I can well understand how the ancients and primitives were terror-stricken at such an experience.

The other trip, an airline-packaged theater tour to London in March 1973, was just fun.

Evelyn and I again set out together in October 1973, this time to the combined AA and Al-Anon convention at Selsey-on-Sea in England. Before the convention we took a charming tour through the Lake District, Yorkshire (Evelyn's birthplace) and Wales. Dorothy H., one of the longest-time English Al-Anon members, made all the arrangements for us.

During the twenty-three years since Bill and I had visited AA in England in 1950, the meetings had changed very little; but members, although still reserved and very anonymous, had lost their former self-consciousness, and there was much joyous camaraderie.

But what an overall difference there really was! Thousands more had joined AA; there were many more young members; and the whole structure of Al-Anon and Alateen had developed. It was thrilling, and I know Bill would have been thrilled, too.

After the convention we visited Prue S. and Helen M.-S. until it was time to go back to London for the Al-Anon General Service Conference, and then home.

An AA convention in Cork, Ireland, in April 1974 was another highlight. Nell accompanied me to this one. Sackville, Jimmy R., Richard P., Dan B. from Limerick, and I did much warm reminiscing. After it was over, Nell, Jack M. (editor of the *AA Grapevine*), and I toured Ireland. Guards questioned us as we approached the border of Northern Ireland. We peered with curiosity into the now "forbidden" territory as Evelyn and I had earlier into Communist China. We could see no difference between the near and far sides of the border. But in the troubled Northern Ireland of today, as in apartheid-divided South Africa, AA and Al-Anon meetings are among the few places where those of diametrically different political views or of different color can meet in peace and accord.

AA and Al-Anon events closer to home have also been a source of inspiration. The Akron Founders Day celebrations, which I have attended almost every year since Bill's death, have given me a great uplift because of the AAs' and Al-Anons' deep dedication to our principles.

The Sixth International AA Convention, held in Denver in 1975, was a tremendous success. At its impressive opening AAs from twenty-nine countries marched in, each carrying his nation's flag. Then each stepped to the microphone and repeated in his own language the Convention's theme, "Let It Begin with Me." A spiritual meeting at the Convention's close was equally moving in spite of the poor sound system which prevented many of the nearly 20,000 AAs and Al-Anons from hearing well. But we could feel!

As at previous AA International Conventions, Al-Anon had its separate program in Denver, where Al-Anon and Alateen registrations exceeded 5,000. Members from the far corners of the earth took part in the seven large meetings and many Al-Anon and Alateen workshops. There was standing-room-only at the first big meeting, where I greeted everyone before members from Argentina, Australia, Brazil, Costa Rica, England, France, India, Ireland, South Africa, and West Germany shared their experiences.

We get something at these huge, unique gatherings that cannot be gained in any other way. The combined emotional impact of so many people believing and striving for the same ideals is felt by everyone and brings a rich kind of joy.

In Chicago there is a group of AAs who call themselves the Twelve Step

Travelers. Their purpose is to organize trips to visit AAs in far-off, interesting places. They can get reduced rates from the airlines because of the large number of passengers they can guarantee. They have flown three times to Hawaii, once to Bogotá, Colombia, and once to Paris, France. I went with them to Hawaii in 1975 and to Paris in June 1977 and greatly enjoyed the AA and Al-Anon meetings as well as the varied sight-seeing.

In between the trips to Hawaii and Paris, Mary S., then chairman of the Al-Anon Policy Committee, accompanied me to Ponce, Puerto Rico, for Al-Anon's first convention there, in July 1976. It was exciting that Al-Anon was strong enough in Puerto Rico to put on its own convention. In fact it is the only all-Al-Anon three-day convention I know of. At its end the AAs held a large meeting and dinner at San Juan on the other side of the island.

Then in November 1976 I accepted an invitation to speak at an AA convention at Mérida in Yucatán, Mexico. Teresa M., the Spanish translator at Al-Anon's World Service Office, went along to be my companion and to help me cross the language barrier. Such enthusiasm I have never seen. Four hundred AA members met us at the airport.

Although Al-Anon meetings are held there and we went to one, the local Al-Anons are having a hard time establishing their identity.

I hope I understand correctly AA and Al-Anon members' special devotion to me. As the only living survivor of the AA founders and their wives and as Bill's widow, I am a symbol to AAs of their beloved Fellowship. I shall always be grateful for the warmth and acceptance they show me. At conventions I never know whether I'm AA or Al-Anon. AA was my first love. It was in AA that I started my own spiritual striving. So I feel an allegiance to both Societies.

As a cofounder of Al-Anon, I naturally represent our cherished Fellowship to its members. Since I am more active than Anne B., our other cofounder, many members hardly know about her. Those who attended the Denver International, however, had the pleasure of meeting Anne there. Anne, of course, could never retire from Al-Anon, but she prefers to live quietly on the West Coast near one of her two daughters and the daughter's family.

In June of every year since 1952 we have held an Al-Anon picnic and then a meeting here at Stepping Stones, with 100 or 200 attending. While Bill was alive, he always closed the meeting with an inspiring talk. One year he said, "We AAs don't stay away from drinking—we grow away from drinking. And if our spouses don't grow along with us, we grow away from them."

Receiving AAs and Al-Anons here at Stepping Stones, where I have much memorabilia of early Fellowship days, attending policy, executive and trustee meetings at the WSO, visiting groups at home and abroad, working in my garden and writing this book have filled my days since Bill's passing.

I regret that I occasionally lost my temper with Bill. I said earlier that I had it under better control most of the time, and so I did. But in spite of Bill's amiability, at times he tried my patience with his inattention to details, which I had to rectify. The pressure would build up until finally I exploded. Bill hated these episodes and would do almost anything to avoid them, and I tried hard to control myself. So these spats occurred very rarely. However, I remember one which I especially regret. It happened while he was ill in 1970. It helped to clear the air about a certain matter, but I am so sorry that I lost my temper, for I know he was troubled by it.

Thinking back on Bill's and my life together, I am overwhelmed with gratitude for the joys, deep understanding, and companionship that we shared. I truly believe there are few human beings who have as much to be thankful for as I have.

17

The Foundations
of Al-Anon

I n the beginning AA was a family affair. Mates, parents and children attended the meetings, usually held in homes. Many of the wives tried to live by the program themselves and made much progress, but this was in a general way only. There was nothing to help them understand their own reactions nor to realize how similar these were to the feelings of other AA wives. There was little sharing of experience. The later formation of the Family Groups filled this gap.

Back in the early days anyone lucky enough to still have a home shared it with those who had lost theirs. Our house was as busy as an anthill. Such terrific excitement and enthusiasm existed about this wonderful program that, when we were not twelfth-stepping or attending meetings, AA was the enthralling topic of conversation by the whole family, morning, night and noon. A new prospect was treated like a raw diamond. All were anxious to help him get the program.

At that time there was only a pamphlet or two of AA literature, so it was through actual contact with older members that a new AA group got started. There was much visiting between groups and traveling back and forth. As Bill and I were younger (Bill was fifteen years younger than Bob) and more mobile, we visited many more groups than Bob and Annie could.

A bunch in New York would often hop into one member's old jalopy and dash for a meeting in Philadelphia, Washington, Richmond, Akron, Cleveland, or way stations. There was always someone willing to bed us down for a night, often very late, as talk was more important than sleep.

As I reported earlier, the Akron alkies continued to think of themselves as belonging to the Oxford Group long after those in New York. I remember telling my story in Akron in 1939 at an Oxford Group meeting in T. Henry and Clarace Williams's attractive living room and then going downstairs to enjoy the delicious refreshments Clarace and wives of AAs had prepared. Those who met in the Williamses' home later became the King Street AA group. This was probably the first in Akron to call itself Alcoholics Anonymous, although one in Cleveland may have preceded it.

I suppose the seeds of Al-Anon actually germinated when the families of early AA members first felt the stirrings of their own regeneration, and began to do something about it.

Annie had belonged to the Oxford Group before we met her and had felt the need for her own spiritual growth, as I did after the shoe-throwing episode. So whenever we met with the wives of other AAs, we each told them how we had come to the decision to live by the same principles as our mates and how we were now endeavoring to follow these principles.

It wasn't until 1940, however, that constructive gatherings for the families of AAs began to evolve. Soon after the first clubhouse for AAs was opened, in New York at 334½ West 24th Street in June 1940, the AAs felt they needed some meetings for alcoholics only. Therefore, while they met in the assembly room below, a handful of us wives got to know each other in the skylighted studio above. At first we either played bridge or gossiped, but soon we began to discuss our own problems and what we could do about them. I told my story. It was great to find that because others had gone through similar experiences, each of us no longer had to be alone with our troubles.

Our family gatherings were composed mostly of AA wives, with a sprinkling of mothers and daughters. There was one man, Wally S., a father who was trying to get his son into AA.

On the trip Bill and I took around the country in 1943 to visit AA groups, I usually spoke briefly at the large open meetings, thanking the AAs for giving me such a wonderful program to live by. But at teas and luncheons for the families, I tried to make more personal talks, telling how important it was for me to live by the spiritual principles of AA and how I came to discover this. Recently I counted sixty-two places where I made talks during our trips around the country between 1939 and 1951. In some places where we visited, groups of the families of AAs had already been formed.

During our 1948 train trip through Canada, I spoke to 400 people at a meeting in Toronto put on by the Wives' Group and led by Pearl E. A year or so before, Colonel Gibby G., an AA, and his wife, Ione, had visited our home to learn how they could start a family group. Since then Ione and her friend Pearl had done wonders in getting a strong, spiritual group started. Two years later in 1950 three of their members gave inspiring talks at the Family Group sessions of the First AA International Convention, in Cleveland.

At Seattle, where there had been no Family Group when I spoke in 1943, forty members attended a meeting held five years later. At San

Francisco there were eighty-five wives on hand to hear me tell my story. Annie, Bob, Bill and I met in Los Angeles, and Annie and I spoke together at a large meeting for AA families. It was the first and last time Annie and Bob would make such a trip together; she died later in 1949.

Annie's part in the formation of AA and consequently in the foundation of Al-Anon should never be forgotten, especially by Family Group members. Although there were few Family Groups during the thirteen years of her activity, Annie did much to instill the spirit of Al-Anon in many of the families of alcoholics. God bless Annie's memory.

As we visited the groups along the West Coast and at Phoenix, Lubbock, Dallas, St. Louis, and Chicago, I was greatly pleased to see the interest displayed by the families of AAs and to learn that many of them held regular weekly meetings. These gatherings seemed to be for various purposes, sometimes just to serve refreshments to the AAs or perhaps to put up curtains in a club for AAs. We later called these "coffee-and-cake groups." But a number of them met for their own spiritual development.

Probably few present-day Al-Anon members ever heard of Ruth G., but without her early Al-Anon could never have gained the impetus it did. In 1949 she started a small twelve-page monthly magazine called *The Family Forum* for discussion of family problems arising from alcoholism. The wife of an alcoholic on the West Coast, Ruth spent much time and thought on the magazine. Its pumpkin-colored sheets were filled with editorials, correspondence from families of alcoholics, appropriate quotations from the Bible, Marcus Aurelius Antoninus, St. Francis of Assisi, Nietzsche, ancient Chinese philosophers, and even Machiavelli. It also contained some cleverly drawn cartoons.

Ruth sent it to already-formed Family Groups, to anyone she felt needed it and to members of AA groups, asking them to pass it on to their spouses. A note on the last page said that although there was no subscription price, voluntary contributions were welcome. After the Al-Anon office opened in New York, she discontinued her publication.

In 1950 Bill went by himself to the AA groups throughout the States and Canada to find out their feelings about establishing a General Service Conference for AA. He was surprised to run into so many Family Groups.

Returning home, he told me about this budding Fellowship and suggested I open a service office in New York, where these groups could register, receive helpful literature, and become more unified. It would also be a place to which any distracted wife could cry out for help, and from which information could be spread to the public.

Bill's suggestion did not appeal to me at first, because I was still excited about having a home of our own. Starting such an office would take too much time away from working in my garden and making useful things for the house. But as I began to think about the need, the idea grew more and more intriguing. At the close of the 1951 AA General Service Conference, I asked the wives of the delegates to meet at Stepping Stones for lunch with local Family Groups members. All but two or three of the wives belonged to Family Groups in their hometowns and told about their meetings, as did our local members.

It was then that I decided to open our own service office and asked a close friend, another Anne, Anne B., to help me. She had already initiated a Family Group in Westchester County, New York. This was three years after the death of Annie S.

We worked upstairs at Stepping Stones. The AA General Service Office (GSO) gave us a list of eighty-seven nonalcoholic individuals or Family Groups that had written asking for literature and wanting to be listed at GSO. Their letters came from the States, Canada, Australia, South Africa, and Ireland. GSO felt it could not list them, since AA was geared to help the alcoholic, not the family. It simply sent the inquirers encouraging letters with reprints of the chapter "To Wives" from the AA Big Book.

In May 1951 Anne and I wrote to these individuals and groups stating our purpose as follows:

> Dear Friends:
> Since experience has proved that the AA Program is a way of life which can be helpful to the non alcoholic, there are now 87 AA Family Groups (including some Loners) known to the [Alcoholic] Foundation, and perhaps ...many more ..... The purpose of these groups is threefold:
>   1. To give cooperation and understanding to the AA at home.
>   2. To live by the 12 Steps ourselves in order to grow spiritually along with our AA.
>   3. To welcome and give comfort to the families of new AAs.
> The time has come when it seems wise to unify these groups. A post office box in New York City, to be used as a clearing house, has been secured, and Lois W. has volunteered to act as temporary chairman.
>
> The following questions present themselves:
>   1. Do you approve of the name AA Family Group? If not, what do you suggest?
>   2. Should we not adopt the 12 Steps as written for AA, without change or embellishment?
> As this is a clearinghouse, let's have your ideas and suggestions. Please send them to Post Office Box 1475, Grand Central Annex, New York 17, N.Y.
>
> > Very sincerely,
> > Lois W - -,*Chairman
> > Anne B - -,*Secretary

*Actually we signed our full names, but for this book only last initials are used.

Bill and I before the Stepping Stones fireplace, sent as 1970 Christmas card.

The answers came in fast. Of the 87 to whom we had written, 48 replied that their groups would be glad to unite in a fellowship and to have their own service office. (The Chicago group, established since 1941, preferred not to join us.)

Periodic bulletins were sent out, and two pamphlets were written: *One Wife's Story* and *Purposes and Suggestions*. Dreaming big, we ordered a whole thousand of the latter offset from a local printer for fifteen dollars.

A donation of ten dollars from Sam K. in Lynn, Massachusetts, followed by several others, surprised and pleased Anne and me. We had assumed our office would be supported by regular voluntary contributions as the AA office was. Whether or not this would work out we didn't know, as we hadn't yet asked for donations.

In November 1951, here at Stepping Stones, we held a meeting of chairmen and secretaries of our local Family Groups to report the progress of our work and to elect a service committee to advise and help us. Anne and I met at Stepping Stones two days a week, and often there were more letters than we had time to answer.

AA members have always been of tremendous help to Al-Anon, especially in the beginning. They were tireless in answering our many questions on structure and policy; they gave us meeting rooms at their large gatherings; they encouraged us in every way. As the Family Group work became more than Anne and I could handle at Stepping Stones, AA members offered us the use of the large upstairs studio at their West 24th Street club in New York City. Knowing there would be others glad to volunteer at our Fellowship's new service office, we asked Wally S., whose son by this time had joined AA, to drive us around to meetings of the seven Family Groups then in the metropolitan area. We told the members that in less than a year the number of Family Groups had grown from 48 to 200, and we encouraged them to volunteer their services at the office.

So on January 9, 1952, when Anne and I moved our headquarters to the 24th Street Clubhouse, several volunteers joined us at what we called the Clearing House. Irma F., Dot L., and Sue L. were the first. Wally S., always kindly and helpful, put up shelves; the club allowed us to use its old mimeograph machine; and Sue, from some unknown source, supplied us with mimeograph paper.

In March 1952 we felt we had enough information from our questionnaires to report back to the groups. The members, including those who had started groups under other names, such as AA Auxiliary, Triple A, Non-Alcoholics Anonymous, and AA Associates, had selected the name Al-Anon Family Groups. The word "Al-Anon" is simply a derivative of Alcoholics Anonymous, combining the first syllables of each word. Within a few years most groups had given up use of any other name.

It had taken longer to decide on principles, because several groups, notably Richmond, Virginia, had worked out steps on their own. Some of these steps used by other groups were similar to AA's; others were entirely original, a few stating, "admitted we were powerless *over an alcoholic.*" However, in the end the groups had all come to recognize the strength of AA's Twelve Steps, even in the wording itself, and we adopted them for our own guidelines. The only word changed was in the Twelfth Step: "carry this message to *others*" instead of "to alcoholics."

We sent a memorandum to AA asking permission to use its Twelve Steps in our Fellowship. AA agreed unofficially, but its members felt strongly that we should be a separate society and not a subsidiary of Alcoholics Anonymous, and that we should not include "AA" in our name. In addition Bill felt AAs should hold no office in our structure. He often said, "Keep us drunks out of it." In the beginning he had thought perhaps an Al-Anon member should be on the AA board of trustees, but this hasn't worked out so far.

Bill's sister, Helen, was married to an alcoholic by this time, and she became one of our volunteers, as did a new Al-Anon member, Margaret D. Anne and I picked up Margaret and her typewriter as we drove the forty miles to New York each week. Several new volunteers joined us: from New Jersey—Mag V., Eleanor A., Jean B., and later Wanda R.; from Long Island, New York—Evelyn C., Vi F., Clara S., and Henrietta S. We distributed the work according to capability and interests. In March we asked the groups whether they would support the office voluntarily at the rate of approximately one dollar per member semiannually.

Anne continued to do most of the bookkeeping and typing, at first carrying her typewriter weekly from Chappaqua to New York. To ensure that pamphlets were received without damage, I took to the office wrapping paper and cardboards I had saved from Bill's shirts. I think it was a shoe box that served as our first card file. The cards were of various pastel shades to distinguish the status of the group. All useful information we jotted down in a little black book. At first Evelyn took the mail to and from the post office in a small bag, but soon she had to get a shopping cart.

The Second AA General Service Conference met in April 1952 and passed a resolution by standing vote, thanking those who had fostered the Al-Anon Family Groups. We were quite moved and very grateful. I again held a luncheon at Stepping Stones for the AA delegates' wives and our local Al-Anon members. It was a fine opportunity to let the visiting women meet with Al-Anon members, and to tell them about our new service office.

A few members reported that because of the change in their own attitude, a like change had taken place in the alcoholic, who often joined AA. The number of these cases mushroomed as time went on. We were astonished when an inquiry came in about starting a group in Southern Rhodesia.

In June we were able to buy, through Wally, some reasonably priced equipment: a cabinet for supplies; a wall map with pins to show the location of our groups; and most necessary of all, a typewriter and table. But Anne and Margaret still had to lug their machines in from the suburbs. The old mimeograph worked erratically and splashed ink all over Dot's clothes as well as the paper. After much wringing of hands we spent the whole of fifty dollars to have it fixed. By then many groups had expressed their wish to support the office.

We believed that Al-Anon leadership should initiate ideas, offer choices, and perhaps emphasize aspects, but leave it up to the Fellowship to make the decisions. It was in this spirit that we sent out our many questions to the groups. We felt all national publicity should be directed by the office, so we asked and received the groups' approval to handle it.

Before we opened this service office, our membership had been composed mostly of wives of AA members, but our principles stated anyone could belong whose life was being affected by the obsessive drinking of a family member or friend. Publicity would undoubtedly bring in families of non-AA, still-drinking alcoholics, thus broadening the usefulness of Al-Anon.

Among other activities, I had been working on an adaptation of AA's Twelve Traditions. Bill helped me a lot with this. The Al-Anon Traditions, which the groups accepted in September 1952, are the same in spirit and are in the same order as AA's. In other words they are as much like AA's as possible.

One might think that Al-Anon had not yet had enough experience for Traditions to have evolved. But AA had had the experience, and its Traditions had proved so useful for the guidance of its groups that it seemed wise for Al-Anon to adapt and adopt them as soon as practical.

These Traditions were sent not only to the Al-Anon groups but also to many AA groups. We wanted AA's approval of the guiding principles of our Fellowship. We received even more encouragement from AA than we did from our own groups. Maybe most Al-Anon groups were too young in experience to think much about group problems. However, the Al-Anon Traditions would now be there when groups needed them.

Our first price list, mimeographed on only a quarter sheet of paper and enclosed in all communications to the groups, had listed only ten pieces of literature. There were three pamphlets for two cents each: *Purpose and Suggestions*, *One Wife's Story*, and *The Family Groups* (the last by an AA member). Four items were free: the World and Local Directories, Suggested Programs for Meetings, and Suggested Readings. Also on that first list were the AA Big Book, the chapter from it about wives (for ten cents) and "Primer on Alcoholism"; but the distribution of these three by Al-Anon was later discontinued.

Soon we added to the list: a subscription to the *AA Grapevine*; a reprint of an article about alcoholics' families from a 1949 issue of *Coronet*; and *Freedom from Despair*, a pamphlet the San Diego group had written and given us permission to revise and use.

The World Directory was and continued to be a chore to get out; group secretaries were always changing. By the time we got the information, a new secretary had been chosen. The directory could never be kept current until groups rented post office boxes, as we urged them to do. This is still true, and we are still urging each group to acquire one.

Our first directory, published in March 1952, had listings in thirty-six states and in seven of the ten Canadian provinces, one listing in Glebe, Australia, one in Belfast, Ireland, and two in South Africa (Capetown and East London). Rhodesia wasn't heard from again until the next year, when a group was formed. California had the most groups, twenty-seven; New York was the runner-up, with sixteen. Some of the entries in the directory were "loners."

In January 1953 we sent out a bulletin to the groups reporting 441 groups had registered, with 151 of them contributing. Receipts were $2,864.03 and expenditures, $1,540.94.

In 1954, when the Clearing House was able to support a part-time staff worker, Henrietta was chosen. Among her many duties was the compilation of the *Newsletter*, which I had written until that time. In these early issues some items noted were: The first male member had joined the Durban, South Africa, group; any member of the family of any alcoholic, whether in AA or not, was welcome in Al-Anon; and our members were helping the AA prison groups by explaining alcoholism to the families of inmates.

Soon we felt we could support a special editor for the *Newsletter*. Margaret, who had just gotten a YWCA job, agreed to take over the *Newsletter*'s editorship at home. Her first issue was June 1954, and the name was then changed to *Al-Anon Family Group Forum*, with the permission of Ruth G., who by then no longer published *The Family Forum*. Margaret continued to be the editor for twenty years.

For business purposes we incorporated the Clearing House in October 1954 under the name Al-Anon Family Group Headquarters, Inc. An Advisory Committee, which we had instituted a year or so before, appointed a Board of Directors to supervise headquarters. After many letters back and forth to the U.S. Treasury Department, we finally procured tax exemption and the status of a nonprofit corporation. Incorporation scared some members who thought we would become "too organized." But we needed this firm foundation on which to build Al-Anon's future, and over the years it has proved to be a sound move.

In 1953 Al-Anon had begun to win publicity. Without showing my face, I spoke on an inspirational TV program called "Lamp unto My Feet," and the *Christian Herald* carried the first piece about our Fellowship. Then there were write-ups in *Life Romances* and *Life Today*. Bill wrote a message for our Christmas bulletin stating, "Growth of the Family Groups is just about the greatest Christmas present AA could be given." And the radio program "Second Chance" presented a story about Al-Anon.

Like AA, Al-Anon had an article in the *Saturday Evening Post*. Written by Jerome Ellison, ours came out in July 1955, and although there were not the thousands of responses the AA article had had, the article resulted in wide recognition of the value of the Al-Anon program.

A broadcast by Lee Graham with three anonymous Al-Anon members brought 150 inquiries; columnists and feature writers Walter Winchell, Beatrice Fairfax, and Doris Drake made reference to Al-Anon.

We had great hopes for a nationwide radio broadcast by Ted Malone on WABC, tying in local stations across the country. I personally worked hard on this, as it seemed a perfect opportunity to tell Al-Anon's story to thousands of listeners. But for some reason never revealed to us, Ted Malone left WABC not long before the showing date, and the broadcast never materialized. But other good publicity came along. On the *Loretta Young Show*, "The Understanding Heart," a story about Al-Anon, was a great success. Copies of this film were given to Al-Anon by its producer and were circulated among the groups until they wore out. *Showcase* also put on a TV presentation of Al-Anon.

Undoubtedly the most effective publicity we have enjoyed came still later, in columnist Ann Landers's articles. From one in 1962, 4,000 letters poured in. Some time after that her response to a letter from the wife of an active alcoholic also produced an overwhelming influx of inquiries. Over the years Ann Landers's answers to questions from her readers about alcoholism have continued to be very favorable to AA, Al-Anon, and Alateen.

Meanwhile for two years we had struggled to prepare our first book, *The Al-Anon Family Groups*. With Bill's help I wrote the first draft of what we thought was going to be a pamphlet. Then Trudy M., a short-time but most capable volunteer, with Margaret's help, made a connected manuscript out of it. Bill and I went over it again and added some material. Ralph B., an AA writer, edited it, and we sent mimeographed copies to groups selected at random. Many of their suggestions and stories were so good that the pamphlet grew into a book. Finally at the 1955 AA International Convention in St. Louis (where Al-Anon participated in five workshops), the multi-authored book made its appearance and sold quite well.

Our headquarters remained at the 24th Street Clubhouse from 1952 to 1957. The large, bare room where we worked was heated by pipes from a nearby apartment building. Larry M., then in charge of the club, was an artist who often used the skylighted studio to paint. He painted portraits of Bill, Bob and Dr. Silkworth which were hung downstairs around the fireplace. When Larry was there, the room was comfortable and things ran smoothly. But if he was not around to call the janitor, we never were able to find the man and consequently froze. In summer the other volunteers called it "Lois's sweatshop."

Set back from the street, the clubhouse had a long, tunnel-like passageway, which the AAs called "the Last Mile." If the front doorbell rang when one or two of us were there alone, it was spooky to navigate this long hallway to the front door. As a rule AAs did not use the club during the day, but occasionally a drunk would come for help.

Once, late in the day after the last volunteer left, forgetting to lock the front door, Henrietta looked up from her desk to find two disreputable characters who had wandered upstairs. They refused to leave until she phoned the janitor to come over and get them out. Soon, however, Dot and Evelyn were added to the staff, and no one had to be in the building alone.

Because the room was used at night by AAs, we had to put away all our papers and typewriters at the end of each day and bring them out again the next workday. The soft-drink deliveryman always seemed to come to replenish the club's supply on one of the days we were there. There was also the downstairs telephone to answer.

Since we paid only a token rental—at first thirty dollars and then forty a month—for the use of the studio, we felt we couldn't complain. We were so grateful for the use of the club that these small inconveniences didn't bother us. But as the work became heavier, we longed for an office of our own. Finally in early 1957 we felt we were financially able to be independent and looked around for office space.

The clubhouse building had to be torn down in 1959 to make way for a new housing project and Larry had the portraits, furnishings, and paneling put in storage. What happened to them is anyone's guess, for Larry became ill, and there was no one to take responsibility.

Before the AA General Service Conference met in New York in 1957, the Al-Anon office moved to its new quarters at 125 East 23rd Street, in time to welcome the AA delegates' wives. During the Conference there was an Al-Anon meeting for them at the Chelsea School, attended by 300. At a reception for the wives here at Stepping Stones, we discovered that half of them belonged to Al-Anon; Palmira, the Puerto Rican delegate's wife, reported two Al-Anon groups in her homeland. We told the wives about our hope for an annual service conference of our own.

Al-Anon took a step toward this in 1960 at the Long Beach, California, AA International Convention. The members present voted to approve a plan similar to AA's for an annual conference of delegates. Later, upon being polled, the groups affirmed this decision. At the Convention the revised and enlarged edition of the book *The Al-Anon Family Groups* was presented under its new title, *Living with an Alcoholic*.

We held our First World Service Conference in New York in April 1961 with twelve delegates, the Headquarters staff, and the Board of Trustees (which had replaced the Board of Directors). The delegates had been chosen from the twelve states and Canadian provinces having the largest Al-Anon populations: British Columbia, California, Florida, Illinois, Kansas, Michigan, Minnesota, New York, Ohio, Ontario, Pennsylvania, and Texas. A Conference Committee had been appointed with Sue L. as chairman and Holly C. as secretary.

The Conference was at first experimental. Twenty-four delegates were supposed to attend the second year, but one of them couldn't make it and had to send her alternate. The New York delegate became the mother of premature twins the day the Conference opened. The next year at the close of the 1963 gathering, the thirty-six delegates plus the Headquarters contingent voted the Conference be made a permanent part of the Al-Anon structure. Sue resigned as chairman of the Conference in 1967, and Penny B. assumed that responsibility until her resignation in 1976. Jean A. from Toronto was then appointed chairman.

It was easier for Al-Anon to get started than for AA, since AA had already done the spadework when Al-Anon came along. Our Fellowship simply followed in AA's footsteps. And of course Al-Anon's field of potential usefulness was and is very wide. Four or five people are affected by one alcoholic—members of the whole family, close friends, employers and employees, and others, all of whom can be helped by Al-Anon.

I think one reason that AA and Al-Anon have been so successful is that members of our Fellowships never talk down to a prospect. We tell how we, too, have been there in the same apparently hopeless mess. Our approach is one of mutual need, of identification.

By 1963 the number of Al-Anon groups had reached 1,500; they had spread to many distant lands; the groups themselves were taking responsibility for their Fellowship; the Al-Anon office was approaching a sound financial status; and the public was learning about us.

Even we optimists, Bill and I, were surprised at the rate Al-Anon was growing.

18

Alateen – Learning Not to Hate

I have always loved the children of AAs. In the early days young teenagers often attended the meetings with the other members of the family. Their absorption in the program, their interest in the progress of each AA member, and their excitement on the arrival of a newcomer seemed almost as great as, if not greater than, those of some of the adult alcoholics.

The AA program fulfilled the idealism of youth. It not only helped children to understand their alcoholic parents, but also enabled them to apply the principles to themselves, although not always consciously. Later the young people often went to Al-Anon meetings, either because of their own desire or at parental suggestion, and were greatly helped.

Very often they showed more sympathy for the alcoholic than for the other parent. To them the cause of the illness of the alcoholic was clear: too much drinking. But the reasons for the irritability and unreasonableness of the nonalcoholic parent were not so obvious.

Children of alcoholics almost always feel insecure. Many of them, particularly in homes where there is no AA background, develop serious problems of their own: rebellion against any sort of authority, addiction to drugs and alcohol, and even criminal activities.

At the Clearing House we began to recognize the special need of these young people and planned a session for them at the AA International Convention in St. Louis in 1955. This was a great success. Many AAs and Al-Anons, as well as the young people themselves, heard inspiring stories of how children of alcoholics were solving their problems through their use of the program, in the same way that Annie S. and I and the other early wives had before the formation of the Al-Anon Fellowship.

We heard this kind of story at St. Louis:

"When Daddy stumbled up the steps late at night, my little dog Trixie would crawl under the covers at the foot of my bed and shake. I'd cover my own head and pray that Dad would make it up to bed . . . . This stopped after Dad's first AA meeting. I went with him to his second. So did Mother.

"The point I want to make is: start out as a family behind the alcoholic. We all need unity. A child should be given the privilege of finding out alcoholism is a disease, not just lack of willpower. Even a small child can understand the meaning and beauty of the program."*

There was a heavy demand for copies of these teenage St. Louis talks, which were distributed by the Clearing House.

A young man in California wrote that he had started meetings for teenagers, and he suggested that a third division be formed, since their problems were different from those of the members of either AA or Al-Anon. This new section would, of course, be part of Al-Anon and would follow the principles suggested in the Steps.

Another group of young people sprang up in California, and a letter came in from Durban, South Africa, asking for literature for teenagers. The only literature available was a reprint of the young people's talks at the St. Louis Convention and an *AA Grapevine* piece called "It's a Teenage Affair," signed B. L.

So many young people began writing in to the office that we saw a new section was indeed needed. The name Alateen was suggested, and a pamphlet was prepared called *Youth and the Alcoholic Parent*, copies of which were sent with every Al-Anon order to alert our membership about Alateen.

The Al-Anon Twelve Steps did not have to be changed for teenagers, but the Traditions did; so a proposed revision of them was sent to all Alateen groups for suggestions for improvement.

By 1958 our headquarters had appointed Wanda R. chairman of an Alateen Committee and had added a part-time Alateen secretary to the staff. Soon the Al-Anon basic book, *Living with an Alcoholic*, was revised to include a chapter on Alateen.

In 1960 at the AA International Convention in Long Beach, California, workshops were held especially for teenagers. Both AAs and Al-Anons who attended were thrilled by these sessions and reported that the young people seemed to have grasped the program better and with more understanding than they themselves had. Alateen, then numbering about 100 groups, had sprung into being in the five years since the St. Louis Convention.

Al-Anon and the teenagers' parents both insisted that each Alateen group should have a sponsor. Unfortunately there was and is great diffi-

*Excerpts from the books *Living with an Alcoholic* (see *The Al-Anon Family Groups – Classic Edition*) and *Alateen—Hope for the Children of Alcoholics* are used with permission of Al-Anon Family Group Headquarters, Inc.

culty in finding sponsors. AAs are not only willing but happy to serve in this way, but for some reason few Al-Anon parents want to be sponsors. Some even disapprove of their children's attending meetings.

To a certain degree this reaction corresponds to that of some early AAs who didn't like the formation of Al-Anon, perhaps for the same reasons. Quite a number of AAs at first feared that they were being criticized and their escapades recounted at Al-Anon meetings. In reality Al-Anon and Alateen sessions are held for the members' own improvement, and as little as possible is said about the rest of the family.

Many parents, however, are very enthusiastic about Alateen and note a beneficial change in their teenagers' attitudes. One mother wrote thanking headquarters for helping her daughter "embrace such a radiant philosophy." Parents want to be respected by their children, but in many families where there is alcoholism, this respect is lost. Through the practice of Alateen principles members acquire a better understanding of their parents and, even more important, regain their own self-respect. As one says:

"For the first time . . . I'm starting to really care about other people, mainly because I feel like a worthwhile person. I believe . . . you can't love someone until you first care about yourself."

The strongest and most progressive Alateen groups have sponsors. Al-Anon members are the most appropriate sponsors for Alateens since they are part of the same Fellowship, but the problem of finding sponsors continues.

It has proved impractical to have a group sponsored by the parent of a member of that group. Children are often reluctant to speak freely in front of their own parents. Members conduct the meetings themselves, and sponsors are simply there to answer questions and be available in case of trouble. Sponsors can also help the teenagers alert alcoholic clinics and juvenile and family courts about Alateen, can have newspapers publish times and places of meetings, and can help youngsters organize for conventions and other activities.

An article in the Sunday supplement *Parade* was the first publicity to appear about Alateen, followed by many pieces in other magazines and newspapers. These stories were so dramatic and moving that there was a real burst of interest all over the country.

A *Life* Magazine article about Alateen, illustrated with sketches, brought in over 500 inquiries within three weeks. This opened the door to more public information in *Time* Magazine, *American Weekly*, *Children 's Family Digest* and the "Dear Abby" and Ann Landers columns. The World Service Office, or WSO, as we now called our headquarters, distributed 10,000 reprints of a *Guidepost* piece, "My Mother Is an Alcoholic," written by an Alateen. Another Alateen member wrote an article published in *Seventeen* Magazine which brought in 100 letters. WSO had it reprinted and distributed to the groups.

Membership in an Alateen group fluctuates far more than in an adult Al-Anon group. Teenagers grow up; they go away to college or marry; some enlist in military service or take jobs in different areas. When they outgrow Alateen, many of them join Al-Anon and make wonderful sponsors for new teenage groups.

Most Alateen groups are very responsible and wish to pay their own way wherever they go. Some of them have discovered ingenious ways for raising money to make their voluntary contributions to WSO. They find great joy in helping other teenagers who have alcoholic parents, and their attention to these newcomers is most devoted. In letters to WSO they express their gratitude and enthusiasm in glowing terms.

As the groups grew in maturity, they formed committees to visit young people in correctional institutions. Groups were started within the confines. The dramatic effect upon these confused kids is heartwarming.

Alateen groups were soon listed in the annual Al-Anon World Directory and in the local directories of metropolitan Al-Anon information services and intergroups.

Many Alateens had attended AA and Al-Anon conventions. But soon Alateen members on the eastern seaboard wanted to hold conventions of their own. With the help of their sponsors they planned, financed, and managed a get-together in Philadelphia in June 1961, the first of many such gatherings all over the country.

By 1963 over 200 groups were functioning in America. Overseas, new ones had been started in South Africa, India, England, Puerto Rico, and Trinidad. Ann Landers continued to receive inquiries, and in her column she urged youngsters to join Alateen. Articles appeared in the New York *Herald Tribune* and the *Ladies' Home Journal.* To coincide with the publication of the latter article, programs were arranged on WCBS-TV and WJRZ-TV in New York by the WSO Alateen Committee.

By April 1964 a full-time secretary for Alateen was needed, and Timmy W. was added to the WSO staff. One of her duties was to prepare a bimonthly newsletter called *Alateen Talk* through which members could communicate and learn of one another's growth and activities.

At the 1965 AA International Convention in Toronto, Alateens played an active part. We heard:

"One night my mother went out, and I was home alone when my father came home drunk. We had a terrible fight with knives, and I almost killed him. I was so upset—I thought I was crazy. I took off in the car and decided to kill myself.

"I went off a small cliff, but my car stopped just three inches from a tree.

It was a miracle, and I made a decision to return to Alateen. This time I listened and started to open up.

"I will always be grateful for Alateen, because without it I know I wouldn't be here today. Alateen taught me not to be afraid of people. It has taught me to accept myself and my father for what we are, to love him, and to understand him."

Outside agencies were now recognizing Alateen as a vital part of family recovery. For example, the Juvenile Court in St. Paul, Minnesota, asked the local group to be court helpers, and in Canada members were invited to speak at a penitentiary. A class of social workers in Kentucky had Alateen speakers at its graduation.

Many Alateen groups were forming in countries that didn't understand English, so we had to have our literature translated, first into French by Al-Anon's French Literature Committee in Quebec, which served the 35 Alateen groups there and new ones in Switzerland, France, and Belgium. Then our Spanish-speaking staff member translated several Alateen pieces into that language. Finland had already translated *It's a Teenage Affair* and *Step Four Inventory for Alateens* into its own language, as had a Flemish translator for Belgian groups.

Two pieces written by Alateen members themselves were added to the WSO price list, and titles of Al-Anon's literature were changed to include our younger section. In order to improve communications an Alateen member and an Alateen sponsor were appointed to the WSO Alateen Committee.

The young people's groups became interested in their assembly structure and elected group representatives (GRs) and district representatives (DRs) to go to Al-Anon assemblies, thus tying their relationship with Al-Anon even closer. Together with the WSO Alateen Committee they made great preparations for the 1970 AA International Convention in Miami, where they held three inspiring workshops.

There we heard such things as: "I try to overcome attacks of self-pity by concerning myself with others—not just within the program, but everywhere—at school, at home, in the neighborhood. Compassion, the program, and help from my Higher Power pull me through."

Two years later an eleven-year-old boy wrote Ann Landers a moving letter asking her how he could learn not to hate his drunken father. Her answer brought 300 inquiries to WSO. That same year the White House in Washington, D.C., held a conference on children and youth. An Alateen member and a sponsor were selected to represent the by-then 1,000 Alateen groups.

The annual Al-Anon picnic at Stepping Stones has been attended by toddlers, teenagers, grandmas, and AAs as well as Al-Anons. After lunch we have a short meeting at which members are asked to speak. While Bill was still here, his greeting always climaxed the meeting. But lately it is the Alateens who really make the day with their enthusiastic, honest, and imaginative talks. Here are two examples:

"A few months ago I was turned on to the most beautiful way of life in the world—for me the only way—Alateen. Through Alateen and a drug meeting I attend, I got off drugs and began coping with my family problem in the right way . . . . For once in my life I really felt like someone. The most beautiful thing I found was God. This is the supreme thing you can get out of Alateen, and I'm thankful I found Him."

And, "About two months after I joined Alateen, I hit bottom. All of a sudden I realized that I wasn't really following the program, that I was sick. I had never admitted that before, but I'm glad I do now, because I can start practicing the program without being phony. I thank God for letting me slip—He let me see how badly I needed Alateen."

Can you see why I love the kids?

19

A Regenerating Force

The maturing of Al-Anon gathered momentum. I suppose it was natural that at first we should place the emphasis on the alcoholic in our lives. After all we are an offshoot of Alcoholics Anonymous, and having an alcoholic in the family is our common bond. In our earliest pamphlet, *Purpose and Suggestions,* the first item in our threefold purpose was "to give encouragement and understanding to the AA in the home"; then came "to welcome and give comfort to the families of AAs"; and last "to grow spiritually through living by the Twelve Steps of AA." However, we changed this order soon, placing our own growth first, and soon after that changed "AA" in the first two purposes to "alcoholic(s)."

In Al-Anon's early adaptation of the AA Traditions, the first one stated, "Our common welfare and that of AA should come first," and continued, "our effectiveness in helping families . . . depends upon our cooperation with AA." And in Tradition Twelve we used the phrase "as in AA anonymity." But we soon found our field of usefulness extended beyond the families of AAs. So by 1955 we dropped any unnecessary reference to AA. Our new First Tradition said simply, "Our common welfare should come first."

By degrees we began to emphasize that Al-Anon was for those affected by another person's drinking, whether or not the drinker even acknowledged a problem.

Incidentally, not until 1961 did we recognize the existence of TV, for until then our Eleventh Tradition mentioned only "press, radio and films" as places where anonymity should not be broken.

In the early days of Al-Anon we felt we should learn as much as possible about alcoholism, so we could help our mates. But again by degrees the emphasis began to shift toward detachment-*with-love* from the alcoholic. The idea was not only that the latter could not learn from mistakes if nursed and protected, but that the nonalcoholic should strive for spiritual development first and foremost. No one can directly change anyone but oneself.

However, detachment-*with-love* does not exclude knowledge about alcoholism, and such knowledge can be helpful as long as the spouse does detach with love. But the idea of "detachment" can be misunderstood and overemphasized. "With-love" is the important part of this idea. True love does what is believed to be best for the person loved, not what is easiest at the moment. Spoiling and pampering do not spring from love, but from lack of knowledge or from lack of discipline in the "spoiler." This is where many of us made our mistakes. For example, in protecting the one I loved from the consequences of his own actions, I was not helping Bill.

Most people come to Al-Anon meetings to get the alcoholic in their lives sober and are shocked to learn they themselves need to change. It is sometimes harder for them to recognize that they are part of the problem than it is for drinkers to admit their own alcoholism.

The fundamentals of our program can be learned from our general literature. However, we soon realized that for people in certain relationships, such as male spouses, parents and children of alcoholics, specific literature would be helpful, and we started preparing it. The male spouse was often reluctant to join a group of females, so in addition to literature for men, stag groups evolved.

Some members called Al-Anon a "sister fellowship" to AA. At the 1965 Al-Anon Annual Conference a male delegate identified himself as "one of the shaving sisters." After much laughter and joking we realized Al-Anon could no longer be called a "sister fellowship." And by the same logic Al-Anon should be represented by no symbol that is inappropriate to either sex. Today most groups include a few men, who feel at home.

Parents of alcoholics, particularly the mothers, have very poignant stories and are helped by trying to live the program as well as by literature telling of others with the same problem.

In 1957 soon after Alateen began, a whole new set of literature was adapted for young people. It seemed we were continually publishing new literature. Up to the present, Al-Anon books or pamphlets have been translated into eight languages, transcribed in Braille and put on tapes for the visually handicapped. Our ten books and their publication dates are: *Al-Anon Family Groups* (1955*), *Al-Anon Faces Alcoholism* (1965), *The Dilemma of the Alcoholic Marriage* (1967), *One Day at a Time in Al-Anon* (1968 *), *Al-Anon's Favorite Forum Editorials* by Margaret D. (1970), *Alateen—Hope for Children of Alcoholics* (1973), *Al-Anon's*

*Revised and expanded in 1960 as *Living With An Alcoholic*; reverted to original title in 1983; and in 2000 the text of the first edition was republished along with an extensive appendix.

Twelve Steps & Twelve Traditions (1981), *A Day at a Time in Alateen* (1983), *As We Understood . . .* (1985), *First Steps: Al-Anon—35 Years of Beginnings* (1986).

The *Dilemma* and *One Day at a Time* are both by our past longtime chairman of the Literature Committee, Alice B. The "ODAT" for short, is a daily reader and is by far our best seller.

The circulation of *The Forum* at present has kept pace with our growth. Since Margaret D. retired in 1974, the editorship has been changed twice. Louise M. took on the job after Margaret left and did very well with it. She remarried in early 1977 and became too busy to carry it on, so she resigned. Hildegard M., replacing Louise, had bright visions for *The Forum*. Her proposal for a pocket-sized magazine with more pages and with illustrations was approved by the Conference in April 1977. Hildegard not only refined the existing format of *The Forum*, but presented a completely new magazine to the Conference of 1978.

Younger and younger spouses had begun to join Al-Anon over the years. It is good to know that these young people do not have to approach the end of the dreary road or reach the bottom of the pit before they turn around. But on the other hand some of them may not feel the overwhelming, fanatical attachment to Al-Anon felt by those of us who experienced utter desolation.

Persons living with an alcoholic as well as those engaged to be married to one now join Al-Anon. Al-Anon welcomes all who feel the need of our program, including friends, employers and employees of alcoholics. It sets no restrictions on color, race, religion, or life-style. It is Al-Anon policy for members to give no personal or marital advice but simply to share their own stories and experience in working the program.

The Federal government has finally awakened to the fact that there is a tremendous alcohol problem among its civilian employees and members of the armed services. It is now ordering literature in large quantities from AA and Al-Anon.

Nevertheless, the number of alcoholics continues to increase, so at last public concern has been aroused. AA has given help to probably over a million and a half drinkers. Committees, commissions and agencies have been springing up everywhere trying to restore the alcoholic as a useful member of society. But some of these well-meaning associations have little real knowledge of or experience with the problem. As AA has long understood, the alcoholic needs more than psychiatric or social-service aid. He or she needs a complete rebirth or "change" as the Oxford Group

---

* In 1980, at the 45th Anniversary International Convention of AA in New Orleans, LA, the one millionth copy was presented to Milton A. Maxwell, Ph.D., nonalcoholic Chairman of AA's General Service Board.

A pastime we both enjoyed.

used the word, has to acknowledge inability to solve the problem alone, and must surrender to a greater Power even if that is only the AA group. The alcoholic must begin to build a whole new life.

So must the families of alcoholics. Therefore associations are being formed to counsel them. The very recognition that the family of an alcoholic does have a special problem is useful. Some of these agencies order Al-Anon literature and advise their clients to attend Al-Anon meetings, and I'm sure many persons are consequently helped.

Sometimes members seek advice from clergymen, psychiatrists, or counselors. Al-Anon is glad to have members adopt any treatment that helps them, but Al-Anon meetings are not the place to discuss these treatments. Religious retreats and marriage-counseling groups, for instance, are not part of Al-Anon. Failure to make this distinction clear could confuse and diffuse our understanding of the Al-Anon program. Our program is built on spiritual principles which contain certain religious and psychiatric truths. It does not compete with any treatment, nor is it a substitute for any treatment, nor can any treatment be a substitute for Al-Anon.

A number of AAs are married to alcoholics, and many of these join Al-Anon as well as AA groups. We call these "double winners" and

Al-Anon has recently published a pamphlet for them. Over the years we have seen many Al-Anon members discover that they need AA. It is wonderful to witness their recovery through the AA program.

In 1971, after fourteen years at 125 East 23rd Street, our quarters again became too restricted. So we moved up the block to 115 East 23rd Street. We felt these commodious new quarters would last us a long period, but in no time we had to take another floor upstairs for the packing, storing, and distributing of books and literature. This department employed four men under Gene, one of the earliest shipping clerks at 125. And then more space was needed for secretaries' offices, for a conference room, and for storage of files, so another floor was leased.

Henrietta had been considering retiring for some time, and about a year before she left, at the close of 1976, she engaged Eleanor O. to train as her replacement. Of course it was impossible for anyone to take Henrietta's place. A volunteer before becoming our first paid staff worker, Henrietta was in at Al-Anon's start and had steered it through its fast-growing years. She had not only a remarkable memory but also a great gift for administration. Among her special interests were the overseas groups, which multiplied many times during her tenure.

Soon after Eleanor took office, we found we had to move again. It took long tough negotiating by our new general secretary, but she pulled us through superlatively. On March 4, 1978, the Al-Anon office was moved to a large area on the second floor of 1 Park Avenue.

This space was selected for several reasons: it is a perfect location, across the street from the AA General Service Office; the building is strong enough (which many office buildings are not) to hold our stacks and stacks of books in the packing department; the space is large enough to allow for future expansion; and above all it permits all our workers, although in separate offices, to be together on one floor for easy communication.

Myrna H., who as senior administrative assistant had worked closely with Henrietta and learned many of the details of the office management, was appointed Eleanor's deputy. When Eleanor decided to resign in the summer of 1978, Myrna was enthusiastically named general secretary at the fall meeting of the Board of Trustees.

During these later years the Al-Anon services are becoming more and more international and intercontinental. Regional trustees from various parts of the United States and Canada help to guide us. Representatives from many overseas countries attend our annual Conference. In the last decade Al-Anon general service offices and national conferences have developed in ten other countries, among them the United Kingdom and Eire, Australia, South Africa, New Zealand, Mexico, and Argentina. Truly Al-Anon is a worldwide movement.

However widely scattered, we remain one Fellowship. The same Twelve Steps show us the way to personal recovery everywhere, and the same Twelve Traditions guard our unity.

In these days when the number of agencies and treatment methods in the alcoholism field is rising so rapidly, our Traditions are more important than ever. A public meeting held in Washington, D.C., early in 1978 by the National Council on Alcoholism illustrated the application of two Traditions: Tradition Six (nonendorsement) and Tradition Eleven (anonymity). A large number of prominent persons who had found sobriety were invited to speak. This was to help lift the stigma from alcoholism by showing that respected people could be recovered alcoholics. None of the speakers said they belonged to AA, though it may reasonably be assumed that many were members. No anonymity was broken in the public media, and no AA endorsement of NCA was implied.

On the other hand there seems to be a trend in certain areas toward an excess of anonymity even within the Fellowships. Al-Anon's Eleventh Tradition states:

"Our public relations policy is based on attraction rather than promotion; we need always maintain personal anonymity at the level of press, radio, TV and films."

Nothing is said about maintaining anonymity within our group, our family, and our circle of friends. Let us not mistake anonymity for secrecy.

The degree of anonymity we practice is a personal matter. Most of us, I believe, do not wish to be anonymous within our own Fellowships. Anonymity here hinders our availability to help our fellow members.

Also, if AA and Al-Anon groups do not let the public know of our presence, perhaps by announcing the time and place of meetings in local newspapers or by some other means, we block ourselves off from those in need.

The stigma of alcoholism still is strong. I believe it to be one of the responsibilities of our Fellowships to try to remove this stigma. To act as if AA and Al-Anon were secret societies only increases the idea of shame.

If we sincerely believe alcoholism to be an illness, just as diabetes is an illness, we can more easily convince others and break down their resistance to an admission of having the disease or of living with one who has it. How can we blame the public for its belief that alcoholism is a moral weakness if we seem to believe it ourselves?

Alcoholism is growing at a tremendous rate, and we AA and Al-Anon members want to do all we can, within the Traditions, to aid the recovery of alcoholics and their families.

There are now (in 1979) 14,000 Al-Anon groups, including 2,200 Alateen groups in seventy countries around the world. To those of us who were in at Al-Anon's beginnings, these figures seem astonishing; but we also know that Al-Anon hasn't scratched the surface. Our responsibilities and opportunities for service extend far into the future.

As our philosophy in action continues to spread, more and more people other than alcoholics will find some sort of rebirth in associations based on the Alcoholics Anonymous program.

Of course, true to my sentimental, optimistic self, I believe there *is* a great future for our Fellowships. It seems to me the world is on a not-so-dry bender and is ready for a regenerating force that can bring the kind of faith, security, and happiness that the "A's" (AA, Al-Anon and Alateen) have found.

But the survival of our "A's" depends on growth—growth in spirit more than in numbers. We believe the principles upon which AA and Al-Anon are founded are fundamental for all time and all people. And yet our individual acceptance and application of these principles must continue to grow or we as societies will perish. For stagnation is retrogression. There is no standing still.

AA and Al-Anon are great demonstrations of the love of one human being for another, of people for people. The joy and empathy felt at one of our gatherings are beyond description. Nowhere else have I seen folks so enjoy being together, and in no church or other assembly have I ever heard a prayer recited more movingly than at our Fellowships' meetings.

What is love? What is it that passes between two people who love each other?

Science has discovered that the emotions of fear and anger actually produce emanations in the human body that can be sensed by other men and women, children, animals, and perhaps plants. But I have never heard that science has studied the great force of love.

I suspect that love, too, is an actual physical emanation as well as a spiritual force—a telepathy of the heart and not just the absence of hurtful emotions.

I deeply believe it *is* love that makes the world go 'round. God is love, and love is the creative force, the force that ties family and friends together. It inspires us to greater endeavor in all fields of activity, in love of God, love of man, love of ideas, love of self, love of things. The well of love refills itself. The more one gives of love, the more one has to give.

Children who are not loved grow up unhappy and rebellious. Even though they may be treated with kindness, that is not enough! They need the positive warmth and security of love. They may even need it physically as well as emotionally and spiritually.

This force, embodied as it is in God's love, kept Bill and me together and finally, through various channels, sobered him up. There are moments even now when the wonder and beauty of Bill's regeneration still fill me with awe.

I used to believe *thinking* was the highest function of human beings. The AA experience changed me. I now realize *loving* is our supreme function. The heart precedes the mind.

Gazing at the sky on a bright starlit night, we are overwhelmed with wonder at the seemingly limitless universe. Our finite minds cannot envision its extent and complexity, much less the possibility of other universes beyond. Likewise our finite minds sometimes question why a loving God seems to permit apparently God-loving and virtuous people to suffer the tragedies that occasionally befall them.

But our hearts do not need logic. They can love and forgive and accept that which our minds cannot comprehend. Hearts understand in a way minds cannot.

AL-ANON and AA
HISTORICAL EVENTS

1934

November   Ebby tells Bill of his "release" from alcohol.

December   Bill has his last drink, in Towns Hospital.

       14   Bill has his spiritual awakening.

       18   Bill leaves the hospital and starts working with other alcoholics.

1935

May 1   Bill goes to Akron on a job of collecting proxies and stays three months.

       12   Bill meets Bob.

June 10   Bob has his last drink and AA begins.

       29   I go to Akron to stay with Bob and Annie on my week's vacation.

November 19   Ebby comes to live with us on Clinton Street.

1935-1941

After throwing my shoe, recognizing my need for the Oxford Group, I become quite pious for a period. When later Bill and I travel to spark new AA groups, I speak at many gatherings of wives and tell of my spiritual need. Annie S. and other wives of early AAs do the same. Groups of the families of AAs begin to form with no clear purpose.

1936

February 23   I quit working at Loeser's.

December   Bill is elated by job offered him by Charles B. Towns as a professional therapist at his Hospital, but AA group puts on the damper.

1937

March   Bill and I still attend Oxford Group meetings.

May   Ebby gets drunk in Albany.

August   We stop going to Oxford Group meetings.

October   In Akron Bill and Bob take stock of growth of movement: 40 sober. They decide movement needs a book and perhaps hospitals. In New York Bill and Hank try to raise money for the book without success. Leonard Strong introduces Bill to the Rev. Willard S. Richardson, spiritual adviser to John D. Rockefeller Jr.

1938

February 1-14 Frank Amos goes to Akron to assess movement and Bob. Reporting favorably, he advises John D. Rockefeller Jr. to give $50,000. Rockefeller disagrees but places $5,000 with Riverside Church for AA's use.

4 Dick Richardson proposes Alcoholic Foundation be formed.

March 13 Large meeting at Hank's in Montclair, NJ.

April 10 Eighteen at the weekly meeting at Clinton Street.

May 20 Bill starts writing the Big Book. As he finishes a chapter he first discusses it in New York and then ships it to Akron.

June 15 The name "Alcoholics Anonymous" is used for the first time. Bill, in reaction to my anger, dashes out to take a drink but goes to an AA member instead.

Hank, Bill and the others unsuccessfully solicit wealthy people on a list provided by Rockefeller friends.

August 11 Alcoholic Foundation holds its first meeting.

AA members, mostly in Akron, write stories for the book.

September 6 Ebby returns to Clinton Street.

Bill and Hank get hopeful assurances from an editor at *Reader's Digest* about their publishing an article on AA.

Frank Amos introduces Bill to the religious editor of Harper Brothers Publishers, who offers Bill $1,500 subsidy while he finishes the book.

21 Instead, to publish the book, Hank and Bill form the Works Publishing Company, in which members can purchase stock. The first two chapters are used for money-raising, without success. Charlie Towns contributes $500.

December Bill writes Twelve Steps. AAs argue about not enough or too much God.

1939

February 400 Multilith copies of book entitled *Alcoholics Anonymous* are sent to doctors, judges, psychiatrists, etc. for criticism.

March 1 *Reader's Digest* turns down article on AA. There are 100 members all told in AA.

April 5,000 copies of "Alcoholics Anonymous" are printed. with two chapters for wives.

Gabriel Heatter interviews Morgan R. about AA on his radio program.

April 26 Bill and I leave Clinton Street for good and begin to "live around" with AAs and our families.

Newark *Sunday Call* is the first newspaper to write about AA.

May 14 AAs subscribe money for us to live on: "Bill and Lois Improvement Fund."

16 AAs meet at Bert's tailor shop on Fifth Avenue, New York City.

June 6 AAs meet at an apartment lent by friends, on 72nd Street, New York City.

16 Bill attends AA meeting at Blythewood Sanitarium in Greenwich, CT; 26 present.

5 New York *Times* writes a good review of the Big Book.

30 Harry Emerson Fosdick writes a good review of the book.

July 4 First meeting is held at Harold S.'s in Flatbush, Brooklyn.

August 1 First meeting is held in Bert's larger tailoring work loft.

18 At a special meeting at Mag's and Bob's in Montclair, NJ, six doctors are present: two from Rockland State Hospital, two from Bellevue, Dr. Silkworth and an AA doctor.

September 5 New meeting place is at Steinway Hall; 60 present

12 At meeting in Montclair at Bob's and Mug's, 55 are present,

26 At New York meeting at Steinway Hall; 70-80 are present.

27 Letters come in from *Liberty* article "Alcoholics and God," by Morris Markey.

October 1 We move back to Green Pond; 40 come to meeting there.

21 First of Cleveland *Plain Dealer* articles, which bring in hundreds.

22 Meetings start in Community House in South Orange, NJ.

November 13 New York AAs ask Bill to continue as guide and leakier of AA movement.

December 6 Bill talks at first meeting of Research Council on Problems of Alcohol. Bert T. loans book company $1,000 on his business, which saves the book venture.

1940

February 8 Along with eight AAs, 60 of Rockefeller's friends attend a dinner given by him at the Union Club.
Six articles on AA, written anonymously by Larry J., appear in the Houston *Press*.

23 Bill and Bob each get $30 a week from response from Rockefeller dinner. (Dinner raised only $2,200, including Rockefeller's $1,000).

27 First meeting in Philadelphia is started by Jimmy B. at George S.'s.

March 16 Bill moves Alcoholic Foundation Office from Newark, NJ., to 30 Vesey Street, New York City.

April 11 Bill and I attend Philadelphia meeting–42 present; 15 four weeks ago.

21 Individual AAs obtain use of Joy Farm (later known as High Watch) Kent, CT, as a rest farm for alcoholics.

May 7 I speak at Steinway Hall; 150 present.

22 The AA book company is incorporated. Bill and Hank give their book stock to Works Publishing, with the stipulation that Bob and Annie have 10% royalties on the book for life.

June 5 Ebby has a job at the New York World's Fair.

18 At the first meeting at the new club, 334½ West 24th Street, New York, 100 are present.

September 12 Eight wives meet, upstairs at the club who first met to play cards, soon try to help each other with problems of living with an alcoholic.

1941-1949

Family Groups get started in: Amarillo, TX; Austin, TX; Birmingham, AL; Capetown, South Africa; Chicago, IL; Denver CO; Edmonton, AB, Canada; Joplin, MO; Long Beach, CA; Memphis, TN; New York, NY; Oklahoma City, OK; Richmond, VA; Rochester, NY; Toronto, ON, Canada, and perhaps other places.

1941-1951

87 relatives of AAs, many of them representing a Family Group, write AA for help in starting groups.

1944

December *AA Grapevine* contains article "Bill's Wife Remembers When He and She and the First AAs Were Very Young."

1949

First Al-Anon publicity; *Coronet's* "New Help for Alcoholics" is about their families.

1949-1951

More Family Groups start, seven in New York metropolitan area.

1949-1955

Ruth G. of San Francisco, CA, writes and distributes a periodical for the families of alcoholics: *The Family Forum*.

1951

May Anne B. and Lois open a Clearing House or Service Office at Stepping Stones for 49 Family Groups, which choose the name Al-Anon Family Groups. The Clearing House writes and sends out *Purposes and Suggestions* and *One Wife's Story*.

1952

January Anne B. and Lois move Clearing House to Old 24th Street Clubhouse. Volunteers come to aid: 200 groups registered by then.

March Clearing House reports to groups on work accomplished and asks if they wish to support the Clearing House financially. Their response is yes.

April AA General Service Conference unanimously passes resolution by standing vote approving activities and purposes of Al-Anon Family Groups. At Stepping Stones Family Group members entertain wives of delegates to the AA Conference—the first move toward a conference for Al-Anon.

May 300 Al-Anon groups are registered and 425 letters received and answered.

June A request for literature comes in from South Rhodesia. Clearing House asks groups for permission to handle all national publicity. It is given.

	September	Al-Anon's Traditions are written and accepted by groups. Several new pieces are published.

September Al-Anon's Traditions are written and accepted by groups. Several new pieces are published.

October 400 Al-Anon groups registered and new equipment for office is bought.

1953

February Report of work during 1952 sent to Al-Anon groups. 151 groups make contributions.

April Lois is on "Lamp Unto My Feet" on CBS. *Christian Herald, AA Grapevine, Life Today, Family Circle, Life Romances* have articles on Al-Anon.

1954

January Henrietta S. starts work as a part-time paid secretary.

June Margaret D. is appointed editor of *Forum.*

July Clearing House is incorporated as the Al-Anon Family Group Headquarters, Inc.

1955

July *Saturday Evening Post* publishes article about Al-Anon by Jerome Ellison. Al-Anon's first hardcover book, *The Al-Anon Family Groups,* is sold at the AA International Convention at St. Louis, MO. At this Convention, Al-Anon holds five workshops, one for children of alcoholics.

1956

April Much preparation is made for Ted Malone show on WABC to tell Al-Anon story, but it is canceled.

1957

September The first Alateen group is started.
Al-Anon Headquarters is moved from 334½ West 24th Street to 125 East 23rd Street.

November AA and Al-Anon work together on *Loretta Young Show.*

1958

Part-time secretary for Alateens is added to Headquarters staff.

1960

March Al-Anon's basic book is revised, enlarged and published as *Living With An Alcoholic.*

July Al-Anon members at AA International Convention at Long Beach, CA, vote to approve a plan for an Al-Anon annual conference, later confirmed by groups.

1961

January 1,500 Al-Anon groups are registered; 97 Alateen groups.

April First annual Al-Anon World Service Conference meets in New York on a trial basis.

1963

April The Conference is made permanent.

1965

July *Al-Anon Faces Alcoholism,* a book for the public, is published and introduced at AA International Convention in Toronto, ON, Canada.

1967

March *The Dilemma of the Alcoholic Marriage* by Alice B. is published.

1968

October A daily reader, *One Day at a Time in Al-Anon* by Alice B. is published.

1970

April The service manual, *Al-Anon's Twelve Concepts of Service* receives Conference approval.

July *Al-Anon's Favorite Forum Editorials* by Margaret D. is published and introduced at AA International Convention in Miami Beach, FL.

1971

June Al-Anon Headquarters moves to 115 East 23rd Street.

1975

July 5,000 Al-Anon/Alateen members attend the AA International Convention in Denver, CO.

1976

Al-Anon celebrates its 25th anniversary.

1978

March Al-Anon Headquarters moves to One Park Avenue.
12,650 Al-Anon groups are registered, 2,050 Alateens.
Nearly a million copies sold of *One Day At a Time in Al-Anon*.

1979

April The establishment of Al-Anon Regional Service Seminars is approved at the WSC.

1980

April The National Public Information Committee Canada (NPIC) is established.

July Al-Anon/Alateen members attend the AA International Convention in New Orleans, LA, and the one millionth copy of *One Day at a Time in Al-Anon* is presented to Alcoholics Anonymous.
A one-day trial World Meeting later called International Al-Anon General Services Meeting (IAGSM) is held the day after the International Convention.

1981

April The book, *Al-Anon's Twelve Steps & Twelve Traditions* is published. Conference approval is given to begin a survey to establish an information profile of Al-Anon/Alateen membership.

1983

April *Alateen—one day at a time*, is published. The book, *Living with an Alcoholic* reverts to its original title, *Al-Anon Family Groups*.

1984

September The International Al-Anon General Services Meeting (IAGSM) becomes a permanent part of Al-Anon's structure.

1985

July Al-Anon holds its First International Convention in Montreal, PQ, Canada. Al-Anon's first spiritual book, *As We Understood . . .*, is introduced at this event.

1986

February Al-Anon Headquarters moves to 1372 Broadway; the Shipping Department is relocated to Long Island City.

April Al-Anon celebrates its 35th anniversary at the World Service Conference. The book, *First Steps: Al-Anon—Thirty-Five Years of Beginnings* is published to commemorate this occasion. The film *Al-Anon Speaks for Itself* is approved for distribution.

September The first permanent International Al-Anon General Services Meeting (IAGSM) was held in Stamford, CT.

November 27,201 Al-Anon Family Groups registered, including 3,196 Alateen.

1990

July The second Al-Anon International Convention is held in Seattle, WA.

December The book *In All Our Affairs: Making Crises Work for You*, is published.

1991

May Al-Anon celebrates its 40th anniversary.

1992

July A second daily reader, *Courage to Change: One Day at a Time in Al-Anon II*, is published.

1993

Feb-May The World Service Conference received over 1,300 letters from individuals in Russia as the result of an interview with a doctor published in a Russian newspaper.

1994

April The World Service Conference authorizes the Board of Trustees to purchase property for the Al-Anon Family Group Headquarters, Inc. on a 15 year trial basis.

August *From Survival to Recovery—Growing Up in an Alcoholic Home*, Al-Anon's first book for and by those who grew up with alcoholism, is published.

1995

April The Word Service Conference approves implementation of a revised committee structure for a three year trial period.

The Executive Committee for Real Property Management is established to oversee management of Headquarters' property.

July	*How Al-Anon Works for Families & Friends of Alcoholics* is introduced at the AA International Convention in San Diego, CA.

1996

May	Al-Anon Family Group Headquarters, Inc. relocates to Virginia Beach, VA.
December	*Courage to Be Me—Living with Alcoholism*, the first new Alateen book in over 20 years, is released.

1997

March	Over 31,000 groups are registered worldwide, including 3,000 Alateen groups. Al-Anon/Alateen groups are established in 112 countries and Conference Approved Literature is printed in 30 languages as well as Braille, audio and videocassette tapes.
April	*Paths To Recovery—Al-Anon's Steps, Traditions, and Concepts*, is released. This book is the first comprehensive study of all of Al-Anon's legacies.

1998

July	Al-Anon holds their third International Convention the first separate from AA in Salt Lake City, UT. *Having Had A Spiritual Awakening . . .* is released.

1999

February	Al-Anon Family Group Headquarters (Canada) Inc. is incorporated as a registered charity in Canada as of this date.

2000

July	Conference Approved Literature is published in 30 languages. Al-Anon's first book is reintroduced as *The Al-Anon Family Groups—Classic Edition* at the AA International Convention in Minneapolis, MN. It includes the original text as written by our cofounders, with footnotes, a new introduction, and appendix.

2001

April	Al-Anon celebrates 50 years of offering hope to families and friends of alcoholics. Celebrations are held worldwide throughout the year. Al-Anon is now in 115 countries. A second daily reader for Alateen, *Living Today in Alateen* is published. A Declaration of Gratitude is passed by the World Service Conference and presented to AA.

Index